Home Cooking

with

THE UNCOMMON GOURMET

ELLEN HELMAN

Published by
Font & Center Press
P.O. Box 95
Weston, MA 02193
www.fontandcenter.com

Library of Congress Cataloging in-Publication Data

Helman, Ellen.

First Printing 2002
Published in the United States of America
1 2 3 4 5 6 7 8 9 10

ACKNOWLEDGEMENTS

Thank you, thank you, thank you!

To my wonderful husband, Bobby, for your love, support,
and willingness to try everything

To my children:

Lee and Amy, for your enthusiasm

Jen and Sam, for your encouragement, brainstorming,
and constructive criticisms

To Cleo for our inspirational walks

To friends, Sylvia D., Marlene F., and Ellen F. for testing recipes

To my grandchildren, Max and Peggy Isabel,
a special dedication to my little darlings

In Praise of Ellen's Works

Nothing is too complicated and everything I make from Ellen's books is absolutely delicious. She has shaped my culinary experiences. She is a fabulous cook and author and I look forward to her new works.—Elysia Oudenians, Maryland

Ellen's books are my bible.—Judi Siskind, Brockton, MA

We have dinner with Ellen every night.—Jennifer Barry, Shrewsbury, MA

I love giving Ellen's books as gifts.—Marsha Goldberg, Brookline, MA

I have 473 cookbooks and Ellen's are the most used by far, most requested by family and friends. Every morning I ask the kids what they want for dinner and they say an Ellen recipe.—Kristin Hughes, Wellesley, MA

Rave Reviews for *The Uncommon Gourmet*

Every recipe fantastic!! I have shared this book with many friends. Every meal is an award winner that I prepare from this book.—A reader from Plymouth, MA

My favorite cookbook by far. I can rely on The Uncommon Gourmet *to prepare impressive meals in little time.*—A reader from Newbury, MA

This is one of my absolute favorite cookbooks of all time. The recipes in this cookbook are elegant and uncomplicated. I have never encountered another cookbook that balances simplicity so well with gourmet taste.—A reader from Washington, D.C.

The best. This is my favorite cookbook in my collection of over 100 cookbooks. I've given it to all my friends and family and they love it as much as I do.—A reader from Portsmouth, NH

Accolades for the *All-Occasion Cookbook*

Sure to excite your taste buds . . . this book is a treasure! This cookbook is sure to be one of those that ends up spattered with stains from being used so often. . . . Rarely have I found a book that contains so many recipes that I want to try.—A reader from Toronto, Canada

This book is elegant, simple, and full of variety. It's one of my very favorite cookbooks . . . it deserves to be a best seller!—A reader from Brooklyn, NY

Creative and easy recipes with menus to match . . . I continue to be impressed with Ellen Helman's cookbooks. . . . This one is a gem.—A reader from MA

Spectacular! Nothing will ever compare!!—A reader from MA

TABLE OF

CONTENTS

INTRODUCTION

POETRY OF THE PALATE

Welcome to *Home Cooking*! This book has been a work of consuming passion that I have lived with in both my waking and sleeping hours for several years. *Home Cooking* presents food for the new millenium. It focuses on Americana—retro recipes, diner foods, and new wave renditions of old traditions—and the creation of exciting dishes in the home kitchen. As we move into the 21st century, we seek pleasure and simplicity in food, be it ethnic, grilled, or interesting combinations. When our souls need soothing, we turn to comfort foods. We seek satisfying, wholesome food and home-cooked classics such as macaroni and cheese, meat loaf, mashed potatoes, pot pies, roast chicken, and puddings. This book was designed to help you take advantage of these fresh-tasting, contemporary flavors and to turn out high quality meals with consistent results. In addition to the scores of mouth-watering recipes, there are helpful menu suggestions for family meals and special occasions.

Taking simple ingredients and magically turning them into fashionable meals is a challenge we all face. How to entice others to sample the food is a complex adventure. The tasting process actually begins before the food graces one's palate. Other senses are involved in the first phase of the process. We taste with our eyes and our nose before we taste with our mouth. The visual appeal of food and how it smells are of utmost importance! As an artist, presentation is a primary concern for me, followed closely by the aroma and flavors of the food. Romance the senses, and I guarantee you'll be delighted with the results.

Everyone always asks me how I got involved with cooking. From the moment I took command of the kitchen as a newly wed, I've always loved cooking and experimenting. The actual recipe testing started as a creative outlet when my children were little and I was an at-home mom. It soon developed into a passionate hobby, and as time passed, it blossomed into a central force in my life. I've spent countless hours clipping recipes, reading cookbooks and food magazines, and dreaming up easy, yet flavorful recipes. I love teaching and creating food for others, offering recipes, and providing advice.

Sharing a part of me with you gives me great pleasure and satisfaction. I hope you enjoy *Home Cooking* as much as I've enjoyed creating it for you.

Wishing you glorious meals and happy times!

Ellen Helman

TABLE OF RECIPES

SENSATIONAL SMOOTHIES

BREAKFAST MUFFINS AND SCONES

SATISFYING SOUPS

SIMMERING SOUPS

CHILLED SOUPS

PASTA PASSION

THE SALAD BOWL

GREEN SALADS

GRAIN AND LEGUME SALAD

MEMORABLE MAINSTAYS

SUMPTUOUS MEATS

BEST OF BIRD

SEAFOOD DELIGHTS

VIBRANT VEGGIES

STYLISH GRAINS

GRAND FINALES

FRUITS AND PUDDINGS

COOKIES AND PASTRIES

SECRETS

This section will acquaint you with background information about *Home Cooking*. These guidelines are designed to help you to take advantage of the recipes in this book.

The Basics outline techniques that will make cooking easier and more enjoyable.

The Pantry Defined details specific product brands.

The Enhancements or basic recipes in this section are important reference material for the home cook.

I hope you'll find pleasure in cooking and that you'll be better equipped in preparing and presenting exciting, well-balanced, savory meals!

GETTING THE MOST OUT OF *HOME COOKING*

I feel it is important to provide some guidelines to get the most out of this cookbook. These tips will ensure more success in the kitchen!

1. Follow a recipe exactly the first time. Once you try it, then you can alter it if you wish.

2. Organize and plan ahead—this is the key to successful entertaining.

3. I've learned there are a lot of things that can be done in advance to make cooking less harried. Prepare all sauces, marinades, and salad dressings in advance and store in the refrigerator until needed. This is a great time-saver!

4. Start with the best quality ingredients you can find. This will ensure better tasting results.

5. Keep your pantry well stocked. This is essential to being spontaneous and creative as well as putting together a meal with relative ease.

6. Have all of the ingredients measured and ready before you actually start cooking to facilitate the process.

7. Cooking is an art; baking is a science. You have more freedom and can take liberties in cooking. Baking is precise and measurements must be exact.

8. Use the correct pan size specified in a recipe. Do not make substitutions, as it will alter your results.

9. I always use aluminum or stainless bakeware for baking pans, cookie sheets, tube pans, and muffin pans. If you use the dark-colored, non-stick bakeware, you must reduce the baking time and lower the oven temperature by 25 degrees, as the dark bakeware bakes faster.

10. All ovens are not created equal and are not consistent. Realize if your oven is fast or slow and make the proper adjustments in a recipe. It's helpful to take the oven's temperature.

11. When baking batches of cookies, cool your cookie sheet between batches by rinsing it under cold water. This will ensure that each batch will bake for the same length of time, providing more consistent results.

12. To properly brown food when sautéing, cook over a high flame and don't crowd the pan.

13. Use sea salt or Kosher salt when cooking. It's important to salt when cooking, as it not only adds its own distinctive taste to the food, but it also enhances the other flavors and causes them to sparkle.

Food that has not been seasoned as such tastes bland and lacks luster. However, I do not recommend salting at the table—it only makes the food taste salty!

14. Use extra-large eggs in all the recipes.

15. Use unsalted butter.

16. Always cook with a wine you would choose to drink. Do not buy cooking wine, as it contains salt.

17. Low fat sour cream and low fat mayonnaise are acceptable substitutions if you're on a restricted diet.

18. Never refrigerate tomatoes—it kills their taste and fragrance.

19. Rehydrate sun-dried tomatoes in hot water before adding them to recipes.

20. Use garnishes to make food look more appealing. They add a finishing touch to the presentation.

21. Be creative—experiment and take pleasure in the art of cooking. Remember, what you cook and create is a personal expression, sharing a part of yourself with others.

22. *Denotes a recipe found in *The Uncommon Gourmet Cookbook*.

23. **Denotes a recipe found in *The Uncommon Gourmet's All-Occasion Cookbook*.

BASICS

There are certain basic techniques that every home cook should know. I hope you'll find these helpful hints useful.

How to peel an onion:
Cut off the stem and root ends of the onion. Hold the onion under warm running water for 1 minute. The skin will toughen and will peel off easily.

How to peel and smash garlic:
Place the unpeeled clove of garlic on a chopping board. Crush or smash the clove with a heavy object, separating the skin from the clove and exposing the flesh.

How to pit Kalamata olives:
Place the olives on a chopping board. Cover with plastic wrap and crush with a heavy object, separating the pit from the flesh.

How to toast nuts:
Spread the nuts out in a single layer on a cookie sheet. Bake in a 350° oven for 5 to 10 minutes until lightly golden. The smaller the nut, the faster it will toast, so you'll have to check the oven every 1 to 2 minutes.

How to test for egg freshness:
Put the eggs in a bowl and cover with 2 inches of water. If the eggs sit on the bottom of the bowl, they are fresh; if they float, they're old!

How to hard-boil eggs:
Put the eggs in a single layer in a saucepan. Cover with 2 inches of cold water. Bring to a boil, lower the heat, and simmer gently for 10 minutes. Pour off the water, then cover the eggs with cold water until cool. Refrigerate until needed.

How to make bread crumbs:
Use leftover bread or rolls. Break the bread up into chunks and place in the bowl of a food processor. Pulse and grind until the desired crumb consistency is reached. Transfer to an airtight container and store in the freezer.

How to melt chocolate:
Use a double boiler so that you don't burn the chocolate. Fill the bottom pan of the double boiler with several inches of water and bring to a slow boil. Break the chocolate up into pieces and put it in the top or smaller saucepan of the double boiler. Place this over the boiling water, making sure no water gets into the chocolate. Using a spatula, stir the chocolate until melted and smooth, then remove from the heat.

THE PANTRY DEFINED

I'm always asked what brand of products I use. These are my preferences because of their consistent quality and availability. If you can not find these, don't panic—use the best that is available. I cannot stress enough the importance of buying the freshest, best quality produce, meats, chicken, fish, and dairy possible. Remember, the end product is only as good as its components!

Artichoke hearts: Pastene artichoke hearts
Beans: Pastene cannellini, chick peas, and black beans
Broth: Swanson's lower sodium chicken broth
Butter: Land O'Lakes unsalted butter
Chili Sauce: Heinz chili sauce
Chocolate: Ghirardelli semi-sweet and bittersweet baking chocolate,
                semi-sweet chocolate chips
           Baker's unsweetened and German's sweet chocolate
Cornmeal: Quaker yellow cornmeal
Crabmeat: Crown Prince lump crabmeat
Flour: Pillsbury all-purpose flour
Herbs and Spices: McCormick dried herbs and spices
Maple Syrup: Maple Grove Farms dark amber pure maple syrup
Mayonnaise: Hellmann's mayonnaise (I use low fat.)
Mustard: Grey Poupon Dijon mustard
Olive Oil: Bertolli or Colavita extra-virgin and classico olive oils
Parmesan Cheese: Parmigiano-Reggiano cheese
Pasta: Barilla pastas
Prosciutto: Prosciutto di Parma
Rice: Imported Arborio rice
      Uncle Ben's long grain white rice
Roasted Peppers: Pastene roasted peppers
Salt: Coarse or Kosher salt
     Alessi Mediterranean sea salt (fine crystals)
Sardines: Crown Prince sardines
Spinach: Green Giant frozen spinach
Tomatoes: Del Monte diced tomatoes
Tuna: Bumble Bee fancy albacore tuna, packed in water
Vinegar: Monari Federzoni balsamic vinegar of Modena
        Progresso red wine vinegar
        Columela sherry vinegar
        Maitre Jacques tarragon wine vinegar

ENHANCEMENTS

BASIC VINAIGRETTE

MEDITERRANEAN
FLAIR

Mesclun Salad with
Basic Vinaigrette
. . .
Grilled Tuna with
Mediterranean Relish
. . .
Pasta Toscano
. . .
Cannoli

This basic vinaigrette serves as both salad dressing for mixed greens and as marinade for meats, poultry, fish, or vegetables before being grilled.

salt and freshly ground pepper to taste
1 clove garlic, smashed
1 teaspoon Dijon mustard
2 tablespoons red wine vinegar
6 tablespoons extra-virgin olive oil

Optional:
1/2 teaspoon dried basil, thyme, or oregano or a combination
2 tablespoons grated Parmigiano-Reggiano cheese

1. In a small bowl, whisk together the salt, pepper, garlic, Dijon, vinegar, and olive oil. (You may add any optional seasonings if you wish.)

2. Store in the refrigerator until needed. This will keep for 5 days. (Remove the garlic after 24 hours.)

Enough dressing for a salad for 6 portions; enough marinade for 2 pounds meat, chicken, fish, or vegetables

GARLIC BREAD

Redolent with freshly crushed garlic and dusted with herbs, this garlic bread gives new definition to the Italian classic. Use it as a side accompaniment to the meal, as a base for grilled burgers, or cut into small pieces for garnishing salads.

about 1 pound loaf Italian bread
¼ cup extra-virgin olive oil
6 large cloves garlic, crushed
¾ teaspoon dried basil
¼ teaspoon dried oregano

1. Preheat the oven to 400°.

2. Split the loaf in half lengthwise as you would to make a sandwich. Cut each half into 3 equal pieces.

3. Brush the olive oil over the cut side of the bread pieces. Spread the garlic over the oil. Sprinkle with the herbs.

4. Bake for 8 to 10 minutes until golden around the edges. Serve hot out of the oven.

6 portions

HOMESTYLE
MEAL

Carlos Salad
. . .
Chicken Parmigiana
. . .
Pasta
. . .
Garlic Bread
. . .
Fresh Fruit

PEANUT SAUCE

Americans are smitten with peanut sauce. This Asian sauce is a flavor sensation. Use it as a dip for crudités or poached shrimp; as a sauce for steamed fish and vegetables, roast pork, or noodles garnished with chopped scallions; as a topping for chicken or beef satay; or as a dressing for an Oriental-style salad. Anyway you use it, you're sure to love it!

1 cup creamy peanut butter
$1/4$ cup water
$1/4$ cup light cream
3 tablespoons soy sauce
2 tablespoons lime juice
2 tablespoons light brown sugar
1 tablespoon grated gingerroot
1 large clove garlic, minced
$1/2$ teaspoon crushed red pepper flakes (or to taste)

In a bowl, combine all of the ingredients and mix until smooth and creamy. Store in the refrigerator until needed.

about 2 cups sauce

PESTO

The infamous, lush Genovese sauce continues to romance our senses. It has become a household staple because of its fabulous flavor and versatility. I have refined this version from the one that appears in *The All-Occasion Cookbook,* making it even better.

1 cup firmly packed fresh basil
¹/₂ cup pine nuts, toasted
2 large cloves garlic, crushed
salt to taste
6 tablespoons grated Parmigiano-Reggiano cheese
¹/₂ cup extra-virgin olive oil

1. Put the basil, pine nuts, garlic, salt, and cheese in the bowl of a food processor and grind to a paste.

2. With the motor running, add the oil in a slow, steady stream until completely incorporated. Transfer the pesto to a container and store in the refrigerator for up to 1 week or longer in the freezer.

1 cup of pesto

CASUAL DINNER
WITH FRIENDS

Mixed Greens with
Basic Vinaigrette
. . .
Chicken Paolo
. . .
Pasta with Pesto
. . .
Pear Crisp

RASPBERRY VINEGAR

HEARTY WINTER FARE

Roasted Chicken with
Winter Vegetables
. . .
Salad Marly with
Raspberry Vinegar
. . .
Arborio Rice Pudding

The exquisite flavor of the queen of berries shines in this homemade vinegar.

3 cups white vinegar
1 cup raspberries
$1/3$ cup sugar

1. Combine the vinegar and raspberries in a covered container and let sit at room temperature for 1 week.

2. After a week, strain the liquid into a non-reactive saucepan. Add the sugar and bring to a boil. Lower the heat and simmer for 10 minutes. Let cool.

3. Transfer the vinegar to a sterile glass bottle and cover tightly. The vinegar is now ready to use or to give as a gift. Store in a cool, dark place.

3 cups

TASTY TIDBITS

Appetizers are the trendy, tasty morsels meant to stimulate and awaken the appetite. They're the whimsical, toothy part of the meal that we devour. Whether snappy wafers to accompany chilled glasses of wine, bruschetta or crostini sporting savory toppings, shellfish treasures, lusty dips, or just tantalizing nibbles, appetizers are fun, savory, and delicious.

Many people would prefer to sample a host of zesty hors d'oeuvres rather than sit down to a formal main-course. For that reason, cocktail parties are a wonderful way to entertain family and friends with hors d'oeuvres being the star actors. The fussier the appetizers look, the more people will want them. The trick is to make them look fabulous without them being labor intense. When I host a cocktail party, I try to serve three hot and three cold appetizers and vary the menu. Balance the scales—make some hors d'oeuvres with vegetables, others with seafood, meats, chicken, or cheese. It's good to serve some things that need no attention, i.e. a basket of crudités with a gusty dip. Allow 2 to 3 pieces of each item per person.

Bring on the hors d'oeuvres and let the good times roll!

DIPS AND SPREADS

HONEY-MUSTARD DIP

GRADUATION
DINNER

Honey-Mustard Dip
with Crudites
. . .
Stuffed Leg of Lamb
. . .
Garlic Mashed Potato
Cakes
. . .
Roasted Asparagus**
. . .
Spice Poundcake

This creamy honey-mustard sauce is not only divine with raw vegetables; it also turns grilled vegetables, shrimp, and chicken into special events.

¹/₂ cup mayonnaise
¹/₄ cup Dijon mustard
¹/₄ cup honey
1 tablespoon dark brown sugar

1. In a bowl, mix the mayonnaise and mustard until evenly blended.

2. Add the honey and brown sugar and mix well. Serve with an assortment of crudités—carrots, red pepper, cucumber, snow peas, mushrooms, cauliflower, celery, asparagus, and zucchini.

1 cup

BLACK BEAN DIP

This snappy black bean purée is lush with Mexican flavors—garlic, cilantro, lime, and olive oil. Serve it surrounded by tortilla chips, wedges of pita bread, or crudités.

15 to 16-ounce can black beans, rinsed and drained
salt and freshly ground pepper to taste
2 large cloves garlic, crushed
1/2 teaspoon crushed red pepper flakes
1/3 cup lightly packed fresh cilantro
3 tablespoons lime juice
1/2 cup extra-virgin olive oil

1. Put the beans, salt, pepper, garlic, red pepper flakes, cilantro, and lime juice in the bowl of a food processor and purée.

2. With the motor running, add the oil in a slow, steady stream until it is completely incorporated and the purée is smooth and creamy. Transfer to a bowl and serve. (It may be made 6 to 8 hours in advance and refrigerated; return to room temperature to serve.)

6 to 8 portions

LITTLE MEXICAN
BITES

Guacamole
. . .
Black Bean Dip
. . .
Baked Tortilla Chips
. . .
Quesadillas

WHITE BEAN PURÉE

This thick purée of cannellini beans and carrots is splendid as a spread over slices of crusty bread as well as a dip for crudités. There's no fat or cholesterol in this seductive spread!

1 pound carrots, peeled and cut into $1/2$-inch rounds
19-ounce can cannellini beans, rinsed and drained
salt and freshly ground pepper to taste
$1^1/2$ teaspoons sugar

1. Cook the carrots in boiling salted water until tender, approximately 5 minutes. Drain well and transfer to the bowl of a food processor.

2. Add the remaining ingredients and purée.

3. Transfer to a bowl and serve at room temperature with slices of bruschetta.

approximately 3 cups of purée

GREEN OLIVE TAPENADE

Hailed from Provence, tapenade is the marvelous, rich paste abundant with olives, garlic, anchovies, and capers. Serve the spread on toasted crostini with a crisp white wine.

1 cup green olives, pitted
1 large clove garlic, crushed
freshly ground pepper to taste
4 anchovy filets, rinsed
2 tablespoons capers, rinsed
1 tablespoon lemon juice
$1/3$ cup extra-virgin olive oil

1. Put the olives, garlic, pepper, anchovies, capers, and lemon juice in the bowl of a food processor and purée.

2. With the motor running, add the oil in a slow, steady stream until completely incorporated and the mixture is smooth. Remove to a bowl and serve surrounded by crostini.

1 cup

MEDITERRANEAN PALATE

Grilled Chicken
with Green Olive
Tapenade
. . .
Pasta with Cauliflower
Crumbs
. . .
Mixed Greens with
Basic Vinaigrette

BAKED BRIE OLIVADA

Brie is the elegant, soft-ripening French cheese with a downy white rind. It is noted for its buttery interior and rich taste. When capped with a black olive paste and sun-dried tomatoes, and baked until warm and oozing, it's heavenly!

> *1 pound Brie cheese*
> *$1/2$ cup olivada (see page 14, **The All-Occasion Cookbook**)*
> *$1/3$ cup chopped sun-dried tomatoes, rehydrated in hot water for 1 minute*

1. Preheat the oven to 350°.

2. Place the Brie in a baking dish to fit.

3. In a bowl, mix together the olivada and sun-dried tomatoes. Spread the mixture on top of the cheese.

4. Bake for 15 to 20 minutes until the Brie is warm and melted. Serve with rounds of French bread.

8 or more portions

HUMMUS BI TAHINI

Tahini, ground sesame seed paste, distinguishes this famous creamy Middle Eastern chickpea purée. Serve it with pita wedges or as a dip for crudités.

19-ounce can chickpeas, rinsed and drained
3 large cloves garlic, crushed
$^1/_2$ teaspoon salt
$^1/_4$ cup tahini
$^1/_3$ cup lemon juice
$^1/_4$ cup water
$^1/_4$ cup extra-virgin olive oil
paprika for garnish

1. Put all of the ingredients except the paprika in the bowl of a food processor and purée until smooth and creamy.

2. Remove the hummus to a bowl, dust with paprika, and serve.

$2^2/_3$ cups

MEZE PARTY

Mediterranean Spiced
Olives**
· · ·
Hummus Bi Tahini
· · ·
Baba Ghanoush
· · ·
Pita Bread
· · ·
Tsaziki
· · ·
Stuffed Grape
Leaves**

BABA GHANOUSH

This classic Middle Eastern meze or snack features a purée of roasted eggplant laced with garlic, lemon, and tahini. Tahini is a ground sesame seed paste that imparts a distinctive, nutty essence to the dip.

1 large eggplant
$1/2$ teaspoon salt
$1/4$ teaspoon ground cumin
2 large cloves garlic, crushed
3 tablespoons tahini
3 tablespoons lemon juice
2 tablespoons chopped fresh parsley for garnish

1. Preheat the oven to 400°.

2. Prick the eggplant all over with a fork. Place it in a roasting pan and bake for 40 minutes.

3. Let cool, then peel off the skin. Split the eggplant in half, and place it in a colander to drain. Press gently to remove the excess liquid.

4. Put the eggplant, salt, cumin, garlic, tahini, and lemon juice in the bowl of a food processor and purée until smooth. Transfer to a bowl and garnish with parsley. Serve accompanied by pita wedges.

4 to 6 portions

RED PEPPER HUMMUS

This lush, red-hued chickpea spread is redolent with roasted red pepper. It's fabulous spread over thick slices of peasant bread, as a dip for crudités, or as a topping for grilled chicken. It's also fun to serve the hummus in a hollowed-out bread round.

$1^1/_4$ cups canned chickpeas, rinsed and drained
1 large roasted red pepper, cut into chunks
1 clove garlic, crushed
salt and freshly ground pepper to taste
1 teaspoon paprika
$1^1/_2$ tablespoons lemon juice
3 tablespoons extra-virgin olive oil

1. Put all of the ingredients in the bowl of a food processor and purée.

2. Remove the hummus to a bowl, surround with chunks of bread and vegetables, and serve.

$1^1/_2$ cups

MIDDLE EASTERN
COMFORT FOOD

Red Pepper Hummus
· · ·
Turkish Lamb Burgers
· · ·
Chopped Vegetable
Salad
· · ·
Israeli Couscous

GUACAMOLE

This lively version of the popular Mexican avocado dip has layers of flavor and lots of personality. Use it as a dip with tortilla chips and vegetables or as a sauce atop grilled chicken and seafood.

3 ripe Haas avocados, peeled and pitted
1 medium-size tomato, seeded and diced
¹/₄ cup finely minced onion
1 jalapeño pepper, partially seeded and diced
¹/₄ cup chopped fresh cilantro
2 tablespoons lime juice
salt to taste

1. In a bowl, mash the avocados with a fork.

2. Add the remaining ingredients and mix gently. Serve within 1 hour at room temperature.

approximately 2¹/₂ cups

TSAZIKI

This Greek yogurt and cucumber dish is redolent with garlic and fragrant with dill. It's a stellar appetizer and also doubles as a refreshing salad.

1 quart plain nonfat yogurt
1 seedless cucumber, peeled and coarsely grated
salt and freshly ground pepper to taste
2 to 4 large cloves garlic, finely minced
¹/₄ cup chopped fresh dill
1 tablespoon lemon juice
2 tablespoons olive oil (not extra-virgin)

1. Place the yogurt in a double layer of cheesecloth in a colander and let drain at room temperature for 4 hours.

2. Place the cucumber in a colander and let drain for 30 minutes. Pat dry with a paper towel.

3. In a bowl, combine the yogurt, salt, pepper, garlic, dill, lemon juice, and olive oil and mix well.

4. Just before serving, stir the yogurt, add the cucumber, and mix well. Serve at once with pita bread. (The tsaziki can become watery if left to stand.)

8 or more appetizer portions; 4 salad portions

MEZE PARTY

Mediterranean Spiced
Olives**
. . .
Hummus Bi Tahini
. . .
Baba Ghanoush
. . .
Pita Bread
. . .
Tsaziki
. . .
Stuffed Grape
Leaves**

WAFERS AND CROSTINI

BLUE CHEESE-CHEDDAR WAFERS

Blue cheese aficionados will appreciate these buttery cocktail wafers replete with Roquefort, sharp cheddar, and walnuts.

1/2 cup butter, cut into 8 pieces
1 cup all-purpose flour
2 ounces sharp cheddar cheese, grated
2 ounces Roquefort cheese, crumbled
1/2 teaspoon Worcestershire sauce
1/2 cup very finely chopped walnuts

1. Put the butter, flour, cheeses, and Worcestershire sauce in the bowl of a food processor. Pulse until the dough comes together and forms a ball. Remove the dough and form it into a log—6 inches long and 2 inches in diameter.

2. Sprinkle the walnuts on a piece of wax paper. Roll the dough in the chopped nuts, pressing down firmly. Wrap the dough in plastic wrap and refrigerate for at least 3 hours until well chilled and as much as 2 days.

3. Preheat the oven to 400°.

4. Slice the log into 1/4-inch thick rounds. Place the rounds on ungreased cookie sheets.

5. Bake for 10 to 13 minutes until golden. Remove the wafers from the cookie sheet to a rack to cool slightly. Serve warm or at room temperature. Store any extras in a tin for up to 3 days.

24 wafers

PARMESAN BITES

Laced with the rich, sharp flavor or Parmigiano-Reggiano, the pre-eminent Italian cheese, these toothsome, buttery, flaky cookies are the perfect companion for cocktails.

1/2 cup butter
3/4 cup all-purpose flour
1 cup grated Parmigiano-Reggiano cheese
1/8 teaspoon salt
1/4 teaspoon cayenne pepper
pinch of paprika

1. In a bowl, combine all of the ingredients and mix well until the dough comes together and forms a ball. Form into a log—6 inches long and 1 3/4 inches in diameter. Wrap the log in plastic wrap and refrigerate until well chilled, at least 1 hour and as much as overnight.

2. Preheat the oven to 375°.

3. Slice the dough into 1/4-inch thick rounds. Place the rounds on ungreased cookie sheets.

4. Bake for 10 to 12 minutes until golden. Remove the wafers from the pan to a rack to cool. Serve warm or at room temperature.

24 wafers

SPRING-SUMMER LUNCHEON

Parmesan Bites
. . .
Arugula, Tomatoes, and White Beans
. . .
Deviled Salmon Cakes
. . .
Dessert Cups with Assorted Berries and Whipped Cream

ROSEMARY-WALNUT BISCOTTI

These tasty, crunchy nibbles are a refreshing change to crackers. Scented with rosemary and flavored with Parmesan cheese and walnut oil, they're perfect with drinks and also make a wonderful garnish for salads.

2 cups all-purpose flour
2 teaspoons baking powder
1 teaspoon salt
1/4 teaspoon black pepper
1 teaspoon dried rosemary
1/2 cup grated Parmigiano-Reggiano cheese
1/2 cup walnuts, toasted and finely chopped
6 tablespoons walnut oil
2 tablespoons extra-virgin olive oil
2 eggs, beaten

1. Preheat the oven to 325°. Line two baking sheets with parchment paper.

2. In a large bowl, combine the flour, baking powder, salt, pepper, rosemary, and Parmesan and mix well. Stir in the walnuts.

3. In a separate small bowl, mix the walnut oil, olive oil, and eggs. Add to the flour mixture and stir until the dough comes together.

4. Divide the dough in half. Place each half on a baking sheet and form the dough into a log, 2 1/2 inches wide and 12 inches long.

5. Bake for 30 minutes. Remove from the oven and let rest for 2 minutes. Then with a serrated knife, carefully slice each log into 1-inch wide pieces. Separate the slices so that they're 1 inch apart. Return to the oven and bake for 20 minutes more. Transfer the biscotti to a rack to cool before serving.

24 biscotti

OLIVE BISCOTTI

These biscotti are savory rather than sweet, making them a lovely accompaniment to cocktails. They're studded with Kalamata olives and fragrant with fennel.

2 cups all-purpose flour
1^1/$_2$ teaspoons baking powder
^{1}/$_2$ teaspoon salt
1 teaspoon fennel seeds
^{1}/$_2$ teaspoon dried orange peel
^{1}/$_2$ teaspoon crushed red pepper flakes
^{3}/$_4$ cup pitted Kalamata olives, chopped (see page 5)
^{1}/$_2$ cup extra-virgin olive oil
2 eggs, beaten

1. Preheat the oven to 325°. Line two baking sheets with parchment paper.

2. In a large bowl, combine the flour, baking powder, salt, fennel, orange peel, and red pepper flakes and mix well. Stir in the olives.

3. In a separate small bowl, mix the oil and eggs. Add to the flour mixture and stir until the dough comes together.

4. Divide the dough in half. Place each half on a baking sheet and form the dough into a log, 2^1/$_2$ inches wide and 12 inches long.

5. Bake for 30 minutes. Remove from the oven and let rest for 3 minutes. Then with a serrated knife, carefully slice each log into 1-inch wide pieces. Separate the slices so that they're 1 inch apart. Return to the oven and bake for 20 minutes more. Transfer the biscotti to a rack to cool before serving.

24 biscotti

ITALIAN SUPPER

Olive Biscotti
· · ·
Balsamic-Glazed Veal Chops
· · ·
Pasta with Roasted Peppers and Potatoes
· · ·
Sliced Tomatoes and Buffalo Mozzarella
· · ·
Italian Ices

SEEDED PITA WEDGES

These crispy, savory flat bread triangles are encrusted with a riot of toasted seeds—poppy, sesame, and flax—and make for delicious nibbles with drinks.

2 tablespoons sesame seeds
2 tablespoons poppy seeds
2 tablespoons flax seeds (available in whole foods markets)
4 large (10-inch) pita rounds
1 egg, beaten with 1 tablespoon cold water
1 teaspoon coarse or Kosher salt

1. Preheat the oven to 400°.

2. In a small bowl, combine the sesame, poppy, and flax seeds and mix well.

3. Place each pita round on a separate cookie sheet. Brush each with the egg wash. Sprinkle each with an equal amount of the seed mixture and season each with 1/4 teaspoon salt.

4. With a sharp knife, cut each round into 12 wedges, separating the pieces. Bake for 8 to 10 minutes until crisp and golden. Remove to a platter when done. Serve warm or at room temperature.

48 wedges; allow 3 per person

BAKED TORTILLA CHIPS

This is one of those recipes where no specific amounts are given. The tortillas are baked with a sprinkling of seasonings; the heavier the coating, the bolder the flavor—it's to your discretion. These are great served unadorned with drinks or as a dipper with salsa.

4 (9-inch) fresh flour tortillas, cut into 8 wedges
vegetable oil spray
sea salt
chili powder
grated Parmesan cheese

1. Preheat the oven to 400°. Grease two cookie sheets.
2. Place the tortilla wedges on the cookie sheets, $1/2$-inch apart.
3. Spray the wedges generously with the vegetable oil. Season to taste with salt, chili powder, and Parmesan.
4. Bake for 6 to 8 minutes until lightly golden. Transfer to a rack to cool. Serve warm or at room temperature.

32 wedges; 6 to 8 portions

LITTLE MEXICAN
BITES

Guacamole
· · ·
Black Bean Dip
· · ·
Baked Tortilla Chips
· · ·
Quesadillas

DILLED ONION CROSTINI

These savory puffs, warm out of the oven, make a grand statement at cocktail time. They also make a delicious garnish for a simple green or Caesar salad.

2/3 cup diced Vidalia or other sweet onion
1/2 cup mayonnaise
1/4 cup freshly grated Parmigiano-Reggiano cheese
1/2 teaspoon dried dill
1 loaf French bread, cut into 3/4-inch thick rounds—you'll need 10 slices

1. Preheat the oven to 400°.

2. In a mixing bowl, combine the onion, mayonnaise, cheese, and dill and mix well.

3. Spread approximately 2 tablespoons of the mixture atop each bread round, piling the topping high. Set the rounds on a baking sheet.

4. Bake for 12 to 15 minutes until puffed and golden. Serve hot from the oven.

10 bruschetta

WHITE BEAN CROSTINI

This white bean topping is heady with the flavors of gremolata—garlic, lemon, and parsley. It also makes a lush dip for crudités.

> 15-ounce can cannellini beans, rinsed and drained
> 2 large cloves garlic, crushed
> salt and freshly ground pepper to taste
> 1 tablespoon finely grated lemon peel
> 1 tablespoon lemon juice
> 1/4 cup chopped fresh parsley
> 1 tablespoon extra-virgin olive oil
> large French bread, cut into 3/4-inch thick rounds and toasted

1. Put the beans, garlic, salt, pepper, lemon peel, lemon juice, parsley, and olive oil in the bowl of a food processor and purée.

2. Top each bread round with 1 tablespoon of the bean purée and present.

about 1 1/2 cups purée; 24 crostini

MOZZARELLA CROSTINI

Rounds of French bread are draped with slices of fresh mozzarella, sprinkled with herbs de Provence, then baked until warm and melted. The herbs de Provence reflect the fragrant seasonings typical to southern France. Generally the mixture includes basil, fennel seed, lavender, marjoram, rosemary, sage, savory, and thyme.

15 slices French bread, cut $^3/_4$-inch thick
8 ounces fresh mozzarella, cut into $^1/_2$-inch thick pieces (15 slices). If the
*   mozzarella balls are very large, slice them in half before you cut them*
*   into individual slices.*
1 tablespoon extra-virgin olive oil
$^3/_4$ teaspoon herbs de Provence

1. Preheat the oven to 400°.

2. Arrange the slices of bread on a large baking sheet.

3. Place a piece of cheese atop each bread round. Drizzle each with the olive oil and sprinkle with the herbs.

4. Bake for 10 minutes until the cheese is warm and melted. Serve at once.

15 crostini

OLIVE PUFFS

The characteristic tangy, salty flavor of green olives shines in these cheesy melt-in-your-mouth morsels.

2/3 cup chopped pimiento-stuffed green olives
3/4 cup coarsely grated sharp cheddar cheese
1/2 cup mayonnaise
12 slices French bread, cut 3/4-inch thick

1. Preheat the oven to 400°.

2. In a bowl, combine the olives, cheddar, and mayonnaise and mix well.

3. Spread 1½ tablespoons of the mixture atop each bread round. Place the bread on a baking sheet.

4. Bake for 15 minutes until puffed and golden. Serve at once.

12 puffs; allow 2 to 3 per person

GRAZING PARTY

Artichoke Pillows
. . .
Roquefort-Stuffed
Mushrooms
. . .
Grilled Shrimp with
Pesto Mayonnaise
. . .
Olive Puffs
. . .
Hearty Lentil Soup

BRUSCHETTA WITH DRIED FRUIT MASCARPONE

Mascarpone is the buttery-rich, sweet cream cheese hailed from Italy. It is delicious served unadorned, and exceptional when topped with dried fruits and nuts. These toasted bread rounds spread with mascarpone and crowned with dates, apricots, and walnuts are dazzling!

8 ounces mascarpone cheese
1/4 cup finely chopped walnuts, toasted
6 tablespoons chopped dates
1/4 cup chopped dried apricots
1 tablespoon minced crystallized candied ginger
14 slices French bread (cut 1/2-inch thick on the diagonal), toasted

1. In a small bowl, mix together the mascarpone, walnuts, dates, apricots, and candied ginger.

2. Spread the mixture on the bruschetta and serve.

4 to 6 portions

TOMATO BRUSCHETTA

Long slices of toasted French bread are crowned with a heavenly tomato relish rich with capers, roasted pepper, olives, and onion.

4 plum tomatoes, seeded and chopped
salt to taste
2 tablespoons extra-virgin olive oil
1 tablespoon capers
1/2 yellow pepper, roasted and chopped
2 tablespoons chopped Vidalia (or other sweet) onion
4 Kalamata olives, pitted (see page 5)
4 (1-inch thick) slices French bread, cut on the oblique diagonal, toasted
    (slices should be 5-inches long)

1. Put the tomatoes in a bowl and sprinkle liberally with salt. Drizzle with the olive oil and mix well.

2. Add the capers, roasted pepper, onion, and olives. Let marinate at room temperature for 1 hour for the flavors to mellow.

3. To serve, place a slice of bread on each plate. Top with heaping spoonfuls of the tomato relish, allowing any extra to surround the bread on the plate. Drizzle with the accumulated juices and serve at once.

4 portions

ITALIAN REPAST

Tomato Bruschetta
. . .
Chicken Marcella
. . .
Israeli Couscous
. . .
Tiramisu**

BRUSCHETTA WITH BLACK OLIVE PESTO

This black olive pesto is a cross between the much adored basil pesto and the dazzling olive paste, olivada. The Kalamatas lend a distinctive tang and rich taste to the lush spread. These bruschetta also make a first-rate garnish for green and Caesar salads.

1/2 cup pitted Kalamata olives (see page 5)
1/2 cup packed fresh basil
1/4 cup pine nuts, toasted
1 large clove garlic, crushed
salt and freshly ground pepper to taste
3 tablespoons grated imported Parmesan cheese
1/2 cup extra-virgin olive oil
large French bread, cut into 18 slices (3/4-inch thick)

1. Preheat the oven to 400°.

2. Put the olives, basil, pine nuts, garlic, salt, pepper, and Parmesan in the bowl of a food processor and purée.

3. With the motor running, add the oil in a slow, steady stream until completely incorporated and the pesto is smooth and creamy.

4. Spread 1 tablespoon of pesto atop each bread round. Place the bruschetta on a baking sheet.

5. Bake for 10 minutes and serve.

18 bruschetta

BRUSCHETTA WITH CHÈVRE AND SMOKED SALMON

Rounds of French bread are daubed with goat cheese, draped with smoked salmon, and drizzled with pesto. It's a feast for the eyes as well as the palate!

8 ounces chèvre
large French bread cut into 16 slices (³/4-inch thick)
8 ounces sliced smoked salmon, cut into 16 pieces
about 3 tablespoons pesto (see page 12)

1. Spread about 1 tablespoon of the goat cheese on each bread round.

2. Cover the cheese with a slice of smoked salmon.

3. Garnish each bruschetta with approximately ¹/2 teaspoon dollop of pesto and serve. These may be made 4 to 6 hours in advance and refrigerated. Return to room temperature to serve.

16 bruschetta; allow 2 to 3 per person

BRUNCH BUFFET

Bruschetta with
Chèvre and Smoked
Salmon
. . .
Mocha Latte
Smoothies
. . .
Cinnamon-Pecan
Scones
. . .
Cranberry-Nut Scones
. . .
Mushroom Frittata

PIZZETTA WITH ONION AND FETA

Greek flavors abound in these pita rounds that are lavished with thinly sliced onion, mint, feta, and olive oil and baked to a turn.

> 4 mid-size pita breads (approximately 7-inches in diameter)
> 1 medium to medium-large size Vidalia (or other sweet) onion, sliced into wafer thin rings
> 1 cup crumbled feta cheese
> 1 teaspoon dried mint
> 1/4 cup extra-virgin olive oil

1. Preheat the oven to 400°

2. Place the pita rounds on two baking sheets.

3. Divide the onion slices evenly atop each round. Sprinkle each with 1/4 cup feta and 1/4 teaspoon mint. Drizzle 1 tablespoon olive oil over each pizzetta.

4. Bake for 10 minutes until golden. Slice each round into 6 wedges and serve.

24 wedges; allow 3 wedges per person

IT'S A WRAP

ARTICHOKE PILLOWS

These wonton wraps are plump with a creamy, zesty artichoke purée deviled with Dijon, Worcestershire, and Parmesan. Once you try them, you'll keep coming back for more.

14-ounce can artichoke hearts, drained
1 large clove garlic, crushed
salt and freshly ground pepper to taste
1 teaspoon Dijon mustard
1/2 teaspoon Worcestershire sauce
1 tablespoon lemon juice
1/4 cup grated Parmigiano-Reggiano cheese
3 tablespoons extra-virgin olive oil
1 package wonton skins

1. Preheat the oven to 400°. Grease two baking sheets.

2. Put the artichoke hearts, garlic, salt, pepper, Dijon, Worcestershire, lemon juice, Parmesan, and 2 tablespoons olive oil in the bowl of a food processor and purée.

3. Place a generous 1/2 tablespoon of the filling in the middle of a wonton skin. Wet the edges of two adjacent sides with cold water. Fold over to form a triangle, pressing the edges together to seal. Place on the prepared baking sheet. Repeat with the remaining wonton skins until all the filling has been used.

4. Brush the top of the wontons with 1 tablespoon olive oil. Bake for 10 minutes until golden. Serve at once.

about 24 pillows; allow 2 to 3 per person

SPINACH AND CHÈVRE TURNOVERS

A creamy spinach, goat cheese, and Parmesan mixture makes a savory filling for wonton skins that are baked until puffed and golden.

10-ounce package frozen chopped spinach, thawed and squeezed of all its liquid
5 ounces chèvre
$1/2$ cup grated Parmigiano-Reggiano cheese
$1/4$ cup thinly sliced scallions
1 tablespoon sour cream
salt and freshly ground pepper to taste
1 teaspoon dried dill
1 package wonton skins
1 to 2 tablespoons olive oil (not extra-virgin)

1. Preheat the oven to 400°. Grease two baking sheets.

2. In a bowl, combine the spinach, chèvre, Parmesan, scallions, sour cream, salt, pepper, and dill and mix well.

3. Place a scant tablespoon of the filling in the middle of a wonton skin. Wet the edges of two adjacent sides with cold water. Fold over to form a triangle, pressing the edges together to seal. Place on the prepared baking sheet. Repeat with the remaining wonton skins until all the filling has been used.

4. Brush the top of the wontons with the olive oil. Bake for 10 minutes until golden. Serve at once.

about 40 turnovers; allow 2 to 3 per person

QUESADILLAS

Quesadillas are the Mexican equivalent to the Italian pizza or calzone. The spectrum of fillings for the tortilla turnover is as varied as the imagination. When sliced into wedges, it makes a tantalizing hors d'oeuvre.

LITTLE MEXICAN BITES

Guacamole
. . .
Black Bean Dip
. . .
Baked Tortilla Chips
. . .
Quesadillas

8 large (10-inch) flour tortillas
2 cups grated Monterey Jack cheese
2 cups grated mild sharp cheddar cheese
4-ounce can mild green chilies, chopped
1 small yellow onion, thinly sliced

Garnishes:
sour cream
Salsa Fresca (see page 433)

1. Preheat the oven to 400°.

2. Place the tortillas on a work surface. Sprinkle ¼ cup of Jack cheese and ¼ cup cheddar on half of each round. Distribute equal amounts of chilies and onion over the cheeses on each tortilla. Fold each tortilla in half to enclose the filling. Transfer to baking sheets.

3. Bake for 7 to 8 minutes until tortillas are crisp and lightly golden. Remove from the pans and cut each into quarters. Serve with a dollop of sour cream and Salsa Fresca.

32 wedges; 8 or more portions

APPLE-BRIE STRUDEL

Is it an hors d'oeuvre or is it a dessert? It could easily double as both—either way it's delicious! Grated apples and Brie are a stellar combination. They're further enhanced with dried cranberries and candied ginger, spread with apricot preserves, and wrapped in a puff pastry turnover.

1 pound frozen puff pastry, thawed
$1/2$ cup apricot preserves
3 tablespoons dried cranberries
1 tablespoon minced crystallized candied ginger
$1/2$ pound Brie cheese, frozen for 30 minutes
2 Granny Smith apples
1 egg yolk beaten with 1 tablespoon cold water

1. Roll out the puff pastry on a floured board to form a rectangle 12 x 20 inches. Place it on a large cookie sheet and chill for 30 minutes.

2. Preheat the oven to 350°.

3. In a small bowl, combine the preserves, cranberries, and candied ginger and mix well.

4. Slice the Brie thinly with a cheese slicer.

5. Peel and coarsely grate the apples. Spread them down the center of the length of the dough forming a layer 4 inches wide and extending to within $1/2$-inch of each end.

6. Cover the apples with the slices of Brie. Spread the apricot mixture evenly over the Brie.

7. Fold the dough over like a turnover, overlapping the sides. Crimp the ends together firmly to seal.

8. Brush the pastry with the beaten egg yolk mixture.

9. Bake for 30 minutes until golden. Transfer the loaf to a platter, cut into $1^1/2$ inch wide strips, and serve at once.

8 or more portions

BROCCOLI, HAM, AND CHEESE TURNOVER

This enticing dish features a pastry turnover encasing a toothsome filling of broccoli, ham, and Swiss cheese slathered with honey-mustard and baked until golden. This also makes a spectacular statement for brunch or lunch.

1 pound frozen puff pastry, thawed
1 tablespoon Dijon mustard
1 tablespoon honey
10-ounce package frozen chopped broccoli, thawed and squeezed
    of all its liquid
salt and pepper to taste
$1/4$ pound Swiss cheese, coarsely grated
$1/2$ pound Black Forest baked ham, very thinly sliced
1 egg yolk beaten with 1 tablespoon cold water

1. Roll out the puff pastry on a floured board to form a rectangle 12 x 20 inches. Place it on a large cookie sheet and chill for 30 minutes.

2. Preheat the oven to 350°.

3. In a small bowl, mix the Dijon and honey.

4. Spread the broccoli down the center of the length of the dough forming a layer 4 inches wide and extending to within $1/2$-inch of each end. Season with salt and pepper.

5. Cover the broccoli with half of the Swiss cheese. Lay the slices of ham evenly over the cheese. Spread the honey-mustard over the ham. Cover with the remaining cheese.

6. Fold the dough over like a turnover, overlapping the sides. Crimp the ends together firmly to seal.

7. Brush the pastry with the beaten egg yolk mixture. This will give the loaf a golden glaze.

8. Bake for 30 minutes. Transfer the loaf to a platter, cut into $1^1/2$ inch wide strips, and serve at once.

8 to 10 portions

SANGRÍA

Sangría is the popular sparkling drink from Spain. Favored in warm weather, this refreshing cooler combines red wine, fruit juices, sparkling water, and chunks of fruit.

1 (750 ml) bottle dry red wine
1/4 cup superfine sugar
1 cup sparkling water
1 cup orange juice
2 tablespoons lemon juice
1 ripe peach, pitted and sliced into thin wedges
6 strawberries, hulled and halved
4 thin orange slices with the rind
ice cubes

1. In a large glass pitcher, combine the wine, sugar, water, orange juice, and lemon juice. Mix well until the sugar dissolves.

2. Add the peach wedges, strawberries, and orange slices and stir well. Refrigerate until ready to serve.

3. When ready to serve, pour over ice in large wine glasses.

6 large drinks

CURRIED NUTS

Nuts are definite cocktail fare. Easy to prepare, these peanuts are peppered with curry powder and perfect for casual munching!

1 pound salted cocktail peanuts (not dry roasted) or cashew nuts
1¹/₂ teaspoons curry powder
1 teaspoon ground cumin
2 teaspoons superfine sugar

1. Put the peanuts in a large bowl.

2. In a separate small bowl, mix the curry, cumin, and sugar until evenly combined.

3. Sprinkle the spice mix over the nuts and toss well until the nuts are evenly coated with the seasonings. Store in an airtight container for up to 2 weeks.

3 cups

LUNCH BOX
TREATS

Curried Nuts
. . .
Blue Cheese-Cheddar
Wafers
. . .
Chocolate Chip-
Peanut Butter Muffins
. . .
Max's Vanilla
Cupcakes
. . .
Macadamia Nut
Fudge

CHILI-SPICED MIXED NUTS

These party nuts are addictive nibbles. Pecans, almonds, and walnuts are coated in a sugary, chili-flavored crust. The subtle melding of sweet and spicy results in a blast of flavor! These make a welcome gift, especially at holiday time.

2¹/₂ cups mixed nuts—almonds, pecans, and walnuts
¹/₃ cup sugar
1¹/₂ teaspoons chili powder
1 teaspoon coarse salt
¹/₂ teaspoon ground cumin
heaping ¹/₄ teaspoon cayenne pepper
¹/₄ teaspoon garlic powder
1 egg white from an extra-large egg

1. Preheat the oven to 300°.

2. Put the nuts in a large bowl.

3. In a separate small bowl, mix the sugar, chili powder, salt, cumin, cayenne, garlic powder, and egg white until evenly combined.

4. Pour the seasoning mix over the nuts and toss well. Spread the nuts out in a single layer on a non-stick cookie sheet.

5. Bake for 30 minutes, stirring every 10 minutes. Remove from the oven and stir once more. Let cool and store in a tin for up to 2 weeks.

2¹/₂ cups

PROSCIUTTO-WRAPPED FIGS

The complementary flavors in these roll-ups are exquisite—sweet figs, tangy goat cheese, and salty ham.

18 fresh or dried Calimyrna figs, stems removed
¼ cup balsamic vinegar
4 ounces chèvre
18 paper-thin slices of prosciutto

1. Macerate the figs in the balsamic for 30 minutes. Drain, then slice each fig almost in half lengthwise, leaving the bottom end attached.

2. Stuff each fig with 1 teaspoon goat cheese. Press to close.

3. Wrap each with a slice of prosciutto and secure with a toothpick. Serve at room temperature.

18 figs; allow 3 per person

ELEGANT
EVENING

Prosciutto-Wrapped
Figs
· · ·
Salmon with Pesto
Crumbs
· · ·
Boston Lettuce,
Mushroom, and
Fennel Salad
· · ·
Coffee Mascarpone-
Raspberry Tart

PRUNES PURCELL

These dried plums are stuffed with peanut butter, wrapped in bacon, and baked to a turn. The marriage of flavors in these sweet, savory morsels adds a new dimension to the hors d'oeuvre hour.

24 large, pitted prunes, split almost in half
about 1/2 cup super chunk peanut butter
8 slices bacon, cut into thirds

1. Preheat the oven to 375°.

2. Stuff each prune with about 1 teaspoon of peanut butter. Press together to close. Wrap each prune with 1/3 piece of bacon and secure with a toothpick.

3. Place the stuffed prunes on a baking sheet. Bake for 10 minutes; turn the prunes over and bake for 5 to 10 minutes more until the bacon is cooked and golden. Drain on paper towels and serve.

24 tidbits; allow 2 to 3 per person

DEVILED EGGS REMOULADE

Deviled eggs are an American facvorite. These hard-boiled egg whites are plumped with a piquant, zesty remoulade-flavored filling lush with diced shallots, capers, and cornichons.

6 hard-boiled eggs, shelled
1 tablespoon Dijon mustard
1 tablespoon mayonnaise
1 tablespoon capers
1 tablespoon minced celery
1 tablespoon minced cornichons
2 tablespoons minced shallots
salt and freshly ground pepper to taste
1 teaspoon dried tarragon
1 teaspoon tarragon vinegar

1. Slice the eggs in half lengthwise and remove the yolks. Place the yolks in a bowl and set the whites aside.

2. Mash the yolks with a fork. Add the remaining ingredients and mix well.

3. Spoon the mixture into the reserved egg whites, filling each cavity generously. Serve at room temperature.

12 stuffed egg halves

BRIDAL BRUNCH

Deviled Eggs
Remoulade
. . .
Mango-Lime
Smoothies
. . .
Assorted Bagels
. . .
Cream Cheese
. . .
Salmon Gefilte Fish
. . .
Sliced Tomatoes,
Cucumbers, and Red
Onions
. . .
Blueberry Cheesecake
Bread Pudding

CURRIED CHUTNEY-STUFFED EGGS

Chutney is a spicy Indian condiment resplendent with fruit, vinegar, sugar, and spices. It is a wonderful counterpoint to the curry in these tasty stuffed eggs. Marvelous as an hors d'oeuvre, these tasty morsels also double as a favored picnic food.

6 hard-boiled eggs, shelled
1/4 cup mango chutney
2 tablespoons mayonnaise
salt and freshly ground pepper to taste
3/4 teaspoon curry powder
paprika for garnish

1. Slice the eggs in half lengthwise and remove the yolks. Place the yolks in a bowl and set the whites aside.

2. Mash the yolks with a fork. Add the chutney, mayonnaise, salt, pepper, and curry and mix well.

3. Spoon the mixture into the reserved whites, mounding the filling in each cavity. Dust with paprika. Serve at room temperature.

12 stuffed egg halves

HERB-MARINATED BUFFALO MOZZARELLA

Bite-size pieces of fresh mozzarella are infused with an herb-scented olive oil. After eating the cheese morsels, the scented oil makes a wonderful dipping sauce for baguettes and country breads.

1 pound fresh or buffalo mozzarella, cut into 3/4-inch pieces
3 tablespoons extra-virgin olive oil
salt and freshly ground pepper to taste
1/2 teaspoon dried basil
1/2 teaspoon dried marjoram
1/2 teaspoon dried oregano
1/4 teaspoon crushed red pepper flakes

1. Put the mozzarella in a bowl. Drizzle with the olive oil and sprinkle with the seasonings. Mix well until evenly coated.

2. Let marinate at room temperature for 1 hour and as much as overnight in the refrigerator. Serve at room temperature with crostini.

6 to 8 portions

CHICKEN LIVERS YAKITORI

This classic Japanese dish showcases skewered chicken livers and scallions glazed in a honey-soy sauce. The dish also works well with pieces of boneless chicken.

1/2 cup soy sauce
1/4 cup mirin (available in Oriental markets)
1/4 cup honey
1 pound chicken livers, cut in half
1 bunch scallions, cut into 2-inch lengths

1. Combine the soy sauce, mirin, and honey in a small saucepan and bring to a boil. Lower the heat and simmer for 10 to 15 minutes until the mixture is reduced to half its volume. Let cool. (This may be done up to 24 hours in advance and refrigerated.)

2. Alternate the chicken livers and pieces of scallion on skewers. Pour the cooled sauce over the skewered food.

3. Grill over hot coals, 4 inches from the heat source, 3 to 5 minutes per side, basting with the sauce, until cooked and charred. Serve hot off the grill or let cool to room temperature.

2 main course portions; 4 to 5 appetizer portions

ASPARAGUS BUNDLES

The bright green stalks of the prized perennial plant are big on flavor. When asparagus spears are draped with prosciutto and laced with shaved Parmesan, it's simple perfection. This also makes a lovely presentation as a springtime salad.

1 pound mature asparagus, peeled, and poached for 5 minutes until
*   tender-crisp*
1/4 pound thinly sliced prosciutto
1/4 cup shaved Parmigiano-Reggiano cheese
1 1/2 tablespoons extra-virgin olive oil
freshly ground pepper to taste

1. Divide the asparagus spears into 4 portions.

2. Drape 1 to 2 pieces of prosciutto over each bundle. Sprinkle each with Parmesan, drizzle with olive oil, and season with pepper. Serve at room temperature.

4 portions

SPECIAL
OCCASION
DINNER

Asparagus Bundles
. . .
Soft-Shell Crab
Remoulade
. . .
Corn Soufflé
. . .
Romaine with
Tomato Relish
. . .
Fruits with
Raspberry Sauce

STUFFED ARTICHOKE BOTTOMS

Artichokes are the consummate vegetable for stuffing. I've stream-lined the idea by utilizing only the bottoms of this thistle plant. The cup-like shape of the bottoms provides the perfect vessel to house a mouth-watering bread stuffing resplendent with garlic, Parmesan cheese, pine nuts, and capers. Baked until golden, these pop-in-the-mouth morsels are truly a Tuscan treat.

1 cup fresh French bread crumbs
2 tablespoons pine nuts
1 tablespoon capers
1 medium-size clove garlic, crushed
freshly ground pepper to taste
1/4 cup grated Parmigiano-Reggiano cheese
2 tablespoons finely chopped parsley
6 tablespoon extra-virgin olive oil
2 (14-ounce) cans artichoke bottoms, rinsed and drained

1. Preheat the oven to 400°.

2. In a bowl, combine the bread crumbs, pine nuts, capers, garlic, pepper, Parmesan, parsley, and olive oil. Mix well until evenly moist.

3. Mound the filling in each artichoke bottom, pressing the stuffing firmly in place. Place on a baking sheet.

4. Bake for 10 minutes until golden. Serve hot out of the oven or at room temperature.

6 portions

CORN CAKES WITH SOUR CREAM AND CAVIAR

Corn is an all-American food. These pancakes sport a cornmeal base dotted with corn kernels for double-delicious flavor. Garnished with dollops of sour cream and caviar, they are a gastronomic treat. They're also tasty when served with a maple-sour cream topping for breakfast or brunch.

^{1}/2 cup cornmeal
^{1}/3 cup all-purpose flour
1 teaspoon sugar
^{1}/2 teaspoon baking powder
^{1}/2 teaspoon baking soda
^{1}/2 teaspoon salt
1 egg, beaten
^{3}/4 cup buttermilk
^{2}/3 cup corn kernels
4 tablespoons vegetable oil

Garnishes:
^{1}/2 cup sour cream
2-ounce jar black lumpfish caviar

1. In a large bowl, combine the cornmeal, flour, sugar, baking powder, baking soda, and salt and mix well.

2. In a separate small bowl, stir together the egg, buttermilk, and corn kernels.

3. Add the corn mixture to the dry ingredients, mixing well.

4. Heat 2 tablespoons of oil in a large skillet. Using 2 tablespoons of batter, pour circles of the corn mixture onto the hot pan. Sauté over medium heat until golden on both sides, about 2 minutes per side. Remove to a baking sheet and keep warm in a low oven. Repeat with the remaining oil and batter. (These may be made in advance and refrigerated; return to room temperature before reheating in a 350° oven.)

5. Serve with dollops of sour cream and caviar.

14 corn cakes; 6 to 7 portions

EGG FOO YUNG

Akin to the western omelet, these crispy, Oriental egg pancakes are rich with Asian ingredients. They don't have to be limited to hors d'oeuvre time, they also make a delicious choice for brunch or luncheon.

8 eggs, beaten
salt and freshly ground pepper to taste
1 tablespoon mirin (available in Oriental markets)
1 cup coarsely chopped cooked shrimp
2 cups beansprouts
1/4 pound shiitake mushrooms, stems removed and very thinly sliced
1 cup coarsely chopped scallions
5 tablespoons vegetable oil

1. In a large bowl, combine the eggs, salt, pepper, mirin, shrimp, beansprouts, mushrooms, and scallions and mix well.

2. In a large non-stick skillet, heat $2^1/_2$ tablespoons oil. When hot, add large spoonfuls of the egg mixture, forming the batter into 4-inch rounds. Cook over medium heat until browned on both sides. Keep warm in a low oven while repeating with the remaining oil and batter. Serve hot with duck sauce. (These may be made in advance and reheated in a 400° oven for 5 to 10 minutes.)

12 cakes; allow 2 per person

ROQUEFORT-STUFFED MUSHROOMS

Stuffed mushrooms are the darlings of finger foods! These deep-flavored creminis house a glorious, creamy blue cheese and walnut filling. As well as being a fabulous hors d'oeuvre, they also make a delightful garnish for a green salad.

1/2 cup crumbled Roquefort cheese
1/4 cup cream cheese, at room temperature
1/4 cup toasted walnuts, ground
16 large cremini mushrooms, stems removed

1. Preheat the oven to 400°. Grease a baking sheet.

2. In a small bowl, combine the cheeses and nuts and mix well.

3. Fill each mushroom cap with a heaping spoonful of the cheese mixture. Place the filled caps on the baking sheet.

4. Bake for 10 minutes. Serve hot out of the oven or at room temperature.

16 caps; allow 2 to 3 per person

GRAZING PARTY

Artichoke Pillows
. . .
Roquefort-Stuffed
Mushrooms
. . .
Grilled Shrimp with
Pesto Mayonnaise
. . .
Olive Puffs
. . .
Hearty Lentil Soup

STUFFED PORTOBELLOS

Portobellos, the granddaddy of the mushroom kingdom, are rich and meaty. These giant roasted caps sport a crabmeat, cheese, and roasted pepper filling. They are a great first course, a lavish luncheon, or special dinner fare.

1/2 pound crabmeat
2/3 cup grated Romano cheese
2 scallions, chopped
1 medium-size roasted red pepper, chopped
1/2 cup mayonnaise
freshly ground pepper to taste
6 large portobello caps (4- to 5-inches in diameter), stems removed
6 tablespoons fresh French bread crumbs

1. Preheat the oven to 400°. Grease a large baking sheet.

2. In a bowl, combine the crabmeat, cheese, scallions, roasted pepper, mayonnaise, and pepper and mix well.

3. Mound the filling on each cap. Place the stuffed mushrooms on the baking sheet.

4. Sprinkle the top of each mushroom with 1 tablespoon of bread crumbs.

5. Bake for 20 minutes until browned and bubbly. Serve at once.

3 main-course portions; 6 appetizer portions

ROASTED PORTOBELLOS WITH TOMATO RELISH

GARDEN MEAL

Bruschetta with Dried
Fruit Mascarpone
. . .
Roasted Portobellos
with Tomato Relish
. . .
Israeli Couscous
. . .
Green Beans and
Jicama

Roasting portobellos brings out the rich, intense flavor of these giant mushrooms. The piquant cherry tomato relish further enhances its extraordinary taste.

Tomato Relish:
1 cup quartered cherry tomatoes
1/2 cup coarsely chopped Italian parsley
1 tablespoon capers
salt and freshly ground pepper to taste
1 tablespoon balsamic vinegar
1 tablespoon extra-virgin olive oil

salt and freshly ground pepper to taste
1 tablespoon balsamic vinegar
2 tablespoons extra-virgin olive oil
4 medium-size portobello caps (5-inches in diameter), stems removed
1/4 cup freshly shaved Parmesan cheese

1. Make the Tomato Relish. In a bowl, combine the tomatoes, parsley, capers, salt, pepper, balsamic, and olive oil and mix well. Set aside for flavors to mellow.

2. Preheat the oven to 400°.

3. In a small bowl, whisk together the salt, pepper, balsamic, and olive oil.

4. Brush all surfaces of the mushrooms with the vinaigrette. Place the caps on a baking pan, gill side down.

5. Roast for 20 minutes until tender. Remove to a platter and drizzle with any pan juices. Serve warm or at room temperature topped with spoonfuls of Tomato Relish and sprinkled with shaved Parmesan.

4 portions

SCALLION PANCAKES

These delectable Oriental pancakes are rich with scallions, peppers, and shrimp. They're especially good served with duck sauce. Use the batter as soon as it is mixed, as it gets very thick if left to sit.

1 cup all-purpose flour
1/4 cup cornstarch
1 teaspoon salt
1 cup water
1 egg, beaten
4 scallions, cut into 2-inch lengths
1/4 large green pepper, cut into thin julienne slices
1/4 large red pepper, cut into thin julienne slices
1/4 pound cooked shrimp, chopped (you may substitute crabmeat)
1/4 cup vegetable oil

1. In a large bowl, combine the flour, cornstarch, salt, water, and egg and mix well.

2. Add the scallions, peppers, and shrimp and stir until evenly combined.

3. Heat 2 tablespoons oil in a large non-stick skillet. When hot, add 4 large spoonfuls of batter to the pan. Sauté over medium heat until golden on both sides. Transfer to a baking sheet and keep warm in a low oven. Repeat with the remaining oil and batter. Serve at once with duck sauce.

8 pancakes

POTATO AND GOAT CHEESE FRITTATA

Frittatas are the Italian equivalent to the omelet. The only difference being that the frittata has the ingredients mixed into the eggs rather than folded inside like the omelet. The round egg pie is every bit as delicious and boasts endless combinations of fillings.

1 pound red-skinned potatoes, thinly sliced
2 tablespoons olive oil (not extra-virgin)
salt and freshly ground pepper to taste
2 roasted red peppers, cut into $^1/_2$-inch wide strips
8 eggs
5 ounces goat cheese, crumbled

1. Preheat the oven to 450°. Grease a 9-inch deep-dish pie pan.

2. Layer the potatoes in the pan, drizzling each layer with olive oil and seasoning with salt and pepper.

3. Bake for 30 minutes until the potatoes are tender.

4. Lower the heat to 400°.

5. Arrange the peppers over the potatoes.

6. Beat the eggs and season with salt and pepper. Stir in the goat cheese. Pour the mixture over the peppers.

7. Bake for 20 minutes until puffed and golden. Cut into wedges and serve at once.

6 portions

LUNCH FOR 6

Green Beans and
Tomatoes with Green
Olive Vinaigrette
. . .
Assorted Rolls
. . .
Potato and Goat
Cheese Frittata
. . .
Ginger Crisps
. . .
Lemon Sorbet

MUSHROOM FRITTATA

This egg pie is one of my absolute favorites! The frittata showcases a riot of sautéed, wild mushrooms laced with Provolone cheese and baked until puffed and golden.

BRUNCH BUFFET

Bruschetta with
Chèvre and Smoked
Salmon
· · ·
Mocha Latte
Smoothies
· · ·
Cinnamon-Pecan
Scones
· · ·
Cranberry-Nut Scones
· · ·
Mushroom Frittata

4 tablespoons olive oil (not extra-virgin)
3/4 pound assorted mushrooms (cremini and shiitake), sliced
salt and freshly ground pepper to taste
3/4 teaspoon dried thyme
1 large clove garlic, minced
10 eggs
1/2 cup grated provolone cheese

1. Preheat the oven to 400°. Grease a 9-inch deep-dish pie pan.

2. Heat the oil in a large skillet. Add the mushrooms, season with salt, pepper, and thyme and sauté over medium heat until golden, about 10 to 15 minutes, stirring occasionally. Add the garlic and sauté 1 minute more. Set aside.

3. In a large bowl, beat the eggs. Season with salt and pepper. Add the sautéed mushrooms and cheese and mix well. Turn into the prepared pan.

4. Bake about 20 minutes until puffed and golden. Cut into wedges and serve at once.

6 to 8 portions

LITTLE
SEAFOOD BITES

DEVILED CRAB CAKES

Deviled recipes are seasoned with spicy ingredients. These light, plump cakes are infused with Dijon, Worcestershire sauce, cayenne, and Old Bay Seasoning, lending zip and sparkle to the crab. They're sautéed until golden and served up with dollops of red pepper mayonnaise.

1 pound crabmeat
¹/₄ cup finely diced onion
¹/₃ cup finely diced red pepper
1 egg, beaten
¹/₂ cup mayonnaise
1¹/₂ cups fresh bread crumbs
1 tablespoon Dijon mustard
1 teaspoon Worcestershire sauce
1 teaspoon Old Bay Seasoning
generous pinch of cayenne pepper
freshly ground pepper to taste
¹/₄ cup olive oil (not extra-virgin)
Red Pepper Mayonnaise (recipe follows)

1. In a large bowl, combine the crabmeat, onion, red pepper, egg, mayonnaise, ¹/₂ cup bread crumbs, Dijon, Worcestershire, Old Bay, cayenne, and pepper and mix until evenly blended.

2. Form the mixture into 8 equal-sized cakes. Dip each cake in the remaining 1 cup bread crumbs, coating completely. Refrigerate for 1 hour—this helps the crumbs to adhere better.

3. Heat 2 tablespoons oil in a large skillet. Add half of the cakes and sauté over medium heat until golden brown on both sides, about 3 to 4 minutes per side. Keep warm in a 300° oven while cooking the remaining cakes in the remaining oil. Serve with dollops of the Red Pepper Mayonnaise.

4 main-course portions; 8 appetizer portions

Red Pepper Mayonnaise:
2 red peppers, roasted and puréed
¹/₂ cup mayonnaise
generous pinch of cayenne pepper
salt and pepper to taste

Combine all of the ingredients and mix well. Store in the refrigerator until needed. (This will keep for 1 week.)

HERRING WITH MUSTARD SAUCE

Jarred herring is actually pickled herring that has been marinated in vinegar and spices before being bottled in a wine sauce. The process not only preserves the herring, but also lends a delicate flavor to the fish. When napped with a dill-mustard sauce, the herring is glorious.

16-ounce jar herring in wine sauce
1 tablespoon sugar
2 tablespoons Dijon mustard
1/2 teaspoon freshly ground pepper
2 tablespoons chopped fresh dill
2 tablespoons olive oil (not extra-virgin)

1. Drain the wine sauce from the herring, reserving 2 tablespoons.

2. Put the herring in a bowl.

3. In a separate bowl, whisk together the reserved herring sauce, sugar, Dijon, pepper, dill, and olive oil until thick and creamy.

4. Pour the mustard sauce over the herring, toss well, and let marinate for 1 to 2 hours for flavors to mellow. (This may be made up to 24 hours in advance and refrigerated; return to room temperature to serve.) Present with French bread rounds.

4 portions

LABOR DAY
BRUNCH

Assorted Bagels
· · ·
Cream Cheese
· · ·
Gravlax*
· · ·
Herring with
Mustard Sauce
· · ·
Cucumber Salad
· · ·
Spinach, Feta, and
Rice Bake
· · ·
Fruits with
Raspberry Sauce
· · ·
Streusel Coffeecake

GRILLED MUSSELS GREEN GODDESS

All shellfish are delicious grilled; mussels are no exception. They go directly on the grill in their shell and pop open when done. Served up with dollops of creamy, tarragon-scented green goddess dressing, you're treated to a feast. Any extra sauce makes a savory dressing for a green salad.

Green Goddess Sauce:
3/4 cup mayonnaise
3/4 cup sour cream
1/4 cup thinly sliced scallions
1/4 cup chopped fresh parsley
salt and freshly ground pepper to taste
1 clove garlic, minced
1 teaspoon anchovy paste
1 teaspoon dried tarragon
2 tablespoons tarragon vinegar

4 pounds mussels, scrubbed and debearded

1. In a bowl, combine all of the ingredients of the Green Goddess Sauce and mix well. Cover and refrigerate for 1 to 2 hours for flavors to blend.

2. Put the mussels in a grill basket and place on the grill over a hot fire. (You can also place the shellfish directly on the grill rack.) Grill until the shells pop open—this will only take 3 or 4 minutes. Remove the mussels when they are done. Discard any unopened ones.

3. Serve with the Green Goddess Sauce.

4 to 6 portions

SALMON GEFILTE FISH

Gefilte fish is a popular Jewish dish traditionally served at holiday time. It is actually ground fish mixed with egg, matzo meal, and seasonings which is then formed into balls and simmered in a fish stock, much like quenelles. Left to chill, they are then dressed up with red horseradish. Carp, whitefish, or pike are the classic choices for these fish balls, but I've taken the liberty of using salmon for a more delicate rendition. This also makes a lovely luncheon dish.

Stock:
1 salmon fish head
2 carrots, sliced into ¹/₂-inch thick rounds
1 large Spanish onion, sliced into ¹/₄-inch thick rings
1 tablespoon sugar
1 tablespoon salt
6 peppercorns
3 quarts water

3 pounds salmon filets, skinned, boned, and cut into 1-inch chunks
1 Spanish onion, cut into 1-inch chunks
3 eggs, beaten
2 teaspoons salt
white pepper to taste
¹/₂ cup matzo meal

1. Put all of the stock ingredients in a large stockpot. Bring to a boil, cover, lower the heat, and simmer for 20 minutes. Remove the fish head and skim if necessary.

2. While the stock is cooking, prepare the fish balls. Put the salmon in the bowl of a food processor and finely grind the fish. Transfer to a large bowl.

3. Put the onion in the bowl of the food processor and pulse until finely chopped—do not purée!

4. Add the onion, eggs, salt, pepper, and matzo meal to the salmon and mix well. With moistened hands, use ¹/₄ cup of fish and form into loose balls. Do not pack the mixture tightly as you want the balls to be fluffy.

BRIDAL BRUNCH

Deviled Eggs
Remoulade
. . .
Mango-Lime
Smoothies
. . .
Assorted Bagels
. . .
Cream Cheese
. . .
Salmon Gefilte Fish
. . .
Sliced Tomatoes,
Cucumbers, and
Red Onions
. . .
Blueberry Cheesecake
Bread Pudding

5. Return the stock to a simmer and gently add the fish balls. Simmer over low heat for 30 minutes until the fish balls are cooked through. Transfer the balls to a serving dish. Boil the stock until slightly reduced; then pour the stock over the salmon. Refrigerate for 6 hours or overnight until chilled. Serve at room temperature with horseradish.

30 fish balls; allow 2 per person

SARDINE PUFFS

Sardines will no longer be regarded as those salty or uninteresting little fish! With their packed in deviled flavor, these darlings will disappear like soap bubbles.

3³/₄- to 4³/₄-ounce can sardines, drained and mashed
2 tablespoons finely diced red onion
1¹/₂ tablespoons finely chopped fresh parsley
¹/₄ cup mayonnaise
1¹/₂ tablespoons Dijon mustard
1 tablespoon lemon juice
5 drops Tabasco sauce
3 English muffins, split in half

1. Preheat the oven to 400°.

2. In a bowl, combine the sardines, onion, parsley, mayonnaise, Dijon, lemon juice, and Tabasco and mix well.

3. Spread the mixture evenly atop the English muffin halves. Cut each half into quarters and place them on a baking sheet.

4. Bake for 12 to 15 minutes until puffed and golden. Serve piping hot.

24 puffs; 6 portions

WINE AND . . .

Seeded Pita Wedges
. . .
Sardine Puffs
. . .
Coconut Shrimp with
Mango-Lime Coulis
. . .
Prosciutto-Wrapped
Figs

SCALLOPS SEVICHE

Seviche is a Latin American dish that consists of raw fish marinated in lime juice. The citrus juice actually "cooks" the fish by firming the flesh and turning it opaque. I've enlivened the cooked fish with flavors particular to South-of-the-Border—onion, garlic, jalapeño, and cilantro.

1 pound sea scallops, quartered
$3/4$ cup lime juice
1 medium-size clove garlic, minced
salt and freshly ground pepper to taste
1 jalapeño pepper, seeded and minced
$1/3$ cup thinly sliced red onion
$1/2$ cup loosely packed fresh cilantro, coarsely chopped
2 tablespoons olive oil

1. In a Pyrex or glass bowl, combine the scallops and lime juice. Cover and refrigerate for 6 hours for seafood to "cook". Drain well.

2. In a separate bowl, combine the garlic, salt, pepper, jalapeño, onion, cilantro, and olive oil and mix well.

3. Pour the sauce over the scallops, toss well, and serve.

4 portions

GRILLED SHRIMP WITH PESTO MAYONNAISE

The simplicity of this dish makes it absolutely exquisite!

1/2 cup mayonnaise
1/4 cup pesto (see page 12)
2 pounds raw extra-large shrimp, shelled
2 tablespoons extra-virgin olive oil
salt and freshly ground pepper to taste

1. Make the pesto mayonnaise. In a small bowl, combine the mayonnaise and pesto and mix well. Set aside.

2. Skewer the shrimp. Drizzle with the olive oil and season with salt and pepper.

3. Grill over hot coals, 4 inches from the heat source, about 2 minutes per side, until shrimp turn pink and are lightly charred. (If you wish, you may poach the shrimp rather than grill them.) Remove to a platter and serve with the pesto mayonnaise.

10 to 12 portions

GRAZING PARTY

Artichoke Pillows
· · ·
Roquefort-Stuffed Mushrooms
· · ·
Grilled Shrimp with Pesto Mayonnaise
· · ·
Olive Puffs
· · ·
Hearty Lentil Soup

SHRIMP POPPERS

Poached shrimp are stuffed with a zippy jalapeno cream cheese for those who like it hot!

16 extra-large shrimp, shelled and poached
4 ounces cream cheese, at room temperature
1 large jalapeño pepper, seeded and finely minced
1¹/₂ tablespoons snipped chives

1. On the outer side of each shrimp, slice the shellfish lengthwise, almost in half.

2. In a small bowl, mix together the cream cheese, jalapeño, and chives.

3. Stuff each shrimp with 1¹/2 teaspoons of the cream cheese mixture. Press the shrimp together gently, arrange them on a platter, and serve. (These may be prepared 6 to 8 hours in advance and refrigerated; return to room temperature to serve.)

16 poppers; allow 2 to 3 per person

COCONUT SHRIMP WITH MANGO-LIME COULIS

A sweet, crispy coconut crust adds zip to these shrimp, lending a taste of the tropics. They're further enhanced with a lime-infused mango purée.

> 1 pound raw extra-large shrimp, shelled
> salt and pepper to taste
> 1 egg, beaten
> 1¹/₃ cups sweetened, shredded coconut
> 5 tablespoons butter
> Mango Coulis (recipe follows)

1. Season the shrimp with salt and pepper. Dip the shrimp in the egg, then roll in the coconut to coat completely. Place on a cookie sheet and refrigerate for 30 minutes to help the coconut adhere.

2. Heat the butter in a large non-stick skillet. Add the shrimp and sauté over medium heat, 2 to 3 minutes per side until golden. Serve at once with the Mango Coulis.

4 to 6 portions

> *Mango Coulis:*
> 1 ripe mango, peeled, pitted, and puréed
> 1 teaspoon finely grated lime peel
> 1 tablespoon lime juice
> 1 tablespoon snipped chives
> 1 tablespoon finely chopped fresh cilantro
> salt and freshly ground pepper to taste

Combine all of the ingredients and mix well. Refrigerate until needed. Serve at room temperature.

WINE AND . . .

Seeded Pita Wedges
. . .
Sardine Puffs
. . .
Coconut Shrimp with Mango-Lime Coulis
. . .
Prosciutto-Wrapped Figs

TUNA TARTARE

This dish is sushi at its flavor-packed best. Cubes of tuna, cucumber, and chopped scallions are coated with an Oriental ginger-sesame topping. Remember raw fish is very rich, so less is more!

1 pound very fresh sushi-grade tuna, diced into $1/2$-inch cubes
1 cup seedless cucumber, diced into $1/2$-inch cubes
$1/3$ cup thinly sliced scallions
salt and freshly ground pepper to taste
1 tablespoon grated gingerroot
1 tablespoon sesame seeds, toasted
2 tablespoons soy sauce
1 tablespoon Oriental sesame oil

1. Place the tuna, cucumber, and scallions in a large bowl.

2. In a separate small bowl, mix together the salt, pepper, gingerroot, sesame seeds, soy, and sesame oil.

3. Pour the dressing over the fish mixture, stir until evenly combined, and serve at once on a bed of lettuce.

5 to 6 portions

TUNA MOUSSE

Quick and easy to prepare, this lush and creamy tuna purée struts a tasty Dijon, caper, and balsamic embellishment. This makes a wonderful topping for bruschetta as well as a lusty dip for crudités.

> 6-ounce can tuna, drained
> salt and freshly ground pepper to taste
> 1 tablespoon Dijon mustard
> 1 tablespoon capers
> $1^1/2$ tablespoons balsamic vinegar
> 2 tablespoons olive oil (not extra-virgin)
> $^1/4$ cup heavy cream

1. Put all of the ingredients in the bowl of a food processor and purée until smooth and creamy.

2. Transfer to a bowl and serve with bruschetta. (This may be made up to 8 hours in advance and refrigerated; return to room temperature to serve.)

scant $1^1/4$ cups

THE FLAVORS
OF ITALY

Tuna Mousse
. . .
Penne with Fennel,
Onion, and Artichokes
. . .
5-Star Chopped Salad
. . .
Red and Green Grapes

SENSATIONAL SMOOTHIES

Smoothies are definitely in vogue. They're those luscious, thick, tall, fruity drinks. We can't get enough of them, whether for breakfast, morning snack, or as an energy booster. These refreshing drinks are put together in moments, with just a whirl in a blender or food processor.

Rather than add ice to smoothies, which waters them down as they sit, I add chopped fruit that's been frozen. This provides the necessary quick chill and gives the smoothies their characteristic thick consistency. Use the freshest fruits of the season for peak flavor and enjoyment.

BANANA-RUM RAISIN SMOOTHIE

MID-DAY
PICK-ME-UP

Banana-Rum Raisin
Smoothie
. . .
Peanut Butter-White
Chocolate Chippers

For a special occasion brunch, serve this blissful sipper that's both comforting and delicious. The blend of banana, raisins, and dark rum is sure to enlighten the day.

$1/3$ cup raisins
$1/4$ cup dark rum
1 large banana, peeled, sliced into $1/2$ inch rounds, and frozen until firm
2 cups nonfat vanilla yogurt
$1/2$ teaspoon vanilla

1. Plump the raisins in the rum for at least 30 minutes, and as much as overnight.

2. Put all of the ingredients in a blender or food processor and purée.

3. Pour into tall glasses and serve at once.

2 portions

BLUEBERRY SMOOTHIE

The delightful combination of blueberries and maple syrup makes this smoothie a breakfast treat. Try it teamed with pancakes or waffles.

2 cups blueberries, frozen
1 cup nonfat blueberry yogurt
1/2 cup low-fat milk
1 tablespoon maple syrup

1. Put all of the ingredients in a blender or food processor and purée.
2. Pour into tall glasses and serve at once.

2 portions

AFTERNOON SNACK

Blueberry Smoothie
. . .
Coconut-Currant Scones

MIXED BERRY SMOOTHIE

Whether picking your own summer berries or buying them at a produce stand, save some to enjoy in this fruit-filled, flavor-packed, blueberry and raspberry smoothie.

1 cup blueberries, frozen
1 cup raspberries, frozen
2 cups strawberry sorbet
1 cup low-fat boysenberry yogurt

1. Put all of the ingredients in a blender or food processor and purée.
2. Pour into tall glasses and serve at once.

3 portions

STRAWBERRY-BANANA SMOOTHIE

Lush with fresh strawberries, rich with bananas, and sweetened with honey, this smoothie remains the number one favorite of all.

1 cup hulled and chopped strawberries, frozen until firm
2 large bananas, peeled, sliced, and frozen until firm
1 cup nonfat vanilla yogurt
³/4 cup low-fat milk
1 tablespoon honey

1. Put all of the ingredients in a blender or food processor and purée.

2. Pour into tall glasses and serve at once.

3 portions

BREAKFAST BONANZA

Strawberry-Banana
Smoothie
· · ·
Granola**

STRAWBERRY DAIQUIRI SMOOTHIE

AFTERNOON REFRESHER

Strawberry Daiquiri
Smoothies
. . .
Lemon Icebox
Cookies
. . .
Ginger Crisps

Exotic and tropical, this frothy strawberry, lime, and rum drink will set your taste buds dancing.

> 2 cups strawberries, hulled, chopped, and frozen until firm
> 2 cups strawberry sorbet
> 1/4 cup light rum
> 2 tablespoons lime juice
> 1 tablespoon light corn syrup

1. Put all of the ingredients in a blender or food processor and purée.

2. Pour into tall glasses and serve at once.

2 portions

WIMBLEDON SMOOTHIE

This smoothie captures the luscious flavors of the strawberries and cream theme that has become the classic at the famous tennis tournament.

2 cups strawberries, hulled, chopped, and frozen until firm
2 cups strawberry sorbet
1 cup nonfat vanilla yogurt
$^1/_4$ cup low-fat milk
$^1/_2$ teaspoon vanilla

1. Put all of the ingredients in a blender or food processor and purée.
2. Pour into tall glasses and serve at once.

3 portions

PIÑA COLADA SMOOTHIE

SUNDAY SIPPER

Piña Colada Smoothie
. . .
Seven Layer Bars

This tropical flavored smoothie featuring pineapple and coconut is further enhanced with a splash of rum.

2 cups pineapple chunks, frozen until firm
1/3 cup sweetened, shredded coconut
1 cup nonfat vanilla yogurt
1/4 cup well-stirred coconut milk
3 tablespoons light rum

1. Put all of the ingredients in a blender or food processor and purée.
2. Pour into tall glasses and serve at once.

2 portions

HONEYDEW-LIME SMOOTHIE

The combination of honeydew melon and lime sherbet offers a refreshing pick-me-up on a hot day.

2¹/₂ cups honeydew melon chunks, frozen until firm
2 kiwis, peeled, cut into chunks, and frozen until firm
2¹/₂ cups lime sherbet
3 sprigs mint for garnish

1. Combine the fruits and sherbet in a blender or food processor and purée until smooth.

2. Pour into tall glasses, garnish each with a sprig of mint, and serve at once.

3 portions

SUMMER BREAKFAST

Honeydew-Lime Smoothie
. . .
Strawberry Muffins

MANGO-LIME SMOOTHIE

Mango and lime have a wonderful affinity which was the inspiration for this toothsome drink.

1 mango, peeled, pitted, cut into chunks, and frozen until firm
2 cups mango sorbet (if unavailable use orange sherbet)
1 tablespoon lime juice
1 teaspoon grated lime peel

1. Put all of the ingredients in a blender or food processor and purée.

2. Pour into tall glasses and serve at once.

2 portions

ORANGE CREAMSICLE SMOOTHIE

If you like creamsicles, then you'll love this divine combination of orange sherbet and vanilla yogurt.

2¹/₂ cups orange sherbet
1 cup nonfat vanilla yogurt
¹/₂ cup orange juice

1. Put all of the ingredients in a blender or food processor and purée.

2. Pour into tall glasses and serve at once.

2 portions

ALL-AMERICAN BACKYARD BARBECUE

Grilled Burgers
· · ·
All-American Potato Salad
· · ·
Sweet Pickled Vidalias
· · ·
Watermelon, Cucumber, and Jicama Salad
· · ·
Peanut Butter Swirl Brownies
· · ·
Orange Creamsicle Smoothies

PEACH MELBA SMOOTHIE

**BREAKFAST
IN BED**

Peach Melba
Smoothie
. . .
Blueberry Scones

This smoothie captures the lush flavors of summer—fragrant peaches and ruby-red raspberries—all whirled together for an irresistible treat.

> *2 medium-size peaches, skinned, pitted, chopped, and frozen until firm*
> *³/4 cup raspberries, frozen until firm*
> *¹/2 cup nonfat vanilla yogurt*
> *1 cup low-fat milk*
> *1 tablespoon raspberry preserves or jam*

1. Put all of the ingredients in a blender or food processor and purée.

2. Pour into tall glasses and serve at once.

3 portions

PEANUT BUTTER-BANANA SMOOTHIE

This smoothie struts a peanut butter, banana, and vanilla yogurt base, sweetened with honey for high energy refreshment.

1 large banana, peeled, sliced into ¹/₂-inch chunks, and frozen until firm
2 tablespoons smooth peanut butter
1 cup nonfat vanilla yogurt
¹/₄ cup low-milk
1 tablespoon honey

1. Put all of the ingredients in a blender or food processor and purée.

2. Pour into a tall glass and serve at once.

1 portion

MOCHA LATTE SMOOTHIE

This lavish espresso smoothie is a welcome relief on a hot summer's day. The rich combination of chocolate and coffee will appeal to coffee aficionados.

1 tablespoon instant espresso coffee
$1/2$ cup low-fat milk
2 cups low-fat chocolate frozen yogurt
1 cup nonfat vanilla yogurt

1. Dissolve the espresso in the milk by letting it sit at room temperature for 5 to 10 minutes.

2. Put all of the ingredients in a blender or food processor and purée.

3. Pour into tall glasses and serve at once.

2 portions

KAHLUA AND CREAM SMOOTHIE

The flavors of coffee and Kahlua come together in this decadent and most satisfying tall drink. It's a refreshing treat on a hot summer day.

2 cups coffee low-fat frozen yogurt
1 cup nonfat vanilla yogurt
¼ cup Kahlua

1. Put all of the ingredients in a blender or food processor and purée.
2. Pour into tall glasses and serve at once.

2 portions

BRUNCH IN THE GARDEN

Kahlua and Cream
Smoothies
. . .
Maple-Fig Bread
. . .
Sausages
. . .
Assorted Berries

BREAKFAST MUFFINS AND SCONES

Muffins, scones, and tea breads are glorious breakfast and brunch food. They stimulate the taste buds and make the morning meal shine. Freshly baked, they are aromatic and fragrant. Scented with spices and plump with fruits and nuts, they are the perfect companion to mugs of coffee. Serve them warm from the oven, plain or slathered with butter or jam. They're sure to start your day with a smile.

BOSTON BROWN BREAD

Dating as far back as the Pilgrims, this multi-grain quick bread is sweetened with molasses and studded with raisins. It's delicious with grilled sausages, ribs, burgers and dogs, corned beef, and stews, although it was originally intended to accompany baked beans. It's truly all-American!

$3/4$ cup all-purpose flour
$3/4$ cup cornmeal
$3/4$ cup rye flour
1 teaspoon baking soda
$1/2$ teaspoon baking powder
$1/2$ teaspoon salt
$3/4$ cup raisins
$1/2$ cup dark molasses
$1^1/2$ cups buttermilk
4 tablespoons butter, melted

1. Preheat the oven to 325°. Grease a 9 x 5-inch loaf pan.

2. In a large bowl, combine the flour, cornmeal, rye flour, baking soda, baking powder, and salt. Stir in the raisins and mix well.

3. In a separate small bowl, mix the molasses, buttermilk, and butter.

4. Add the wet ingredients to the flour mixture and mix thoroughly. Turn into the prepared pan.

5. Bake for 45 to 50 minutes until a tester inserted in the middle comes out clean. Remove to a rack to cool slightly before removing the bread from the pan. Serve warm or at room temperature with butter.

1 loaf

IRISH SODA BREAD

Fancied as an Irish classic, this buttermilk-based quick bread has won over the hearts of Americans. This version is plump with sweet, golden raisins and laced with the elusive flavor of caraway seeds. Shaped into a round, with a cross cut on the top, it makes a divine bread for breakfast or tea.

IRISH-STYLE MENU

Glazed Corned Beef
. . .
Irish Soda Bread
. . .
Indian Pudding

2 cups all-purpose flour
3 tablespoons sugar
1 teaspoon baking powder
1 teaspoon baking soda
$1/2$ teaspoon salt
3 tablespoons butter
1 cup buttermilk
2 teaspoons caraway seeds
$1/2$ cup golden raisins

1. Preheat the oven to 375°. Grease a cookie sheet.

2. In a large bowl, combine the flour, sugar, baking powder, baking soda, and salt.

3. Cut the butter into the flour mixture until the texture of peas.

4. Stir in the buttermilk, caraway, and raisins and mix well until dough forms a ball.

5. Turn the dough out onto a lightly floured board and knead 1 minute until the dough is smooth and holds together. Shape into an 8-inch round and place on the prepared baking sheet. With a sharp, floured knife, cut an "X" across the top of the bread, about $1/2$-inch deep.

6. Bake for 35 minutes until the loaf is brown and sounds hollow when tapped on the bottom. Serve hot out of the oven or transfer to a rack to cool. Slice thinly and present.

6 to 8 portions

CORNBREAD

This updated version of cornbread from *The Uncommon Gourmet* is a star-spangled winner—it's sweet, moist, and cake-like. An all-American favorite, it makes a wholesome addition to breakfast, brunch, and barbecues. It also makes a great lunch box treat and totes well to picnics. This is my family's absolute favorite!

1¹/₄ cups all-purpose flour
³/₄ cup cornmeal
³/₄ cup sugar
2 teaspoons baking powder
¹/₂ teaspoon baking soda
¹/₂ teaspoon salt
1 egg
1 cup buttermilk
1 teaspoon vanilla
¹/₄ cup vegetable oil

1. Preheat the oven to 400°. Grease an 8-inch square baking pan.

2. In a large bowl, combine the flour, cornmeal, sugar, baking powder, baking soda, and salt.

3. In a separate small bowl, whisk together the egg, buttermilk, vanilla, and oil.

4. Add the wet ingredients to the flour mixture, mixing gently only until evenly combined. Turn the mixture into the prepared pan.

5. Bake for 20 to 25 minutes until golden and a tester inserted in the center comes out clean. It's delicious warm from the oven, or transfer it to a rack to cool before serving.

9 squares

APPLESAUCE BREAD

This cake-like sweet bread is infused with applesauce and has a delicate cinnamon flavor. Fast and easy to prepare, enjoy it in the autumn when apple season is upon us.

1/2 cup butter
1/2 cup granulated sugar
1/2 cup packed dark brown sugar
2 eggs
2 teaspoons vanilla
2 cups all-purpose flour
1 teaspoon baking powder
1 teaspoon baking soda
1/4 teaspoon salt
1 teaspoon cinnamon
2 cups applesauce

1. Preheat the oven to 350°. Grease two 8 x 4-inch loaf pans.

2. In a large bowl, cream the butter and sugars until fluffy. Add the eggs and vanilla and mix well.

3. Sift together the flour, baking powder, baking soda, salt, and cinnamon. Add the dry ingredients to the batter, mixing until well blended.

4. Stir in the applesauce.

5. Turn the batter into the prepared pans.

6. Bake for 45 to 50 minutes until a tester inserted in the center comes out clean. Remove to a rack to cool in the pans for 30 minutes, then remove the breads from the pans to a rack to cool completely.

2 loaves

HOLIDAY BRUNCH

Assorted Juices—
Orange, Cranberry,
and Mango
. . .
Omelets
. . .
Bacon
. . .
Applesauce Bread
. . .
Vegetable Pancakes
. . .
Heavenly Strawberries
Adorned*

MAPLE-FIG BREAD

This fruity tea bread is packed with dried figs and pecans and laced with maple syrup. Rich in flavor, it's delicious served with cream cheese, but it's also glorious unadorned.

1/2 cup butter
1/2 cup dark brown sugar
1/2 cup pure maple syrup
2 eggs
2 cups all-purpose flour
1 1/2 teaspoons baking powder
1 teaspoon baking soda
1/2 teaspoon salt
1/2 teaspoon cinnamon
3/4 cup milk
1 1/2 cups dried figs, plumped in hot water and chopped
3/4 cup coarsely chopped pecans

1. Preheat the oven to 350°. Grease two 8 x 4-inch loaf pans.

2. In a large bowl, cream the butter and brown sugar. Add the maple syrup and eggs and mix well.

3. Sift together the flour, baking powder, baking soda, salt, and cinnamon.

4. Add the dry ingredients alternately with the milk to the batter, mixing until combined. Stir in the figs and pecans.

5. Turn the batter into the prepared pans. Bake for 45 to 50 minutes until a tester inserted in the center comes out clean. Remove to a rack to cool in the pans for 30 minutes, then remove the breads from the pans to a rack to cool completely.

2 loaves

BAKED FRENCH TOAST

In our house, French toast has become synonymous with Sunday breakfast. In this version, plump slices of country bread are soaked in a rich egg and milk bath, sweetened with brown sugar, and perfumed with vanilla. Baked to a crispy turn, it's cloaked with maple syrup and served up warm.

2 tablespoons granulated sugar
$1/2$ teaspoon cinnamon
$2/3$ cup whole milk
2 eggs
1 teaspoon vanilla
2 tablespoons packed dark brown sugar
5 slices country-style white bread or challah, cut into 1-inch thick pieces
2 tablespoons butter, melted

1. Preheat the oven to 400°. Grease a baking sheet.

2. In a small bowl, combine the sugar and cinnamon, stirring until evenly mixed. Set aside.

3. In a flat container, beat the milk, eggs, vanilla, and brown sugar.

4. Dip the bread into the custard mixture, soaking both sides well. Place on the prepared baking sheet.

5. Brush the slices with the melted butter. Sprinkle with the cinnamon-sugar mixture.

6. Bake for 20 to 25 minutes until golden. Serve warm with maple syrup.

3 to 5 portions

SUNDAY BRUNCH

Wimbledon
Smoothies
· · ·
Baked French Toast
· · ·
Bacon
· · ·
Melon Wedges

OATMEAL MUFFINS

POWER BREAKFAST

Peanut Butter-Banana
Smoothie
. . .
Oatmeal Muffins

Akin to the popular oatmeal cookie, these muffins are rich, dark, and fruity. These wholesome and nutritious morning muffins are distinguished by oatmeal, brown sugar, cinnamon, and raisins.

1/2 cup butter
1/2 cup granulated sugar
1/2 cup packed dark brown sugar
2 eggs
1 teaspoon vanilla
1 cup all-purpose flour
2 teaspoons baking soda
1/2 teaspoon salt
2 teaspoons cinnamon
1 cup buttermilk
1 cup quick oats
1/2 cup raisins dusted with 1 1/2 teaspoons flour

1. Preheat the oven to 400°. Line a 12-cup muffin pan with paper baking cups.

2. In a large bowl, cream the butter and sugars until fluffy. Add the eggs and vanilla and mix well.

3. Sift together the flour, baking soda, salt, and cinnamon. Add the dry ingredients alternately with the buttermilk to the batter.

4. Stir in the oats and raisins and mix well.

5. Spoon the batter into the muffin cups.

6. Bake for 20 minutes, until a tester inserted in the center comes out clean. Remove the muffins from the pan to a rack to cool.

12 muffins

STRAWBERRY MUFFINS

Fragrant with the lushness of ripe strawberries, these plump, fruity muffins will elevate the breakfast meal to new heights.

2 cups chopped strawberries
1/2 cup butter
1 cup sugar
2 eggs
1 teaspoon vanilla
1/2 cup sour cream
2 cups plus 2 teaspoons all-purpose flour
1 teaspoon baking powder
1/2 teaspoon baking soda
1/2 teaspoon salt
2 tablespoons sugar for garnish

1. Preheat the oven to 375°. Line a 12-cup muffin pan with paper baking cups.

2. Mash 1/2 cup of the chopped berries and set aside.

3. In a large mixing bowl, cream the butter and sugar until fluffy. Add the eggs and vanilla and mix well.

4. Stir in the sour cream and mashed berries with their juices.

5. Toss the remaining strawberries with 2 teaspoons flour.

6. Sift together the flour, baking powder, baking soda, and salt. Add the dry ingredients to the batter, stirring until evenly combined.

7. Fold in the chopped strawberries.

8. Pile the batter high into 11 of the muffin cups. Sprinkle 2 tablespoons sugar over the tops of the muffins.

9. Bake for 20 to 23 minutes, until a tester inserted in the center comes out clean. Remove the muffins from the pan to a rack to cool.

11 plump muffins

SUMMER
BREAKFAST

Honeydew-Lime
Smoothie
. . .
Strawberry Muffins

APRICOT CHEESECAKE MUFFINS

CASUAL FAMILY DINNER

Salad Mezzaluna
. . .
Baked Bluefish with
Olive Crumbs
. . .
Couscous Genovese
. . .
Apricot Cheesecake
Muffins

Apricot and almond have a wonderful affinity. These muffins strut a moist, almond-scented cream cheese batter that's dappled with apricot preserves. Once sampled, they're always savored!

1/2 cup butter
1 cup sugar
4 ounces cream cheese, at room temperature
2 eggs
1/2 cup apricot preserves
1 teaspoon vanilla
1 teaspoon almond extract
2 cups all-purpose flour
1 tablespoon baking powder
1/2 teaspoon salt
1/2 cup milk

1. Preheat the oven to 375°. Line a 12-cup muffin pan with paper baking cups.

2. In a large bowl with an electric mixer, cream the butter, sugar, and cream cheese. Add the eggs, preserves, and vanilla and almond extracts and beat until smooth.

3. Sift together the flour, baking powder, and salt. Add the dry ingredients alternately with the milk to the batter.

4. Fill each muffin cup with the batter.

5. Bake for 20 to 25 minutes, until a tester inserted in the center comes out clean. Remove the muffins from the pan to a rack to cool.

12 muffins

CHOCOLATE CHIP-PEANUT BUTTER MUFFINS

The pairing of chocolate and peanut butter is a heavenly combination. These brown sugar-sweetened muffins are similar in taste to peanut butter cookies, infused with chocolate chips for an all-time flavor treat.

1/2 cup butter
1 cup firmly packed dark brown sugar
1/2 cup super chunk peanut butter
2 eggs
1 teaspoon vanilla
1 3/4 cups all-purpose flour
2 teaspoons baking powder
1/2 teaspoon baking soda
1 teaspoon salt
3/4 cup buttermilk
2/3 cup semi-sweet chocolate chips

1. Preheat the oven to 375°. Line a 12-cup muffin pan with paper baking cups.

2. In a large bowl, cream the butter, sugar, and peanut butter. Add the eggs and vanilla and mix well.

3. Sift together the flour, baking powder, baking soda, and salt. Add the dry ingredients alternately with the buttermilk to the batter.

4. Stir in the chocolate chips.

5. Spoon the batter into the muffin cups.

6. Bake for 20 to 23 minutes, until a tester inserted in the center comes out clean. Remove the muffins from the pan to a rack to cool.

12 muffins

LUNCH BOX
TREATS

Curried Nuts
· · ·
Blue Cheese-Cheddar
Wafers
· · ·
Chocolate Chip-
Peanut Butter Muffins
· · ·
Max's Vanilla
Cupcakes
· · ·
Macadamia
Nut Fudge

CARROT CAKE MUFFINS

Related in kind to the delicious cake, these large muffins are rich with grated carrots, dotted with raisins, and swirled with a dollop of cheesecake batter. Try them at any time—for breakfast, brunch, or snack!

1/2 cup butter
1 cup sugar
2 eggs
1 teaspoon vanilla
1 1/2 cups all-purpose flour
1 teaspoon baking powder
1 teaspoon baking soda
1/2 teaspoon salt
1 teaspoon cinnamon
1/2 teaspoon ground ginger
1 1/2 cups grated carrots
1/4 cup raisins, dusted with 1 teaspoon flour
Cream Cheese Filling (recipe follows)

1. Preheat the oven to 375°. Line a 12-cup muffin pan with paper baking cups. Grease the top of the muffin pan.

2. In a large bowl, cream the butter and sugar until fluffy. Add the eggs and vanilla and mix well.

3. Sift together the flour, baking powder, baking soda, salt, cinnamon, and ginger. Add the dry ingredients to the batter.

4. Stir in the carrots and raisins.

5. Spoon the batter into 10 of the muffin cups. Wet the back of a teaspoon and use it to make a well in the top of each muffin. Put a dollop of the Cream Cheese Filling in each well.

6. Bake for 25 minutes, until a tester inserted in the center comes out clean. Use a knife to release the muffin tops from the pan; remove the muffins to a rack to cool.

10 plump muffins

Cream Cheese Filling:
4 ounces cream cheese, at room temperature
1/4 cup sugar
1 egg yolk
1/2 teaspoon vanilla

With an electric mixer, beat the cream cheese, sugar, egg yolk, and vanilla until fluffy.

LINZER TORTE MUFFINS

The flavors of the infamous torte are locked up in these luscious sour cream-laced muffins that are topped with a spoonful of raspberry preserves.

1/2 cup butter
1/2 cup sugar
2 eggs
1 1/2 cups all-purpose flour
1 1/2 teaspoons baking powder
1/4 teaspoon baking soda
1/4 teaspoon salt
1 teaspoon cinnamon
1 cup sour cream
1/4 cup toasted, slivered almonds, finely chopped
about 1/3 cup raspberry preserves

1. Preheat the oven to 375°. Line a 12-cup muffin pan with paper baking cups.

2. In a large bowl, cream the butter and sugar until fluffy. Add the eggs and mix well.

3. Sift together the flour, baking powder, baking soda, salt, and cinnamon. Add the dry ingredients alternately with the sour cream to the batter.

4. Fold in the chopped nuts.

5. Spoon the batter into 10 of the muffin cups. Wet the back of a teaspoon and use it to make a well on the top of each muffin. Fill each well with 1 1/2 teaspoons preserves.

6. Bake for about 20 minutes, until muffins are golden and a tester inserted in the center comes out clean. Remove the muffins from the pan to a rack to cool.

10 muffins

COFFEE AND . . .

Streusel-Topped
Muffins
. . .
Lemon-Poppy
Seed Biscotti
. . .
Linzer Torte Muffins

PISTACHIO-WHITE CHOCOLATE MUFFINS

COFFEE BREAK

Coffee
. . .
Pistachio-White
Chocolate Muffins

Pistachio nuts and white chocolate team up for the ultimate flavor combination that will knock off your socks! These are a truly outrageous morning treat.

$^1/_2$ cup butter
1 cup sugar
2 eggs
$1^1/_2$ teaspoons vanilla
2 cups all-purpose flour
1 tablespoon baking powder
$^1/_4$ teaspoon salt
1 cup milk
$^2/_3$ cup coarsely chopped pistachio nuts
$^3/_4$ cup white chocolate chips

1. Preheat the oven to 375°. Line a 12-cup muffin pan with paper baking cups.

2. In a large bowl, cream the butter and sugar until fluffy. Add the eggs and vanilla and mix well.

3. Sift together the flour, baking powder, and salt. Add the dry ingredients alternately with the milk to the batter.

4. Gently stir in the nuts and chips.

5. Spoon the batter into the muffin cups, filling each completely.

6. Bake for 18 to 20 minutes, until a tester inserted in the center comes out clean. Remove the muffins from the pan to a rack to cool.

12 muffins

GINGERBREAD MUFFINS

Mimicking the flavors of the popular, old-fashioned gingerbread cake, these double ginger-scented muffins are moist and fragrant. They're particularly good spread with cream cheese.

1/2 cup butter
1/2 cup firmly packed dark brown sugar
2 eggs
1/2 cup molasses
2 cups all-purpose flour
2 teaspoon baking soda
1/2 teaspoon salt
2 teaspoons ground ginger
1 teaspoon cinnamon
3/4 cup milk
3 tablespoons finely chopped crystallized candied ginger

1. Preheat the oven to 350°. Line a 12-cup muffin pan with paper baking cups.

2. In a large bowl, cream the butter and sugar. Add the eggs and molasses and mix until evenly blended.

3. Sift together the flour, baking soda, salt, ginger, and cinnamon. Add the dry ingredients alternately with the milk to the batter.

4. Stir in the candied ginger.

5. Fill each muffin cup with the batter.

6. Bake for 20 minutes, until a tester inserted in the center comes out clean. Remove the muffins from the pan to a rack to cool.

12 plump muffins

BREAKFAST ON THE RUN

Mixed Berry Smoothie
. . .
Gingerbread Muffins

S'MORE MUFFINS

These muffins bear the ingredients of the classic s'more—chocolate, marshmallows, and graham crackers. They're sure to be a favorite with young and old alike.

1/2 cup butter
1 cup sugar
2 eggs
1 teaspoon vanilla
1 3/4 cups all-purpose flour
2 teaspoons baking powder
pinch of salt
1 cup milk
1/2 cup coarsely crushed graham crackers
1/2 cup milk chocolate chips
2/3 cup mini marshmallows

1. Preheat the oven to 375°. Line a 12-cup muffin pan with paper baking cups.

2. In a large bowl, cream the butter and sugar until fluffy. Add the eggs and vanilla and mix well.

3. Sift together the flour, baking powder, and salt. Add the dry ingredients alternately with the milk to the batter.

4. Fold in the graham cracker crumbs, chocolate chips, and marsh-mallows.

5. Fill each muffin cup with the batter.

6. Bake for 17 to 20 minutes, until a tester inserted in the center comes out clean. Remove the muffins from the pan to a rack to cool.

12 muffins

DOUBLE CHOCOLATE MUFFINS

If chocolate is your passion, then these decadent muffins will certainly appeal. They boast a rich cocoa batter that's further enhanced with chocolate chips for a double chocolate experience! These are definite snacking material.

1 1/2 cups all-purpose flour
1 cup sugar
1/2 cup unsweetened cocoa (not Dutch)
2 teaspoons baking powder
1/2 teaspoon salt
1 egg
3/4 cup milk
1/3 cup vegetable oil
2/3 cup semi-sweet chocolate chips

1. Preheat the oven to 350°. Line a 12-cup muffin pan with paper baking cups.

2. In a large bowl, combine the flour, sugar, cocoa, baking powder, and salt and mix well.

3. In a separate small bowl, whisk together the egg, milk, and oil.

4. Add the egg mixture to the dry ingredients, mixing well.

5. Stir in the chocolate chips.

6. Fill 9 muffin cups with the batter.

7. Bake for 20 to 23 minutes, until a tester inserted in the center comes out clean. (If you want them fudgy, cook them a shorter amount of time.) Remove the muffins from the pan to a rack to cool.

9 muffins

PICNIC FARE

Rosemary-Walnut
Biscotti
. . .
Vegetables Niçoise
. . .
Prosciutto-Wrapped
Figs
. . .
Herb-Marinated
Buffalo Mozzarella
. . .
Double Chocolate
Muffins
. . .
Iced Tea and
Iced Coffee

STREUSEL-TOPPED MUFFINS

Reminiscent of the taste of coffeecake, these spice-scented muffins are encrusted with a brown sugar-pecan streusel. They're particularly good with mugs of hot coffee.

1/2 cup butter
1 cup sugar
2 eggs
1 1/2 teaspoons vanilla
2 cups all-purpose flour
2 teaspoons baking powder
1/4 teaspoon baking soda
1/4 teaspoon salt
1 teaspoon cinnamon
1/2 teaspoon nutmeg
3/4 cup milk
Streusel Topping (recipe follows)

1. Preheat the oven to 375°. Line a 12-cup muffin pan with paper baking cups.

2. In a large bowl, cream the butter and sugar until fluffy. Add the eggs and vanilla and mix well.

3. Sift together the flour, baking powder, baking soda, salt, cinnamon, and nutmeg. Add the dry ingredients alternately with the milk to the batter.

4. Spoon the batter into the muffin cups, filling each 3/4 full. Place a heaping teaspoonful of streusel atop each muffin.

5. Bake for 20 to 25 minutes, until a tester inserted in the center comes out clean. Remove the muffins from the pan to a rack to cool.

12 muffins

Streusel Topping:
1/4 cup packed dark brown sugar
1/4 cup all-purpose flour
1/2 cup chopped pecans
3 tablespoons butter, melted

In a bowl, combine all of the ingredients and mix well.

MUFFIN MIX-INS

To your favorite basic muffin recipe, try adding any of these mix-ins for flavor-packed treats!

- Crushed Vienna Fingers or vanilla sandwich cookies
- Crushed Oreo Cookies
- Rocky Road mix—chocolate chips, marshmallows, and nuts
- M & M's
- Crushed Heath Bars
- Favorite preserves
- Crystallized candied ginger
- Dried fruits—cranberries, cherries, apricots, pineapple, mango, figs
- Chopped Reese's Peanut Butter Cups
- Peanut butter mixed with mascarpone cheese
- Cream cheese and strawberry jelly
- Chocolate chips, butterscotch chips, or peanut butter chips
- Chocolate covered raisins or peanuts

BUTTERMILK-SCALLION SCONES

Puffed and golden, these savory scones make a great partner for soup or salad. Quick and easy to make, enjoy them straight out of the oven or at room temperature.

> 2 cups all-purpose flour
> 1 tablespoon baking powder
> 1/2 teaspoon salt
> 2 tablespoons sugar
> 1/2 cup butter
> 1/4 cup thinly sliced scallions
> 2/3 cup buttermilk

1. Preheat the oven to 425°. Grease a large cookie sheet.

2. In a large bowl, combine the flour, baking powder, salt, and sugar. Using a pastry blender or fork, cut in the butter until the texture of coarse meal.

3. Stir in the scallions.

4. Add the buttermilk, mixing until the dough is evenly moist. Turn the dough out onto a floured board and knead a few times until smooth. Shape into a 7-inch square, 3/4-inch thick. Cut into 9 pieces and place on the prepared baking sheet, 2 inches apart.

5. Bake in the upper half of the oven for 15 to 17 minutes until puffed and golden. Serve at once.

9 scones

CHEESE SCONES

These scones are a cross between biscuits and rolls. Packed with zesty, cheese flavor, they grace the table with savory delight.

2 cups all-purpose flour
2 teaspoons baking powder
$^1\!/_2$ teaspoon baking soda
$^1\!/_2$ teaspoon salt
1 teaspoon sugar
generous pinch of cayenne pepper
$^1\!/_2$ cup grated Parmigiano-Reggiano cheese
$^1\!/_4$ cup grated Pecorino Romano cheese
$^1\!/_2$ cup butter
$^1\!/_2$ cup buttermilk

1. Preheat the oven to 400°. Grease a large cookie sheet.

2. In a large bowl, combine the flour, baking powder, baking soda, salt, sugar, cayenne, and cheeses. Using a pastry blender or fork, cut in the butter until the texture of coarse meal.

3. Add the buttermilk, mixing until the dough is evenly moist. Turn the dough out onto a floured board and knead a few times until smooth. Shape into a 7-inch square, $^3\!/_4$-inch thick. Cut into 9 pieces and place on the prepared baking sheet, 2 inches apart.

4. Bake in the upper half of the oven for 16 to 18 minutes until puffed and golden. Serve hot out of the oven, or remove the scones from the pan to a rack to cool.

9 scones

APRÈS SKI
GATHERING

Prunes Purcell
. . .
Cheese Scones
. . .
Portuguese Kale Soup
. . .
Buttermilk Poundcake

COCONUT-CURRANT SCONES

AFTERNOON SNACK

Blueberry Smoothie
· · ·
Coconut-Currant
Scones

Scones, of Scottish origin, have captured the hearts of Americans. Although not overly sweet, they strut a tender dough surrounding a host of fruits and nuts—in this case, coconut and currants—making them the perfect companion for breakfast or tea.

2 cups all-purpose flour
1 tablespoon baking powder
$1/2$ teaspoon salt
$1/3$ cup sugar
generous pinch of nutmeg
$1/2$ cup butter
$1/2$ cup currants
$1/2$ cup sweetened, shredded coconut
$2/3$ cup light cream

1. Preheat the oven to 425°.

2. In a large bowl, combine the flour, baking powder, salt, sugar, and nutmeg. Using a pastry blender or fork, cut in the butter until the texture of coarse meal.

3. Stir in the currants and coconut.

4. Add the cream, mixing until the dough is evenly moist. Turn the dough out onto a floured board and knead a few times until smooth. Shape into a round, $3/4$-inch thick. Cut into 8 wedges and place on an ungreased cookie sheet, 2 inches apart.

5. Bake in the upper half of the oven for 15 to 17 minutes until golden and springy to the touch. Remove the scones from the pan to a rack to cool slightly. Serve warm, either plain, or with butter or jam.

8 scones

BLUEBERRY SCONES

Plump with blueberries, these scones capture the best of summer's bounty. They rival blueberry muffins!

2 cups all-purpose flour
2 teaspoons baking powder
$^1/_2$ teaspoon baking soda
$^1/_2$ teaspoon salt
$^1/_3$ cup sugar
$^1/_2$ cup butter
1 cup blueberries
$^1/_2$ cup buttermilk
1 teaspoon vanilla
confectioners' sugar for garnish

1. Preheat the oven to 425°. Grease a baking sheet.

2. In a large bowl, combine the flour, baking powder, baking soda, salt, and sugar. Using a pastry blender or fork, cut in the butter until the texture of coarse meal.

3. Fold in the blueberries.

4. Combine the buttermilk and vanilla and add to the batter, mixing until the dough is evenly moist. Turn the dough out onto a floured board and knead a few times until smooth. Shape into a round, $^3/_4$-inch thick. Cut into 8 wedges and place on the prepared baking sheet, 2 inches apart.

5. Bake in the upper half of the oven for 12 to 14 minutes until lightly golden. Remove the scones to a rack to cool slightly, sprinkle with confectioners' sugar, and serve.

8 scones

BREAKFAST IN BED

Peach Melba Smoothie
. . .
Blueberry Scones

CINNAMON-PECAN SCONES

Perfumed with cinnamon and brown sugar, studded with pecans, and napped with a maple glaze, these scones are extraordinary!

2 cups all-purpose flour
2 teaspoons baking powder
1/2 teaspoon baking soda
1/4 teaspoon salt
1/4 cup packed dark brown sugar
1 teaspoon cinnamon
1/2 cup butter
1/2 cup chopped pecans
2/3 cup light cream
Maple Glaze (recipe follows)

1. Preheat the oven to 425°.

2. In a large bowl, combine the flour, baking powder, baking soda, salt, brown sugar, and cinnamon. Using a pastry blender or fork, cut in the butter until the texture of coarse meal.

3. Stir in the pecans.

4. Add the cream, mixing until the dough is evenly moist. Turn the dough out onto a floured board and knead a few times until smooth. Shape into a round, 3/4-inch thick. Cut into 8 wedges and place on an ungreased cookie sheet, 2 inches apart.

5. Bake in the upper half of the oven for 15 to 17 minutes until golden and springy to the touch. Remove the scones from the pan to a rack to cool. When cool, spread the Maple Glaze over the tops of the scones.

8 scones

Maple Glaze:
1/2 cup confectioners' sugar
3 tablespoons pure maple syrup

Mix the sugar and syrup together until smooth.

CRANBERRY-NUT SCONES

These spice-scented, dried cranberry, orange, and walnut scones are perfect for the Thanksgiving and Christmas holidays. They're great for celebrating and gift giving!

2 cups all-purpose flour
1 tablespoon baking powder
1/2 teaspoon salt
1/3 cup sugar
1/2 teaspoon cinnamon
1/4 teaspoon nutmeg
pinch of cloves
1 tablespoon grated orange peel
1/2 cup butter
1/2 cup dried cranberries
1/2 cup toasted walnuts, chopped
2/3 cup light cream

1. Preheat the oven to 425°.

2. In a large bowl, combine the flour, baking powder, salt, sugar, cinnamon, nutmeg, cloves, and orange peel. Using a pastry blender or fork, cut in the butter until the texture of coarse meal.

3. Stir in the cranberries and nuts.

4. Add the cream, mixing until the dough is evenly moist. Turn the dough out onto a floured board and knead a few times until smooth. Shape into a round, 3/4-inch thick. Cut into 8 wedges and place on an ungreased cookie sheet, 2 inches apart.

5. Bake in the upper half of the oven for 15 to 17 minutes until golden and springy to the touch. Remove the scones from the pan to a rack to cool slightly. Serve warm or at room temperature.

8 scones

BRUNCH BUFFET

Bruschetta with
Chèvre and
Smoked Salmon
. . .
Mocha Latte
Smoothies
. . .
Cinnamon-Pecan
Scones
. . .
Cranberry-Nut
Scones
. . .
Mushroom Frittata

CHOCOLATE CHIP-ORANGE SCONES

These light-textured scones are punctuated by chocolate chips and orange essence, giving rise to a fabulous flavor combination. Buttery rich, scones make an ideal choice at breakfast and snack time.

> 2 cups all-purpose flour
> 1 tablespoon baking powder
> $1/4$ teaspoon salt
> $1/4$ cup sugar
> 1 tablespoon grated orange peel
> $1/2$ cup butter
> $1/2$ cup semi-sweet chocolate chips
> $2/3$ cup light cream

1. Preheat the oven to 425°.

2. In a large bowl, combine the flour, baking powder, salt, sugar, and orange peel. Using a pastry blender or fork, cut in the butter until the texture of coarse meal.

3. Stir in the chocolate chips.

4. Add the cream, mixing until the dough is evenly moist. Turn the dough out onto a floured board and knead a few times until smooth. Shape into a round, $3/4$-inch thick. Cut into 8 wedges and place on an ungreased cookie sheet, 2 inches apart.

5. Bake in the upper half of the oven for 15 to 17 minutes until golden and springy to the touch. Remove the scones from the pan to a rack to cool slightly. Serve warm with butter or orange marmalade.

8 scones

GINGER SCONES

These scones are defined by a double-ginger infusion. Ground ginger and crystallized candied ginger are paired, resulting in a most aromatic, heavenly scented breakfast food.

2 cups all-purpose flour
1 tablespoon baking powder
1/2 teaspoon salt
1/3 cup sugar
1 teaspoon ground ginger
1/2 cup butter
1/3 cup diced crystallized candied ginger
2/3 cup plus 1 tablespoon light cream

1. Preheat the oven to 425°.

2. In a large bowl, combine the flour, baking powder, salt, sugar, and ground ginger. Using a pastry blender or fork, cut in the butter until the texture of coarse meal.

3. Stir in the candied ginger.

4. Add the 2/3 cup cream, mixing until the dough is evenly moist. Turn the dough out onto a floured board and knead a few times until smooth. Shape into a round, 3/4-inch thick. Cut into 8 wedges and place on an ungreased cookie sheet, 2 inches apart. Brush the tops with the 1 tablespoon cream.

5. Bake in the upper half of the oven for 15 to 17 minutes until golden and springy to the touch. Remove the scones from the pan to a rack to cool slightly. Serve warm or at room temperature.

8 scones

TEA FOR 12

Chili-Spiced
Mixed Nuts
· · ·
Cucumber
Sandwiches
· · ·
Curried Tuna Salad
· · ·
Ginger Scones
· · ·
Lemon-Poppy
Seed Scones
· · ·
Stuffed Strawberries
· · ·
Assorted Teas

LEMON-POPPY SEED SCONES

These scones take center stage with their light, cake-like texture, and lemony, nutty taste. They give new definition to the infamous Scottish quick bread.

> 2 cups all-purpose flour
> 1 tablespoon baking powder
> $1/2$ teaspoon salt
> $1/3$ cup sugar
> 1 tablespoon grated lemon peel
> $1/4$ cup poppy seeds
> $1/2$ cup butter
> $2/3$ cup light cream
> Lemon Glaze (recipe follows)

1. Preheat the oven to 425°.

2. In a large bowl, combine the flour, baking powder, salt, sugar, lemon peel, and poppy seeds. Using a pastry blender or fork, cut in the butter until the texture of coarse meal.

3. Add the cream, mixing until the dough is evenly moist. Turn the dough out onto a floured board and knead a few times until smooth. Shape into a round, 3/4-inch thick. Cut into 8 wedges and place on an ungreased cookie sheet, 2 inches apart.

4. Bake in the upper half of the oven for 15 to 17 minutes until golden and springy to the touch. Remove the scones from the pan to a rack to cool. When cool, spread the Lemon Glaze over the tops of the scones.

8 scones

> **Lemon Glaze:**
> $1/2$ cup confectioners' sugar
> 1 tablespoon lemon juice

Mix the sugar and lemon juice together until smooth.

SATISFYING SOUPS

Soup is magical. A bowl of soup is nourishment for the soul. It has restorative powers and makes us feel better when we're down. A pot of simmering soup warms the cockles of the heart and is relaxing in the winter; chilled soups are refreshing and pleasing in the dog days of summer.

Soup can be a complete meal. It's the perfect food for either a casual supper or a formal dinner. Everyone has special favorites, connected to family traditions.

The beauty of soup preparation is in the flexibility it offers. Soups are very forgiving—a little extra of one ingredient, a little less of another, or substitutions—and without compromising the quality, you'll still have a winner. Once put together, they need little attention while they simmer and fill the kitchen with their aroma.

Simple or hearty, cream or tomato-base, vegetable or seafood, chunky or puréed, chowder or stew, there's a soup for every occasion and an occasion for every soup.

SIMMERING SOUPS

CARROT AND PARSNIP SOUP

Once overlooked, the parsnip is finally getting its just recognition as a delectable root vegetable. Both the carrot and the parsnip impart an illustrious, sweet flavor to this smooth and creamy purée. Scented with the essence of ginger and spiced with curry and cumin, this soup embraces the senses.

2 tablespoons butter
1 large yellow onion, chopped
1 large clove garlic, minced
2 tablespoons grated gingerroot
4 cups chicken broth
1 pound carrots, peeled and coarsely chopped
1 pound parsnips, peeled and coarsely chopped
$1/2$ teaspoon curry powder
$1/4$ teaspoon ground cumin
generous pinch of cayenne pepper
salt and freshly ground pepper to taste
$1/2$ cup light cream

1. Heat the butter in a large stockpot. Add the onion and sauté over medium heat until soft and translucent.

2. Add the garlic and ginger and sauté for 1 minute more.

3. Add the broth, carrots, parsnips, and seasonings. Bring to a boil, cover, lower the heat, and simmer for 30 minutes until the vegetables are very tender.

4. Transfer the soup in batches to a food processor and purée. Return the purée to the stockpot.

5. Stir in the cream and heat gently. Serve at once.

6 portions

CORN CHOWDER

This simple, yet satisfying soup captures the essence of sweet corn. Although it's best made with fresh corn on the cob, canned or frozen kernels are an acceptable substitute in this all-American favorite.

2 tablespoons butter
1 large yellow onion, chopped
1 large Idaho potato, diced into ¹/₂-inch cubes
2 cups milk
5 cups corn kernels (fresh, frozen, or canned)
2 cups half and half
salt and freshly ground pepper to taste

1. Heat the butter in a large saucepan. Add the onion and cook over medium heat until soft and translucent.

2. Add the potato and milk and simmer for 10 minutes until the potato is tender.

3. While the potato is cooking, put 2 cups corn kernels and the half and half in a blender or food processor and purée.

4. Add the corn purée along with the remaining whole corn kernels to the soup. Season with salt and pepper. Heat gently until piping hot. Serve at once.

8 soup portions

SPECIAL
BIRTHDAY
CELEBRATION

Corn Chowder
. . .
Mesclun Salad with
Toasted Goat Cheese
. . .
Nubble Light
Seafood Bake
. . .
Rum Cake

CREAM OF CELERY SOUP

**LADIES
LUNCHEON**

Corn Cakes with Sour
Cream and Caviar
· · ·
Cream of Celery Soup
· · ·
Mixed Greens with
Pears and Brie
· · ·
Sourdough Bread
· · ·
Lemon Coolers
· · ·
Raspberry Sorbet

This delicate, heavenly soup is redolent with sautéed celery, onion, and the essence of fennel, laced with tarragon, and finished with a light cream broth. It makes a delectable luncheon or first course soup.

6 tablespoons butter
1 large Spanish onion, chopped
1 large bunch celery, peeled and chopped
1/2 large fennel bulb (fronds removed), sliced
1 large clove garlic, minced
1 teaspoon dried tarragon
1 bay leaf
1 teaspoon salt
freshly ground pepper to taste
5 cups chicken broth
1 cup light cream

1. Heat the butter in a large stockpot. Add the onion, celery, and fennel and sauté over medium heat until onion is soft and translucent, stirring occasionally. Add the garlic and sauté for 1 minute more.

2. Add the tarragon, bay leaf, salt, pepper, and broth. Bring to a boil, cover, lower the heat, and simmer for 10 to 15 minutes until the vegetables are tender.

3. Remove half of the solids to a food processor and purée. Return the purée to the stockpot, mixing well.

4. Stir in the cream and heat gently until piping hot. Serve at once.

6 to 8 portions

POTATO-LEEK-FENNEL SOUP

This rustic soup is teeming with sautéed leeks, red-skinned potatoes, and the delicate, anise-flavored fennel bulb. Finished with a sprinkling of Parmesan, this makes for memorable eating!

4 tablespoons butter
2 large shallots, sliced
3 cups sliced leeks (white part only)
1 medium fennel bulb (fronds removed), thinly sliced
1 pound new or red-skinned potatoes, cut into 3/4-inch chunks
6 cups chicken broth
salt and freshly ground pepper to taste
1/2 cup grated Parmigiano-Reggiano cheese

1. Heat the butter in a large stockpot. Add the shallots, leeks, and fennel and sauté over medium heat until golden, about 10 minutes.

2. Add the potatoes, broth, salt, and pepper. Bring to a boil, lower the heat, and simmer uncovered until the potatoes are tender, about 10 to 15 minutes.

3. Stir in the cheese, mix well, and serve.

6 to 8 portions

WINTER LUNCH

Potato-Leek-Fennel
Soup
· · ·
Peasant Bread

CREAM OF MUSHROOM SOUP

SUNDAY NITE SUP

Cream of
Mushroom Soup
. . .
Oven-Fried Chicken
. . .
Horseradish-Mashed
Yukon Golds
. . .
Sautéed Spinach

Chock full of the rich flavors of wild mushrooms—shiitake and cremini—and delicately seasoned with tarragon, this soup is elegant and most satisfying.

4 tablespoons butter
2 large shallots, minced
1 large clove garlic, minced
1 pound assorted mushrooms (shiitake and cremini), thinly sliced
1 teaspoon dried tarragon
salt and freshly ground pepper to taste
4 cups chicken broth
3/4 cup light cream

1. Heat the butter in a large saucepan. Add the shallots and sauté over medium heat until soft, about 2 minutes. Add the garlic and sauté for 1 minute more.

2. Add the mushrooms. Season with the tarragon, salt, and pepper and sauté until the mushrooms are golden, stirring occasionally.

3. Add the chicken broth and cream. Heat gently for 5 to 10 minutes until piping hot, allowing the cream to take on the flavor of the mushrooms. Serve at once.

4 to 6 portions

CURRIED SWEET POTATO SOUP

This golden-hued soup boasts a thick, creamy purée of sautéed leeks, apples, and sweet potatoes scented with curry. Even though this vegetable potage looks and tastes rich, it's a lean choice, as it contains no cream.

4 tablespoons butter
3 leeks (white part only), chopped
2 large cloves garlic, minced
2 large Granny Smith apples, peeled and coarsely chopped
2 pounds sweet potatoes, peeled and coarsely chopped
4 cups chicken broth
1 tablespoon curry powder
1/2 teaspoon ground cumin
1 teaspoon salt
freshly ground pepper to taste

1. Heat the butter in a large stockpot. Add the leeks and sauté over medium heat until the leeks are tender. Add the garlic and sauté for 1 minute more.

2. Add the apples, sweet potatoes, broth, and seasonings.

3. Bring to a boil, cover, lower the heat, and simmer for 20 to 25 minutes until the apples and potatoes are tender.

4. Transfer the solids to a food processor and purée in batches. Return the purée to the stockpot, stirring until evenly combined. Heat gently and serve.

6 to 8 soup portions; 4 to 6 main-course portions

HARVEST MEAL

Curried Sweet
Potato Soup
. . .
Roasted Cornish Hens
. . .
Maple-Parsnip Purée
. . .
Roasted Green Beans

CABBAGE SOUP GRATINÉE

Akin to onion soup, cabbage is the star in this peasant dish. Teeming with cabbage, carmelized onion, and the smokey taste of bacon, the soup is crowned with slices of pumpernickel bread and grated cheese. Run under the broiler until brown and bubbly, this comfort food is sure to please.

4 tablespoons butter
1 large Spanish onion, thinly sliced
1 teaspoon sugar
6 cups thinly sliced cabbage (cut into $1/4$-inch wide strips)
$1/4$ pound bacon, cooked and coarsely chopped
7 cups chicken broth
1 cup dry sherry
1 teaspoon salt
freshly ground pepper to taste
6 slices pumpernickel bread, toasted
$1^1/2$ cups grated Swiss cheese

1. Heat the butter in a large stockpot. Add the onion, sprinkle with the sugar, and sauté over medium-high until golden, stirring occasionally.

2. Add the cabbage, broth, sherry, salt, and pepper. Bring to a boil, cover, lower the heat, and simmer for 20 to 30 minutes until the cabbage is tender. (Up to this point may be done in advance and refrigerated; return to room temperature before continuing.)

3. Spoon the soup into individual crocks. Cover each with a slice of bread. Sprinkle with the cheese. Bake in a preheated 350° oven for 15 minutes. Run under the broiler until brown and bubbly. Serve at once.

6 portions

SWEET AND SOUR CABBAGE SOUP

The classic sweet and sour flavors of brown sugar, raisins, and lemon juice are captured in this tomato-based, shredded cabbage soup. Although vegetarian in design, meatballs may be added to further enhance the soup.

2 tablespoons olive oil (not extra-virgin)
1 large yellow onion, chopped
1 large clove garlic, crushed
28-ounce can crushed tomatoes
2 tablespoons lemon juice
1/4 cup packed dark brown sugar
1/2 cup golden raisins
6 cups beef broth
1 teaspoon ground ginger
salt and freshly ground pepper to taste
1 small to medium-size head cabbage, cut into 1/2-inch wide strips

1. Heat the oil in a large stockpot. Add the onion and sauté over medium heat until soft and translucent. Add the garlic and sauté for 1 minute more.

2. Add the tomatoes, lemon juice, brown sugar, raisins, broth, ginger, salt, and pepper. Bring to a boil, cover, lower the heat, and simmer for 20 to 30 minutes.

3. Add the cabbage*, return the soup to a boil, cover, and simmer for 20 minutes more until the cabbage is soft. Serve piping hot.

6 to 8 hearty portions

*Meatballs may be added at this time if desired.

COLD WEATHER COMFORT

Sweet and Sour Cabbage Soup with Meatballs

. . .

Dark Rye or Pumpernickel Bread

. . .

Indian Pudding

CHINESE HOT AND SOUR SOUP

Probably the most beloved of Chinese soups, this classic takes only minutes to prepare. White pepper and vinegar are the vital ingredients that distinguish this soup, providing the hot and sour tastes respectively. The rich combination of ingredients ranging from mushrooms and bamboo shoots to julienned pork, tofu, and egg, tantalizes the taste buds.

6 cups chicken broth
1 slice gingerroot, 1/2-inch thick
1/4 cup wood ears, soaked in hot water for 15 minutes, drained and sliced
   in half (optional)*
6 medium to large shiitake mushrooms (stems removed), thinly sliced
1/2 cup bamboo shoots, rinsed, drained, and julienned
1 tablespoon soy sauce
3 tablespoons white vinegar
1 teaspoon white pepper
1/2 teaspoon salt or to taste
1/2 pound boneless pork, cut into julienne slices
1/2 pound firm tofu, cut into 1/2-inch thick strips
3 tablespoons cornstarch mixed with 1/4 cup cold water
2 eggs, beaten
1 teaspoon Oriental sesame oil
2 tablespoons sliced scallions for garnish

1. Put the broth, gingerroot, wood ears, shiitakes, and bamboo shoots in a large saucepan. Bring to a boil, lower the heat, and simmer for 5 minutes.

2. Add the soy sauce, vinegar, pepper, and salt and simmer for 2 minutes more.

3. Add the pork and tofu. Simmer for 2 minutes.

4. Add the cornstarch mixture to the soup, stirring constantly until evenly combined.

5. Slowly pour the eggs into the soup, stirring gently. Remove the soup from the heat.

6. Stir in the sesame oil and garnish with the scallions. Serve at once.

6 portions

*Available in Oriental markets

OLD-FASHIONED CREAM OF TOMATO SOUP

This old-fashioned, homestyle soup has its roots in the 40's. Still retaining its original integrity, this updated version showcases a creamy base with bits of tomatoes, seasoned with garlic and herbs. It continues to be an irresistible comfort food.

2 tablespoons butter
1 large yellow onion, chopped
2 large cloves garlic, crushed
35-ounce can Italian tomatoes, coarsely chopped with their juice
3 cups tomato juice
pinch of sugar
2 teaspoons dried basil
1/2 teaspoon dried marjoram
1 bay leaf
salt and freshly ground pepper to taste
1 cup light cream

1. Heat the butter in a large saucepan. Add the onion and sauté over medium heat until soft and translucent. Add the garlic and sauté for 1 minute more.

2. Add the tomatoes, tomato juice, and seasonings. Bring to a boil, cover, lower the heat, and simmer for 30 minutes.

3. Remove 1/2 of the soup to a food processor and purée. Return the purée to the saucepan.

4. Add the cream and heat gently. Serve at once.

6 portions

OLD-FASHIONED
COMFORT MEAL

Old-Fashioned Cream
of Tomato Soup
. . .
Macaroni and Cheese
. . .
Grapes
. . .
Assorted Cookies

ITALIAN TOMATO AND BREAD SOUP

This simple, peasant soup pairs two of my favorite ingredients, lusty tomatoes and bread! This great bread soup from southern Italy is fragrant with tomatoes, garlic, onion, basil, and a drizzle of extra-virgin olive oil. Thickened with day-old bread, it's heavenly.

2 tablespoons extra-virgin olive oil
1 large yellow onion, chopped
3 large cloves garlic, minced
28-ounce can Italian crushed tomatoes
4 cups water
3 tablespoons chopped fresh basil
2 tablespoons chopped fresh parsley
salt and freshly ground pepper to taste
2 cups (1-inch chunks) day-old Italian bread
2 tablespoons extra-virgin olive oil for garnish

1. Heat 2 tablespoons olive oil in a large stockpot. Add the onion and sauté over medium heat until soft and translucent. Add the garlic and sauté for 1 minute more.

2. Add the tomatoes, water, and seasonings. Bring to a boil, cover, lower the heat, and simmer for 20 minutes.

3. Add the bread and simmer for 15 minutes until bread is soft. Remove the pot from the heat and let stand at least 5 minutes to allow the bread to absorb most of the liquid. The soup will be quite thick. Serve hot, warm, or at room temperature, drizzled with the 2 tablespoons extra-virgin olive oil.

4 to 6 portions

POTATO-CHEESE SOUP

This soul-soothing, puréed soup is steeped in the flavors of the classic fondue—garlic, Gruyère cheese, and white wine—enhanced by the smokey taste of bacon and the creamy texture of Yukon Gold potatoes. It's sure to take the chill out of an autumn night.

APRÈS SKI LUNCH

Shredded
Romaine Salad*
. . .
Potato Cheese Soup
. . .
French Bread

1/4 pound bacon, chopped
1 large sweet onion (Vidalia, Maui, Texas, or Spanish), chopped
1 large clove garlic, minced
1 teaspoon dry mustard
1 1/2 pounds Yukon Gold potatoes, chopped into 3/4-inch pieces
4 cups chicken broth
1/2 cup dry white wine
salt and freshly ground pepper to taste
1 1/2 cups grated Gruyère cheese

1. In a large stockpot, cook the bacon over medium-low heat until crisp and browned. With a slotted spoon, remove the bacon to a plate and reserve.

2. Add the onion to the stockpot and sauté over medium-low heat until soft and translucent. Add the garlic, bacon, and mustard and cook for 1 minute more.

3. Add the potatoes, broth, wine, salt, and pepper. Bring to a boil, cover, lower the heat, and simmer about 15 minutes until the potatoes are tender.

4. Transfer the soup in batches to a food processor and purée. Ladle into bowls, sprinkle with the cheese, and serve at once.

6 to 8 soup portions; 4 main-course portions

BLACK BEAN CHILI

Infused with the bold, assertive flavors of chili—garlic, chili powder, cumin, crushed red pepper, and tomatoes—this zesty, vegetarian soup rich with black beans will warm and soothe the soul. Serve it fireside over cooked white rice.

3 tablespoons olive oil (not extra-virgin)
2 cups chopped yellow onion
4 large cloves garlic, minced
28-ounce can diced tomatoes
4 cups chicken broth
1 tablespoon chili powder
1 tablespoon ground cumin
1 teaspoon dried oregano
1 teaspoon crushed red pepper flakes
1 teaspoon salt
freshly ground pepper to taste
2 (19-ounce) cans black beans, rinsed and drained

Garnishes:
1/4 cup chopped fresh cilantro
1/2 cup sour cream

1. Heat the oil in a large stockpot. Add the onion and sauté over medium heat until soft and translucent. Add the garlic and sauté for 1 minute more.

2. Add the tomatoes, broth, and seasonings. Bring to a boil, cover, lower the heat, and simmer for 20 minutes.

3. Add the black beans, heat for 5 to 10 minutes and serve at once. Garnish each portion with some cilantro and a dollop of sour cream.

6 portions

CHICKPEA SOUP

Italian in design, chickpeas and tomatoes are surrounded by a host of chunky vegetables for a most savory potage. Chickpeas are a type of legume that have a firm texture and a slightly, nutty taste, are low in fat and high in fiber, making them a sound nutritional choice.

1/4 cup extra-virgin olive oil
2 large yellow onions, chopped
2 large carrots, chopped
1 large stalk celery, chopped
2 large cloves garlic, crushed
28-ounce can Italian tomatoes, coarsely chopped with their juice
4 cups chicken broth
2 tablespoons chopped Italian parsley
1 bay leaf
salt and freshly ground pepper to taste
2 (19-ounce) cans chickpeas, rinsed and drained

1. Heat the oil in a large stockpot. Add the onions, carrots, and celery and sauté over medium heat until the vegetables are soft, about 10 to 15 minutes, stirring occasionally. Add the garlic and sauté for 1 minute more.

2. Add the tomatoes, broth, and seasonings. Bring the soup to a boil, cover, lower the heat, and simmer for 20 minutes.

3. Add the chickpeas, heat for 5 to 10 minutes and serve at once.

6 to 8 portions

HALE AND HEARTY

Chickpea Soup
. . .
Garlic Bread
. . .
Sausage, Peppers, and Potatoes
. . .
Congo Bars

CANNELLINI AND SPINACH SOUP

Cannellini, or white kidney beans, and leafy, green spinach are paired in this quick-to-fix soup. Flavored with the smokey taste of bacon and finished with a dusting of Parmesan, it is both enticing and nutritious.

> *4 slices bacon, coarsely chopped*
> *1 large yellow onion, chopped*
> *2 large cloves garlic, crushed*
> *6 cups chicken broth*
> *1 bay leaf*
> *salt and freshly ground pepper to taste*
> *2 (19-ounce) cans cannellini beans, rinsed and drained*
> *10 ounces fresh spinach (stems removed), coarsely chopped*
> *1/3 cup grated Parmigiano-Reggiano cheese*

1. Cook the bacon in a large stockpot over medium heat until crisp. Using a slotted spoon, transfer the bacon to a plate.

2. Add the onion to the bacon fat in the pot and cook over medium heat until soft and translucent. Add the garlic and cook for 1 minute more.

3. Add the broth, bay leaf, salt, pepper, and reserved bacon. Bring to a boil, add the beans and spinach, and simmer for 2 to 3 minutes until the spinach is wilted.

4. Stir in the cheese and serve at once.

6 portions

HEARTY LENTIL SOUP

Resplendent with a host of vegetables, thick with lentils, and enhanced by the hickory taste of bacon, this homestyle soup is designed with busy cooks in mind.

3 slices bacon, chopped
1 large yellow onion, chopped
2 large carrots, chopped
1 large stalk celery, chopped
1 leek (white part only), chopped
$^1/_4$ small head cabbage, chopped
2 large cloves garlic, minced
$2^1/_2$ quarts chicken broth
$1^1/_2$ cups dried brown lentils
1 teaspoon dried thyme
1 bay leaf
$^1/_4$ cup chopped fresh parsley
salt and freshly ground pepper to taste

1. Put the bacon, onion, carrots, celery, leek, and cabbage in a large stockpot. Sauté over medium heat for 10 minutes until vegetables are soft, stirring occasionally. Add the garlic and sauté for 1 minute more.

2. Add the broth, lentils, and seasonings. Bring the soup to a boil, cover, lower the heat, and simmer until lentils are tender, about 40 minutes. Serve piping hot.

8 or more portions

GRAZING PARTY

Artichoke Pillows
. . .
Roquefort-Stuffed Mushrooms
. . .
Grilled Shrimp with Pesto Mayonnaise
. . .
Olive Puffs
. . .
Hearty Lentil Soup

PORTUGUESE KALE SOUP

There are probably as many versions of this soup as there are cooks who make it. Linguica, a garlic-flavored Portuguese sausage, is the vital ingredient that distinguishes this hearty, somewhat spicy, kale, potato, and red kidney bean soup.

2 tablespoons olive oil (not extra-virgin)
2 pounds linguica or chorizo sausage, cut into 1/2-inch thick rounds
1 Spanish onion, chopped
4 large cloves garlic, chopped
3 Idaho potatoes, cut into 3/4-inch cubes
3 quarts chicken broth
1 bay leaf
1/2 teaspoon crushed red pepper flakes
salt and freshly ground pepper to taste
12 cups coarsely chopped, packed kale (stems removed)
2 (15-ounce) cans red kidney beans, rinsed and drained

1. Heat the oil in a large stockpot. Add the linguica and onion and sauté over medium heat until onion is soft and translucent. Add the garlic and sauté for 1 minute more.

2. Add the potatoes, broth, and seasonings. Bring to a boil, lower the heat, and simmer for 15 minutes until potatoes are tender.

3. Add the kale and kidney beans and simmer for 10 minutes more until kale is tender. Serve at once.

8 portions

SALMON CHOWDER

Delicate, yet brimming with flavor, this chowder features the fabulous combination of salmon, corn, potatoes, and sautéed onions in a light dill and sherry-scented, creamy base.

4 tablespoons butter
2 large yellow onions, chopped
1 large stalk celery, diced
³/4 pound new or red-skinned potatoes, cut into ¹/2-inch cubes
1 bay leaf
1 teaspoon dried dill
1 teaspoon salt
freshly ground pepper to taste
3 cups water
1 cup dry sherry
1¹/2 cups fresh or frozen corn kernels
2 pounds salmon filets, skinned, boned, and cut into 2-inch chunks
2 cups evaporated milk

1. Heat the butter in a large stockpot. Add the onion and celery and sauté over medium heat until the onion is golden.

2. Add the potatoes, bay leaf, dill, salt, pepper, water, and sherry. Bring to a boil, cover, lower the heat, and simmer for 10 to 15 minutes until the potatoes are tender.

3. Add the corn and salmon. Bring the soup to a boil, lower the heat, and simmer gently until the fish is cooked, about 4 to 5 minutes.

4. Stir in the evaporated milk and heat gently until piping hot. Ladle spoonfuls of hot chowder into bowls and serve at once.

8 to 10 soup portions; 6 main-course portions

BEST OF
CHOWDER

Salad Campagna
. . .
Salmon Chowder
. . .
Buttermilk-Scallion
Scones
. . .
Lemon Icebox Cookies

THAI HOT AND SOUR SHRIMP SOUP

This light, flavorful soup boasts a lime-chili infused broth embellished with rice noodles, shrimp, and assorted vegetables. It's best served the same day as made.

6 cups chicken broth
$1/2$-inch piece of gingerroot, sliced into 4 rounds
1 tablespoon soy sauce
1 tablespoon fish sauce*
2 tablespoons fresh lime juice
$1/2$ teaspoon chili paste* (or more to taste if you like it hot)
$1/2$ teaspoon sugar
6 medium-size shiitake mushrooms, sliced
4 ounces dried rice noodles, soaked in hot water for 30 minutes until soft
    and drained
$1/2$ pound raw medium-size shrimp, shelled
8 cherry tomatoes, halved
$1/2$ cup sugar snap peas

Garnishes:
2 tablespoons thinly sliced scallions
$1^1/2$ cups beansprouts
$1/4$ cup coarsely chopped fresh basil

1. In a large stockpot, bring the broth, ginger, soy, fish sauce, lime juice, chili paste, sugar, and mushrooms to a boil. Simmer for 5 minutes.

2. Add the noodles, shrimp, tomatoes, and sugar snap peas. Simmer for 2 to 3 minutes until the shrimp turn pink.

3. Stir in the scallions, beansprouts, and basil and serve at once.

4 to 6 portions

*Available in Oriental markets

MUSSEL CHOWDER

Move over clam chowder—you've met your match! This chowder is the stuff of which dreams are made; it's chunky with sweet, succulent mussels and creamy Yukon Gold potatoes in a white wine-cream broth.

3 pounds mussels, scrubbed and debearded
2 cups dry white wine
2 cups water
2 tablespoons butter
1 large yellow onion, chopped
1 large stalk celery, diced
1 large clove garlic, minced
1 pound Yukon Gold potatoes, diced into $1/2$-inch cubes
1 bay leaf
$1/2$ teaspoon dried thyme
splash of Worcestershire sauce
salt and freshly ground pepper to taste
2 cups half and half

1. Put the mussels, wine, and water in a large stockpot. Cover and steam over high heat until mussels open, about 3 minutes. Drain and shell mussels, reserving the broth. Filter the broth through a double layer of cheese cloth or coffee filter and set aside.

2. Rinse out the stockpot to remove any sand. Heat the butter in the stockpot. Add the onion and celery and sauté over medium heat until the onion and celery are soft. Add the garlic and sauté for 1 minute more.

3. Add the reserved broth, potatoes, and seasonings. Bring the mixture to a boil, cover, lower the heat, and simmer until the potatoes are tender, about 10 to 15 minutes.

4. Add the cooked, shelled mussels and half and half. Heat gently and serve.

8 to 10 soup portions; 4 to 6 main-course portions

SEAFOOD
SAMPLER

Mussel Chowder
· · ·
French Bread
· · ·
Striped Bass Provençal
· · ·
Parmesan-Crusted
Zucchini
· · ·
Mixed Berry Galette

SHRIMP AND CRAB GUMBO

From the heart of the Bayou, this stew-like soup is a staple of Cajun cuisine. Basic to gumbo is the roux, a slow-cooked mixture of oil and flour, which acts as a thickener. Okra adds another distinctive flavor dimension as well as body to the soup. Teeming with shrimp and crabmeat, this gumbo is glorious ladled over cooked white rice.

1/4 cup vegetable oil
1/4 cup all-purpose flour
2 large yellow onions, chopped
1 large green pepper, chopped
1 large red pepper, chopped
2 large stalks celery, chopped
3 large cloves garlic, minced
28-ounce can Italian tomatoes, coarsely chopped with their juice
2 cups fresh or frozen okra, cut into 1/2-inch thick rounds
2 bay leaves
1 teaspoon dried thyme
1/2 teaspoon crushed red pepper flakes
1 tablespoon Worcestershire sauce
salt and freshly ground pepper to taste
4 cups water
2 pounds raw extra-large shrimp, shelled
1 pound crabmeat
1/2 cup chopped fresh parsley

1. Warm the oil in a large stockpot. Add the flour and cook over medium-low heat, stirring constantly, until mixture is a nutty, golden brown color, about 5 to 10 minutes.

2. Add the onions, peppers, and celery and cook, stirring until vegetables are tender, about 10 minutes. Add the garlic and cook for 1 minute more.

3. Add the tomatoes, okra, and seasonings, and simmer for 5 minutes. Slowly add the water, stirring constantly, until all the liquid has been added. Simmer uncovered for 30 minutes. (Up to this point may be done several hours and even 24 hours in advance and refrigerated. Return to room temperature before proceeding; then heat until hot.)

4. Add the shrimp, crab, and parsley and simmer for about 5 minutes until shrimp are cooked. Ladle the gumbo over cooked white rice and serve at once.

8 portions

CHILLED SOUPS

BORSCHT

SUMMER
SOLSTICE

Borscht
· · ·
Chopped Tuna Salad
· · ·
French Bread
· · ·
Assorted Melons

I have very fond memories of eating borscht as a child. This butter-milk-based version is defined by sweet, red-hued beets, cucumber, and dill.

4 medium-size beets, scrubbed
1 quart buttermilk
1 cup sour cream
1 large pickling cucumber, coarsely grated
¹/₄ cup snipped chives
¹/₄ cup chopped fresh dill
1 teaspoon sugar
salt and freshly ground pepper to taste

1. Place the beets in a saucepan and cover generously with water. Bring to a boil and simmer for 35 to 40 minutes until tender. Remove the beets from the pot to cool, reserving 1 cup of the cooking liquid.

2. Peel the cooled beets and coarsely grate them into a large bowl.

3. Add the reserved beet cooking liquid, along with the remaining ingredients. Mix well until evenly combined. Refrigerate for 4 to 6 hours to allow flavors to mellow. Serve chilled.

4 portions

COLD CUCUMBER SOUP

This thick purée is light and ever so refreshing on a hot day. Cucumber, dill, mint, scallions, and buttermilk are all whirled together in the blender, resulting in a subtle melding of flavors.

3 cups buttermilk
1/2 cup sour cream
2 cucumbers, peeled and chopped
3 tablespoons chopped fresh dill
3 tablespoons finely chopped fresh mint
1/2 cup thinly sliced scallions
1/2–1 teaspoon salt
freshly ground pepper to taste

1. Combine all of the ingredients in a blender or food processor and purée. (It may be necessary to do it in several batches.)

2. Let marinate in the refrigerator for 2 to 3 hours and as much as overnight for flavors to blend. Serve chilled.

4 to 6 portions

AL FRESCO
DINNER

Cold Cucumber Soup
. . .
Potato and
Mussel Salad
. . .
Sourdough Bread
. . .
Orange Tea Cakes
. . .
Assorted Berries

ICED AVOCADO SOUP

Modeled after the classic Mexican dip, guacamole, this chunky cold soup of avocado, sour cream, lime, garlic, tomato, and spices results in a blast of flavor.

2 ripe Haas avocados, peeled, pitted and mashed
$1/2$ cup sour cream
2 tablespoons lime juice
2 cups chicken broth
1 large clove garlic, minced
2 large tomatoes, chopped
$1/4$ cup diced red onion
1 jalapeño pepper, seeded and minced
2 tablespoons finely minced fresh cilantro
$1/2$ teaspoon ground cumin
salt and freshly ground pepper to taste

1. Mix the avocado and sour cream in a large bowl.

2. Add the remaining ingredients and mix well. Refrigerate for 3 to 4 hours for flavors to blend. Serve chilled or at room temperature.

4 portions

GAZPACHO LATINO

This spicy South-of-the-Border version of the infamous soup show-cases a lively tomato-based potage spiked with jalapeño, cumin, and cilantro and embellished with crabmeat.

28-ounce can Italian tomatoes with their juice
1 large green pepper, cut into chunks
1/2–1 jalapeño pepper, seeded and finely diced (Use the whole pepper
    if you like it hot.)
1 medium-size cucumber, peeled and cut into chunks
1 small red onion, diced
1 large clove garlic, crushed
2 tablespoons extra-virgin olive oil
2 tablespoons lime juice
1 1/2 teaspoons ground cumin
3 tablespoons finely chopped fresh cilantro
salt and freshly ground pepper to taste
2 cups V-8 juice
8 ounces crabmeat

1. Put the tomatoes, peppers, cucumber, onion, garlic, oil, lime juice, and seasonings in the bowl of a food processor. Pulse to a chunky consistency.

2. Transfer the soup to a large bowl and stir in the V-8 juice. Gently mix in the crabmeat. Let marinate for 1 to 6 hours in the refrigerator. Serve at room temperature.

6 portions

MEXICAN FLAIR

Gazpacho Latino
. . .
Carne Asada
. . .
Rice with Green
Chilies
. . .
Ice Cream

MINTED PEA SOUP

The delicate flavor of peas is accented with mint in this velvety soup. It makes an elegant beginning to a meal and is most glorious as a luncheon dish.

1 tablespoon butter
1 large yellow onion, chopped
4 cups chicken broth
3 cups fresh or frozen peas
3 tablespoons finely chopped fresh mint
salt and freshly ground pepper to taste
1 cup light cream
3 tablespoons snipped chives for garnish

1. Heat the butter in a stockpot. Add the onion and sauté over medium heat until soft and translucent.

2. Add the chicken broth, peas, mint, salt, and pepper. Simmer for 4 to 5 minutes. Let cool.

3. Purée the soup in batches in a food processor. Transfer the purée to a large bowl.

4. Stir in the cream and garnish with the chives. Chill for 1 to 2 hours and as much as overnight for flavors to blend. Serve at room temperature.

6 to 8 portions

PASTA PASSION

Pasta, pasta, and more pasta. Pasta has 1,000 personalities. No matter what you crave, you can create a pasta dish to match the mood. This complex carbo still reigns supreme. It offers a quick, easy to fix, comforting meal. The myriad of shapes and sizes and the countless ways to sauce the pasta make it appealing and versatile. The various shapes are actually better suited to specific types of toppings.

Fresh pastas are softer and therefore, rich sauces with butter and cream cling best to these.

Dried pastas are better nests for olive oil and tomato-based toppings or vegetable sautés.

Strands—spaghetti, linguine, and fettuccine—are best for simple tomato and light-bodied sauces.

Tubular or twisted pastas—rigatoni, ziti, fusilli, and farfalle—hold chunky, peasant sauces and pestos best.

No matter what the shape, pasta brimming with a delectable sauce is satisfying and lip-smacking good.

ZITI BAKE

This is one of my daughter's favorite recipes. It's actually a light, vegetarian version of lasagne and is comfort food at its best. Ziti is lavished with an herbed marinara sauce, encrusted with mozzarella cheese, and baked to a turn. The sauce freezes well, so make up a batch to keep on hand.

3 tablespoons extra-virgin olive oil
1 large yellow onion, diced
2 large cloves garlic, minced
28-ounce can crushed tomatoes
1 teaspoon dried basil
$1/2$ teaspoon dried oregano
pinch of sugar
$1/4$ cup chopped Italian parsley
salt and freshly ground pepper to taste
1 pound ziti
$1/2$ pound mozzarella cheese, grated

1. Heat the olive oil in a large saucepan. Add the onion and sauté over medium heat until soft and translucent. Add the garlic and sauté for 1 minute more.

2. Add the tomatoes and seasonings. Bring to a boil, cover, lower the heat, and simmer for 20 minutes.

3. Preheat the oven to 400°. Grease a 9 x 13-inch baking dish.

4. While the sauce is cooking, prepare the pasta according to the package directions. Drain well.

5. Add the pasta to the sauce and mix well. Turn into the prepared pan. Top with the cheese.

6. Bake for 15 to 20 minutes until brown and bubbly. Serve piping hot.

8 main-course portions; about $3^1/2$ to $3^3/4$ cups sauce

PENNE WITH MUSHROOM RAGOUT

EASY DOES IT

Balsamic-Glazed
Veal Chops
. . .
Penne with
Mushroom Ragout
. . .
Mesclun Salad with
Toasted Goat Cheese
. . .
Lemon Sorbet with
Raspberries

Tubular pasta is cloaked in a thick ragout of herb-scented, sautéed wild mushrooms. This Italian-style sauce is also delicious over sautéed chicken breasts, veal chops, and grilled steak.

> 3 tablespoons extra-virgin olive oil
> 1 pound assorted wild mushrooms (cremini, shiitake, portobello), sliced
> salt and freshly ground pepper to taste
> 1 large clove garlic, minced
> 1 1/2 cups crushed Italian tomatoes (fresh or canned)
> 1 teaspoon dried basil
> 1/2 teaspoon dried thyme
> 1/4 cup chopped fresh parsley
> 1 pound penne

1. Heat the oil in a large saucepan. Add the mushrooms and season with salt and pepper. Sauté over medium heat until golden, stirring occasionally. Add the garlic and sauté for 1 minute more.

2. Add the tomatoes, basil, thyme, and parsley. Bring to a boil, cover, lower the heat, and simmer for 15 minutes.

3. While the sauce is simmering, cook the pasta according to the package directions. Drain well and transfer to a large bowl. Pour the ragout over the freshly cooked pasta, toss well, and serve.

6 to 8 portions

PASTA AND ARTICHOKE HEARTS

Strands of linguine are embellished with a gusty topping of marinated artichoke hearts defined by Dijon, capers, and lemon juice. Try the marinated artichoke hearts as a topping for bruschetta or as a dressing for a simple green salad.

1 large clove garlic, smashed
1¹/₂ teaspoons Dijon mustard
1 tablespoon capers
1 teaspoon dried oregano
salt and freshly ground pepper to taste
2 tablespoons lemon juice
¹/₂ cup extra-virgin olive oil
2 (14-ounce) cans artichoke hearts, rinsed, drained, and cut into quarters
1 pound linguine

1. In a bowl, combine the garlic, Dijon, capers, oregano, salt, pepper, and lemon juice. Whisk in the oil until thick and creamy.

2. Add the artichoke hearts and let marinate for 6 hours and as much as overnight in the refrigerator. Return to room temperature to serve.

3. When you are ready to partake, cook the linguine according to the package directions. Drain well and transfer to a large bowl.

4. Pour the artichoke hearts and sauce over the freshly cooked pasta, toss well, and serve warm or at room temperature.

8 side portions

MACARONI AND CHEESE

This old-fashioned favorite is the quintessential comfort food. The timeless classic doesn't get better than this homestyle version!

Topping:
$1/2$ fresh bread crumbs
1 tablespoon butter, melted
$1/2$ cup grated Parmigiano-Reggiano cheese

3 tablespoons butter
3 tablespoons all-purpose flour
$2^1/2$ cups whole milk
$1/2$ teaspoon dry mustard
pinch of cayenne pepper
salt and freshly ground pepper to taste
$2^1/4$ cups grated sharp white cheddar cheese
2 cups (8 ounces) elbow macaroni, cooked according to the
*   package directions*

1. Preheat the oven to 375°. Grease a 2-quart casserole.

2. Prepare the topping. In a bowl, toss together the bread crumbs and melted butter until evenly combined. Mix in the Parmesan cheese and set aside.

3. In a medium-size saucepan, heat the butter over medium heat. When hot, add the flour and cook for 1 minute, stirring constantly.

4. Slowly whisk in the milk. Cook, stirring often, until the mixture bubbles and thickens. Remove from the heat.

5. Add the mustard, cayenne, salt, pepper, and cheddar and mix well. Stir in the cooked macaroni. Turn into the prepared pan. Sprinkle with the buttered crumbs.

6. Bake for 25 to 30 minutes until golden. Let cool for 5 minutes before serving.

6 side portions; 4 main-course portions

OLD-FASHIONED
COMFORT MEAL

Old-Fashioned Cream
of Tomato Soup
. . .
Macaroni and Cheese
. . .
Grapes
. . .
Assorted Cookies

PENNE WITH ROASTED ASPARAGUS AND PROSCIUTTO

I love the nuances of flavors in this glorious dish! Penne struts a topping of oven-roasted asparagus, a balsamic vinaigrette, thin slices of delicately flavored, imported prosciutto, and a dusting of nutty-tasting Parmigiano-Reggiano cheese.

Balsamic Vinaigrette:
salt and freshly ground pepper to taste
2 tablespoons balsamic vinegar
5 tablespoons extra-virgin olive oil

12 ounces penne
$3/4$ pound asparagus, peeled and cut into 2-inch lengths
2 tablespoons extra-virgin olive oil
salt and freshly ground pepper to taste
$1/4$ pound thinly sliced imported prosciutto, cut into $1/2$-inch strips
$1/2$ cup coarsely grated Parmigiano-Reggiano cheese

1. Prepare the balsamic vinaigrette. In a small bowl, whisk together the salt, pepper, vinegar, and olive oil. Set aside.

2. Preheat the oven to 400°.

3. Cook the pasta according to the package directions. Drain well and transfer to a large bowl.

4. While the pasta is cooking, prepare the asparagus. Put the asparagus in a bowl. Drizzle with the olive oil and toss until evenly coated. Season with salt and pepper. Spread the pieces out on a baking sheet. Roast for 15 minutes, shaking the pan after 10 minutes.

5. Add the roasted asparagus along with any pan juices to the freshly cooked pasta.

6. Pour the vinaigrette over the pasta and toss until evenly mixed. Top with the prosciutto and cheese and serve warm or at room temperature.

6 portions

FARFALLE WITH TUNA AND WHITE BEANS

Pantry ingredients—tuna, cannellini beans, roasted red peppers, and Kalamata olives—define this colorful and hearty pasta dish that's dressed in a Dijon vinaigrette.

1 pound farfalle
12 to 13-ounce can tuna, drained and broken into chunks
14 to 15-ounce can cannellini beans, rinsed and drained
2 roasted red peppers, coarsely chopped
2/3 cup pitted Kalamata olives (see page 5)

Dijon Vinaigrette:
1 teaspoon salt
freshly ground pepper to taste
1 teaspoon dried basil
1 1/2 tablespoons Dijon mustard
3 tablespoons red wine vinegar
2/3 cup extra-virgin olive oil

1. Cook the pasta according to the package directions. Drain well and transfer to a large bowl.

2. Add the tuna, beans, roasted peppers, and olives to the pasta.

3. In a separate bowl, whisk together the salt, pepper, basil, Dijon, vinegar, and olive oil.

4. Pour the vinaigrette over the pasta, toss well, and serve warm or at room temperature.

8 or more portions

PASTA PARTY

Pasta and Grilled
Chicken Puttanesca
. . .
Pasta with Spinach
and Chèvre
. . .
Farfalle with Tuna
and White Beans
. . .
Greens with
Walnut Vinaigrette
. . .
Red and
Green Grapes

PASTA ROSA

Penne is teeming with slices of grilled chicken, lavished with pesto, and garnished with sun-dried tomatoes and goat cheese in this mouth-watering pasta ensemble.

2 whole boneless, skinless chicken breasts, split in half
2 tablespoons extra-virgin olive oil
salt and freshly ground pepper to taste
12 ounces penne or rotini
$^1/_2$ cup coarsely chopped sun-dried tomatoes, rehydrated in hot water
$^3/_4$ cup pesto (see page 12)
4 ounces goat cheese, crumbled

1. Brush the chicken with the oil. Season with salt and pepper.
2. Grill over hot coals, 4 inches from the heat source, 4 to 5 minutes per side. Slice the breasts on the diagonal into thin strips. Cover to keep warm and moist.
3. Cook the pasta according to the package directions. Drain well and transfer to a large platter or bowl.
4. Top the pasta with the chicken and any accumulated juices. Sprinkle with the sun-dried tomatoes.
5. Spoon the pesto over the chicken and garnish with the goat cheese. Toss well until evenly coated and serve warm or at room temperature.

4 to 6 portions

PASTA WITH ROASTED PEPPERS AND POTATOES

ITALIAN SUPPER

Olive Biscotti
. . .
Balsamic-Glazed
Veal Chops
. . .
Pasta with Roasted
Peppers and Potatoes
. . .
Sliced Tomatoes and
Buffalo Mozzarella
. . .
Italian Ices

The popular Italian combination of roasted peppers and potatoes stars in this lusty pasta dish that's finished with a dusting of Parmesan.

3/4 pound red-skinned potatoes, cut into 3/4-inch cubes
6 tablespoons extra-virgin olive oil
1/2 teaspoon dried basil
1/2 teaspoon dried thyme
1/2 teaspoon dried oregano
salt and freshly ground pepper to taste
12 ounces gemelli or fusilli
2 large roasted red peppers, cut into 3/4-inch squares
1/2 cup coarsely grated Parmesan cheese

1. Preheat the oven to 400°. Grease a baking pan.

2. Place the potatoes in the pan and drizzle with 2 tablespoons of the olive oil, mixing well until evenly coated. Season with basil, thyme, oregano, salt, and pepper. Bake for 20 minutes until cooked and golden.

3. While the potatoes are roasting, cook the pasta according to the package directions. Drain well and transfer to a large bowl.

4. Add the potatoes with any of the pan scrapings and the roasted peppers.

5. Add the remaining 1/4 cup olive oil, season with salt and pepper, and dust with Parmesan. Toss until evenly combined and serve at once or at room temperature.

6 portions

PASTA MARCO

The colors of this vibrant dish mimic the colors of the Italian flag—red, white, and green. Penne is surrounded by baby spinach, sun-dried tomatoes, and feta cheese and lightly dressed in a mustard-balsamic vinaigrette. It tastes as good as it looks.

WARM WEATHER PLEASERS

Grilled Salmon
Marinated in
Basic Vinaigrette
. . .
Pasta Marco
. . .
Grilled Asparagus
. . .
Assorted Melons

Mustard-Balsamic Vinaigrette:
salt and freshly ground pepper to taste
1 teaspoon Dijon mustard
1 teaspoon sugar
2 tablespoons balsamic vinegar
1/4 cup extra-virgin olive oil

12 ounces penne or mini-penne
5 ounces fresh baby spinach
3/4 cup sun-dried tomatoes, coarsely chopped and rehydrated in hot water
1 cup crumbled feta cheese

1. Prepare the vinaigrette. In a small bowl, whisk together the salt, pepper, mustard, sugar, vinegar, and olive oil. Set aside.

2. Cook the pasta according to the package directions. Drain well and transfer to a large bowl.

3. Add the spinach, sun-dried tomatoes, and feta.

4. Pour the vinaigrette over the pasta, toss until evenly mixed, and serve warm or at room temperature.

6 portions

SPAGHETTI AND MEATBALLS

I am hard-pressed to come up with another recipe that has as wide-spread appeal as spaghetti and meatballs. It's Italian comfort food, but has become an all-American favorite, continuing to get rave reviews. This homestyle recipe uses the basic marinara sauce found in the ziti bake recipe with the addition of red wine. The sauce may be prepared in advance and refrigerated for 1 to 2 days or frozen until needed.

Marinara Sauce:
3 tablespoons extra-virgin olive oil
1 large yellow onion, diced
2 large cloves garlic, minced
28-ounce can crushed tomatoes
1/2 cup dry red wine
1 teaspoon dried basil
1/2 teaspoon dried oregano
pinch of sugar
1/4 cup chopped Italian parsley
salt and freshly ground pepper to taste

1. Heat the olive oil in a large saucepan. Add the onion and sauté over medium heat until soft and translucent. Add the garlic and sauté for 1 minute more.

2. Add the tomatoes, wine, and seasonings. Bring to a boil, cover, lower the heat, and simmer for 20 minutes.

Meatballs:
3/4 pound ground beef
3/4 pound ground pork
2 eggs, beaten
1/2 cup dry red wine
2/3 cup fresh bread crumbs
1 small yellow onion, finely diced
2 large cloves garlic, crushed
salt and freshly ground pepper to taste
1/4 cup chopped Italian parsley
1/2 cup freshly grated Parmesan cheese

1 pound spaghetti

1. Preheat the oven to 400°. Grease a large baking sheet.

2. In a large bowl, mix the beef and pork Add the eggs and wine and stir until evenly combined.

3. Add the bread crumbs, onion, seasonings, and cheese and mix well.

4. With moistened hands, using 2 tablespoons of the mixture, form into golf-ball size nuggets. Place on the prepared baking sheet.

5. Bake in the upper third of the oven until cooked through and browned, about 15 to 20 minutes.

6. While the meatballs are baking, prepare the pasta according to the package directions. Drain well and transfer to a large bowl.

7. Add the cooked meatballs along with any pan scrapings to the Marinara Sauce. Simmer for 5 minutes. Pour over the freshly cooked pasta and serve at once.

28 meatballs; 6 to 8 portions

PASTA WITH ARUGULA PESTO

Arugula, also known as rugula, rocket, and rucola, has a peppery mustard taste I find irresistible. It makes an assertive pesto that will liven up any pasta dish. For a heartier meal, top the pasta with grilled chicken.

2 cups packed arugula, heavy stems removed
1 to 2 large cloves garlic, chopped
$1/2$ cup coarsely chopped walnuts, toasted
3 tablespoons grated imported Parmesan cheese
salt and freshly ground pepper to taste
$1/3$ cup extra-virgin olive oil
12 ounces spaghetti
freshly shaved imported Parmesan cheese for garnish

1. Put the arugula, garlic, $1/4$ cup walnuts, Parmesan, salt, and pepper in the bowl of a food processor. Pulse until the mixture forms a thick paste.

2. With the motor running, add the oil in a slow, steady stream until it is completely incorporated. Set aside.

3. Cook the pasta according to the package directions. Drain well and transfer to a large bowl.

4. Add the pesto to the pasta, tossing until evenly coated. Garnish with the remaining $1/4$ cup walnuts and shaved Parmesan. Serve warm or at room temperature.

4 to 6 portions

BON APPÉTIT

The 47 House Salad
· · ·
Chicken with
Mushroom Ragout
· · ·
Pasta with
Arugula Pesto
· · ·
Almond Cream Cake

ZITI WITH SAUSAGES AND ARTICHOKES

A symphony of Mediterranean flavors flourishes in this toothy, robust pasta dish. Ziti is coated with an embracing garlic and fennel-scented tomato sauce and is layered with sausages and artichoke hearts.

1 tablespoon extra-virgin olive oil
1 pound sweet Italian sausages (I use chicken sausages), cut into
   ³/₄-inch thick rounds
1 large yellow onion, chopped
2 large cloves garlic, minced
28-ounce can diced tomatoes
1 teaspoon fennel seeds
salt and freshly ground pepper to taste
1 tablespoon capers
¹/₂ cup dry red wine
14-ounce can artichoke hearts, drained and quartered
12 ounces ziti, cooked according to the package directions

1. Heat the oil in a large saucepan. Add the sausages and sauté over medium-high heat until browned. Remove the sausages to a plate and set aside. Drain off all but 1 tablespoon of oil from the pan.

2. Add the onion and sauté over medium heat until soft and translucent. Add the garlic and sauté for 1 minute more.

3. Add the tomatoes, fennel, salt, pepper, capers, and wine. Cover and simmer for 20 minutes.

4. Add the sausages and artichokes. Simmer for 5 minutes more.

5. Add the ziti, heat through, and serve piping hot.

4 portions

LINGUINE WITH MUSSELS

Reminiscent of the ever-popular linguine with white clam sauce, this pasta dish has a seductive topping. Sautéed leeks, garlic, and fennel share the limelight with mussels, the darlings of shellfish, in a delicate white wine sauce.

12 ounces linguine
1/4 cup extra-virgin olive oil
2 leeks (white part only), chopped
1/2 fennel bulb, thinly sliced
2 large cloves garlic, minced
1 cup white wine
1 tablespoon lemon juice
1 bay leaf
2 pounds mussels, scrubbed and debearded
1/4 cup chopped Italian parsley
salt and freshly ground pepper to taste

1. Cook the linguine according to the package directions. Drain well.

2. While the pasta is cooking, prepare the sauce. In a large saucepan or stockpot, heat the olive oil. Add the leeks and fennel and sauté over medium-low heat until soft, about 5 to 10 minutes. Add the garlic and sauté for 1 minute more.

3. Add the wine, lemon juice, and bay leaf and simmer for 2 to 3 minutes.

4. Add the mussels, parsley, salt, and pepper. Cover and simmer for 4 to 5 minutes, just until the mussel shells open. Transfer the mussels to a bowl, discarding any unopened ones.

5. Remove all but a dozen mussels from their shells, reserving the rest for garnish. Return the shelled mussels to the sauce along with the freshly cooked pasta. Heat through for 1 minute. Garnish with the mussels in their shells and serve at once.

4 to 6 portions

PASTA PLEASER

Linguine with Mussels
. . .
Garlic Bread
. . .
5-Star Chopped Salad
. . .
Cannoli

PASTA TOSCANO

Each spoonful of this dish unearths another level of complex, mouth-watering flavors. Fusilli boasts a topping of crispy, roasted prosciutto, sautéed shiitake mushrooms, roasted red peppers, and a sprinkling of provolone cheese. Roasting the prosciutto gives it a delicate crispness much like bacon. It can also be used in sandwiches and salads.

1/4 pound thinly sliced imported prosciutto
12 ounces fusilli
6 tablespoons extra-virgin olive oil
1/4 pound shiitake mushrooms, sliced
2 roasted red peppers, sliced into 1/2-inch wide strips
2 large cloves garlic, crushed
salt and freshly ground pepper to taste
1/2 cup coarsely grated provolone cheese

1. Preheat the oven to 375°. Line a baking sheet with parchment paper.

2. Place the prosciutto in a single layer on the parchment paper. Bake about 15 to 16 minutes until crisp. Let cool, then break into bite-size pieces.

3. Cook the pasta according to the package directions. Drain well and transfer to a large bowl.

4. While the pasta is cooking, prepare the topping. Heat the olive oil in a medium-size skillet. Add the mushrooms, peppers, and garlic. Season with salt and pepper and sauté over medium heat until the mushrooms are golden, stirring occasionally.

5. Add the sautéed vegetables to the pasta along with all of the oil. Sprinkle with the prosciutto and cheese, toss until evenly mixed, and serve warm or at room temperature.

4 to 6 portions

PASTA WITH CAULIFLOWER CRUMBS

Cauliflower is an elegant member of the cabbage family, resembling a large flower. It is characterized by a creamy white head of tightly packed flowerets that are slightly sweet and nutty. This pasta topping of flowerets lavished with toasted bread crumbs, garlic, and Parmigiano-Reggiano cheese is sure to capture your fancy.

12 ounces orecchiette (little ears)
1 1/2 pounds cauliflower, cut into small flowerets
1/2 cup fresh, coarse bread crumbs, toasted
1 large clove garlic, minced
1/2 cup grated Parmigiano-Reggiano cheese
salt and freshly ground pepper to taste
1/2 cup extra-virgin olive oil

1. Cook the pasta according to the package directions. Drain well and transfer to a large bowl.

2. While the pasta is cooking, prepare the topping. Steam the cauliflower until tender, about 5 minutes. Add to the pasta along with the bread crumbs, garlic, cheese, salt, pepper, and olive oil. Mix until evenly combined. Serve warm or at room temperature.

4 portions

MEDITERRANEAN
PALATE

Grilled Chicken
with Green Olive
Tapenade
. . .
Pasta with
Cauliflower Crumbs
. . .
Mixed Greens with
Basic Vinaigrette

PASTA WITH DEVILED CRAB

Flavors sparkle in this zesty, luxurious pasta sauce from the heart of the Bayou. Fresh lump crabmeat is bathed in a devilishly delicious wine-cream sauce that's spiked with Worcestershire and cayenne. It's lip-smacking good!

1 pound fettuccine
4 tablespoons butter
2 medium-size yellow onions, chopped
2 large cloves garlic, minced
1 medium-size red pepper, chopped
1 medium-size green pepper, chopped
2 large stalks celery, chopped
1$^{1}/_2$ teaspoons Worcestershire sauce
$^{1}/_8$ teaspoon cayenne pepper
salt and freshly ground pepper to taste
$^{3}/_4$ cup light cream
$^{3}/_4$ cup white wine
12 ounces lump crabmeat

1. Cook the pasta according to the package directions. Drain well and transfer to a large bowl.

2. While the pasta is cooking, prepare the sauce. In a large saucepan, heat the butter. Add the onion, garlic, peppers, celery, Worcestershire, cayenne, salt, and pepper. Sauté over medium heat until the vegetables are tender, about 10 minutes, stirring occasionally.

3. Combine the cream and wine. Add the mixture to the sauce and simmer for 2 to 3 minutes.

4. Add the crab and heat through. Pour over the freshly cooked pasta, toss gently, and serve at once.

6 to 8 portions

LEMON-POPPY SEED NOODLES

Lemon and poppy seeds have a natural affinity. Teamed with sour cream, it provides a delicate topping for pasta.

12 ounces wide egg noodles
2 tablespoons lemon juice
3 tablespoons butter, melted
2 tablespoons poppy seeds
salt and freshly ground pepper to taste
1 cup sour cream

1. Cook the noodles according to the package directions. Drain well and transfer to a large bowl.

2. While the pasta is cooking, prepare the sauce. In a small bowl, combine the lemon juice, butter, poppy seeds, salt, pepper, and sour cream and mix well.

3. Pour the topping over the freshly cooked pasta and serve.

6 portions

FRESH AND EASY

Roasted Cornish Hens

. . .

Lemon-Poppy
Seed Noodles

. . .

Zucchini Mandoline*

. . .

Butterscotch
Pudding Cake

PASTA, MUSSELS, AND TOMATOES

I love the simplicity and subtlety of this heavenly dish. Fusilli is teamed with freshly cooked mussels, chopped tomatoes, and chopped sweet onions. Sprinkled with fresh basil and dressed in a light balsamic vinaigrette, it's especially good served al fresco on a warm summer's night.

1 pound fusilli
4 pounds mussels, scrubbed and debearded
2 cups water
3 cups halved cherry tomatoes
1/2 cup chopped Vidalia or other sweet onion
1/2 cup chopped fresh basil
1/4 cup chopped Italian parsley

Balsamic Vinaigrette:
salt and freshly ground pepper to taste
3 tablespoons balsamic vinegar
1/4 cup extra-virgin olive oil

1. Cook the pasta according to the package directions. Drain well and transfer to a large bowl.

2. While the pasta is cooking, prepare the mussels. Put the mussels and water in a large stockpot. Cover, bring to a boil, and simmer gently just until the mussels open, 4 to 5 minutes. Transfer the mussels to a colander to drain, discarding any unopened ones. Remove the mussels from their shells.

3. Add the mussels, tomatoes, and onions to the freshly cooked pasta. Sprinkle with the basil and parsley.

4. In a separate small bowl, whisk together the salt, pepper, balsamic, and olive oil.

5. Pour the vinaigrette over the pasta and toss gently until evenly combined. Serve warm or at room temperature.

4 to 6 main-course portions

PENNE WITH FENNEL, ONION, AND ARTICHOKES

Fennel's delicate anise flavor lends an aromatic quality to this pasta dish. Thinly sliced fennel, red onion, and artichoke hearts are sautéed with garlic and finished with an orange-scented wine sauce that's magical atop penne.

> 12 ounces penne
> 1/4 cup orange juice
> 1/4 cup white wine
> 1/4 cup extra-virgin olive oil
> 1 fennel bulb (fronds removed), thinly sliced
> 1 large red onion, thinly sliced
> 1 teaspoon finely grated orange peel
> salt and freshly ground pepper to taste
> 2 large cloves garlic, minced
> 14-ounce can artichoke hearts, rinsed, drained, and quartered

1. Cook the pasta according to the package directions. Drain well and transfer to a large serving bowl.

2. While the pasta is cooking, prepare the sauce. In a small bowl, combine the orange juice and white wine and set aside.

3. Heat the olive oil in a large skillet. Add the fennel and red onion and season with the orange peel, salt, and pepper. Sauté over medium heat, stirring occasionally, until the vegetables are tender, about 10 to 15 minutes. Add the garlic and artichoke hearts and sauté for 1 minute more.

4. Add the wine sauce and simmer for 2 to 3 minutes. Pour the sauce over the freshly cooked pasta, toss well, and serve at once.

6 portions

THE FLAVORS
OF ITALY

Tuna Mousse
. . .
Penne with Fennel,
Onion, and Artichokes
. . .
5-Star Chopped Salad
. . .
Red and Green
Grapes

PASTA POSITANO

Pure and simple in design, this medley of Mediterranean ingredients—pasta, chickpeas, tomatoes, and olives—combines to excite the palate and soothe the soul.

12 ounces medium-size shells
19-ounce can chickpeas, rinsed and drained
1¹/2 cups chopped cherry tomatoes
¹/2 cup pitted Kalamata olives, halved (see page 5)
¹/2 cup loosely packed Italian parsley leaves
salt and freshly ground pepper to taste
2 tablespoons balsamic vinegar
¹/4 cup extra-virgin olive oil

1. Cook the pasta according to the package directions. Drain well and transfer to a large bowl.

2. Add the chickpeas, tomatoes, olives, and parsley.

3. In a separate small bowl, whisk together the salt, pepper, balsamic, and olive oil. Pour the vinaigrette over the freshly cooked pasta and toss until evenly mixed. Serve warm or at room temperature.

6 portions

PASTA WITH YELLOW PEPPER RELISH

A potpourri of herbs enhances the sweet, rich flavor of roasted yellow peppers in this savory relish that graces farfalle. This makes a great summertime repast.

3 large yellow peppers, roasted and chopped (see page 243, **The Uncommon Gourmet**)
1 plum tomato, chopped
1/4 cup coarsely chopped Italian parsley
1/2 teaspoon dried basil
1/2 teaspoon dried oregano
1/2 teaspoon dried thyme
salt and freshly ground pepper to taste
1 tablespoon balsamic vinegar
2 tablespoons extra-virgin olive oil
8 ounces farfalle (bow ties)

1. In a bowl, combine the roasted peppers, tomato, parsley, basil, oregano, thyme, salt, pepper, balsamic, and olive oil. Let marinate at room temperature for 30 to 60 minutes.

2. Cook the pasta according to the package directions. Drain well and transfer to a large bowl.

3. Top the pasta with the relish, toss until evenly combined, and serve at room temperature.

4 portions

PASTA WITH ESCAROLE AND ASIAGO

Escarole, actually a type of endive, has broad, pale green leaves and a mild flavor. Sautéed with toasted walnuts and finished with a sprinkling of Asiago cheese, the touted Italian cheddar, it makes a seductive topping for pasta.

12 ounces orecchiette (little ears)
1/4 cup extra-virgin olive oil
9 cups coarsely chopped escarole
1 large clove garlic, crushed
salt and freshly ground pepper to taste
1/2 cup toasted walnuts, coarsely chopped
3/4 cup grated Asiago cheese

1. Cook the pasta according to the package directions and drain well.

2. While the pasta is cooking, prepare the topping. Heat the oil in a large skillet. Add the escarole, garlic, salt, and pepper. Sauté over medium heat, stirring constantly until the escarole wilts, about 2 to 3 minutes. Add the nuts and freshly cooked pasta and mix well.

3. Sprinkle with the cheese, toss gently, and remove from the heat. Serve at once.

4 to 6 portions

PASTA AND EGGPLANT PROVENÇAL

Shells are enlivened with a thick tomato-eggplant ragout rich with the herbs and flavors of Provence.

2 tablespoons extra-virgin olive oil
1 large yellow onion, chopped
2 large cloves garlic, minced
1 large eggplant (about 1½ pounds), peeled and diced into ¾-inch cubes
28-ounce can Italian tomatoes, coarsely chopped with their juice
½ cup dry red wine
1 teaspoon dried basil
½ teaspoon dried thyme
½ teaspoon dried marjoram
1 bay leaf, crushed
¼ cup chopped fresh parsley
salt and freshly ground pepper to taste
1 tablespoon capers
12 ounces medium-size shells

1. Heat the oil in a large saucepan. Add the onion and sauté over medium heat until soft and translucent. Add the garlic and sauté for 1 minute more.

2. Add the eggplant and sauté for 3 minutes, stirring occasionally.

3. Add the tomatoes, wine, seasonings, and capers. Cover and simmer for 30 minutes.

4. While the sauce is simmering, cook the pasta according to the package directions and drain well.

5. Add the pasta to the sauce, stir through until evenly mixed, and serve at once.

4 to 6 portions

PRE-THEATER
DINNER

Parmesan-Crusted
Chicken
. . .
Pasta and Eggplant
Provençal
. . .
Rum Cake

LINGUINE WITH WALNUT CRUMBS

Linguine is embraced by the mellow, nutty taste of toasted walnuts and the tangy zip and characteristic saltiness of Romano cheese in this simple pasta dish. It's sure to become a favorite!

12 ounces linguine
lots of freshly ground pepper
1 tablespoon lemon juice
3 tablespoons walnut oil
$^1/_2$ cup toasted walnuts, finely chopped
$^3/_4$ cup grated Pecorino Romano cheese

1. Cook the pasta according to the package directions. Drain well and transfer to a large bowl.

2. While the pasta is cooking, prepare the sauce. In a small bowl, whisk together the pepper, lemon juice, and walnut oil.

3. Pour the walnut vinaigrette over the freshly cooked pasta and mix well. Add the walnuts and cheese and toss until evenly coated. Serve warm or at room temperature.

4 to 6 portions

PENNE WITH TOMATOES AND WHITE BEANS

This quick, easy, and colorful pasta dish showcases penne adorned with cherry tomatoes, cannellini beans, and a drizzle of basil oil.

12 ounces penne
1 cup lightly packed fresh basil
1 tablespoon balsamic vinegar
salt and freshly ground pepper to taste
5 tablespoons extra-virgin olive oil
1^1/$_2$ cups halved cherry tomatoes
1^1/$_2$ cups canned cannellini beans, rinsed and drained

1. Cook the pasta according to the package directions. Drain well and transfer to a large bowl.

2. While the pasta is cooking, prepare the sauce. Put the basil, vinegar, salt, and pepper in the bowl of a food processor and purée. With the motor running, add the oil in a slow, steady stream until completely incorporated.

3. Add the tomatoes, beans, and basil oil to the freshly cooked pasta. Toss well until evenly combined. Serve warm or at room temperature.

4 to 6 portions

LIGHT REPAST

Minted Pea Soup
. . .
Grilled Salmon
. . .
Penne with Tomatoes
and White Beans
. . .
Chocolate
Pudding Cake

LINGUINE PICCATA

Fashioned after the famous Italian veal in lemon sauce, this pasta dish is light, lemony, and delicate. The simple sauce is made from butter, lemon, and parsley and punctuated with capers. You can expand the flavors by garnishing the pasta with freshly grated Parmesan and Romano cheeses.

12 ounces linguine
4 tablespoons butter, melted
3 tablespoons lemon juice
1 teaspoon grated lemon peel
salt to taste
$1/2$ teaspoon freshly ground black pepper
3 tablespoons chopped fresh parsley
2 tablespoons capers

1. Cook the pasta according to the package directions. Drain well and transfer to a large bowl.

2. While the pasta is cooking, prepare the sauce. In a small bowl, combine the butter, lemon juice, peel, salt, pepper, parsley, and capers.

3. Pour the lemon-butter sauce over the freshly cooked pasta, toss well, and serve.

4 to 6 portions

PASTA WITH ROASTED WINTER VEGETABLES

This hearty vegetarian dish stars fusilli adorned with a host of roasted root vegetables. It's winter comfort food that's sure to warm and delight you. If you like, you can add a sprinkling of imported Parmesan or Romano cheese as a garnish.

COLD WEATHER COMFORTS

Chicken Gigi*
· · ·
Pasta with Roasted Winter Vegetables
· · ·
Indian Pudding

2 medium-size leeks (white part only), cut into 1-inch chunks
2 large carrots, halved lengthwise, and cut into 1-inch chunks
(Do not use peeled baby carrots.)
2 large parsnips, halved lengthwise, and cut into 1-inch chunks
1 pound turnips, peeled and cut into 1-inch chunks
1 small sweet potato, cut into 1-inch chunks
8 Brussel sprouts, trimmed and cut into half through the core
1 cup chicken broth
1/4 cup extra-virgin olive oil
1/2 cup dry white wine
1 1/2 teaspoons Old Bay Seasoning
salt to taste
1 pound fusilli

1. Preheat the oven to 400°. Grease a large roasting pan.

2. Heap the vegetables in the prepared pan.

3. Combine the broth, olive oil, and wine. Pour the mixture over the vegetables. Sprinkle with Old Bay and season with salt. Roast for 45 minutes, stirring every 15 minutes.

4. While the vegetables are roasting, cook the pasta according to the package directions. Drain well and transfer to a large bowl.

5. Pour the roasted vegetables and pan juices over the pasta and mix well. Serve warm or at room temperature.

8 or more portions

PASTA WITH SPINACH AND CHÈVRE

Spinach and goat cheese are a dynamic duo. The vibrant green leaves and heady cheese dressed in a warm mustard vinaigrette adds luster to fusilli.

6 tablespoons extra-virgin olive oil
2 tablespoons sherry vinegar
1 clove garlic, smashed
1 teaspoon Dijon mustard
1/2 teaspoon mustard seeds
pinch of sugar
salt and freshly ground pepper to taste
12 ounces fusilli
10 ounces spinach, coarsely chopped
4 ounces chèvre, crumbled
1/3 cup slivered almonds, toasted

1. Prepare the vinaigrette. In a small bowl, combine the olive oil, vinegar, garlic, Dijon, mustard seeds, sugar, salt, and pepper and mix well.

2. Cook the pasta according to the package directions. Drain well and transfer to a large bowl.

3. Heat the mustard vinaigrette in a large skillet. When hot, add the spinach and stir-fry over high heat for about 1 minute until wilted.

4. Pour the spinach and any pan juices over the pasta. Garnish with the goat cheese and nuts. Toss well until evenly mixed and serve.

4 to 6 portions

PASTA SETTO MEZZO

Bask in the glory of this savory fresh pasta sauce. Lush cherry tomatoes, Vidalia onion, and Kalamata olives top gemelli for a simple, yet sumptuous dish. It's a light meal for warm weather.

1 pound cherry tomatoes, halved
1 small Vidalia (or other sweet) onion, chopped
1/2 cup pitted Kalamata olives, coarsely chopped (see page 5)
salt and freshly ground pepper to taste
1 1/2 tablespoons balsamic vinegar
1/4 cup extra-virgin olive oil
12 ounces gemelli or fusilli

1. In a large bowl, combine the tomatoes, onion, and olives.

2. In a separate small bowl, whisk together the salt, pepper, balsamic, and olive oil. Pour the vinaigrette over the tomato mixture, toss well, and let marinate at room temperature for 30 to 60 minutes.

3. While the tomatoes are marinating, cook the pasta according to the package directions and drain well. Add the pasta to the marinated tomatoes, toss thoroughly, and serve warm or at room temperature.

4 to 6 side portions

**DINING
AL FRESCO**

Mixed Greens with
Balsamic Vinaigrette*
. . .
Grilled Chicken with
Salsa Verde
. . .
Pasta Sette Mezzo
. . .
Raisin Poundcake
à la Mode

PASTA WITH OVEN-BRAISED FENNEL

Fennel, also know as anise or finocchio, has a broad bulbous base with celery-like stems or fronds, sporting feathery tops. When braised, this fragrant vegetable is especially delicate with an elusive flavor. Set atop linguine and finished with a Parmesan garnish, this dish is sure to effect smiles.

2 large fennel bulbs (fronds removed), cut into quarters through the core
1 cup chicken broth
6 tablespoons extra-virgin olive oil
salt and freshly ground pepper to taste
12 ounces linguine
1/2 cup grated Parmigiano-Reggiano cheese

1. Preheat the oven to 450°. Grease a 9 x 13-inch baking dish.

2. Place the fennel in the prepared pan. Pour the broth over the fennel and drizzle with 4 tablespoons of the olive oil. Season with salt and pepper.

3. Roast for 30 minutes, basting after 15 minutes, until the fennel is tender when pierced with a fork.

4. While the fennel is roasting, cook the pasta according to the package directions. Drain well and transfer to a large serving bowl. Drizzle with the remaining 2 tablespoons olive oil and toss until evenly coated.

5. Chop the cooked fennel and add it to the pasta along with any pan juices. Sprinkle with the cheese and serve at once.

4 portions

PASTA Y FAGIOLI

U sually presented as a soup, this Italian-inspired dish stars the winning combination of pasta and white beans. Cloaked in a heavenly, herb-scented tomato sauce it's sure to satisfy and comfort you.

2 tablespoons extra-virgin olive oil
1 large yellow onion, chopped
3 large cloves garlic, minced
28-ounce can crushed tomatoes
1 1/2 teaspoons dried basil
1 teaspoon dried thyme
1 teaspoon dried sage
1/4 teaspoon dried rosemary
salt and freshly ground pepper to taste
14 to 15-ounce can cannellini beans, rinsed and drained
12 ounces farfalle

1. Heat the oil in a large saucepan. Add the onion and sauté over medium heat until soft and translucent. Add the garlic and sauté for 1 minute more.

2. Add the tomatoes, herbs, salt, and pepper. Simmer uncovered for 15 minutes. Add the beans and heat through.

3. While the sauce is simmering, cook the pasta according to the package directions. Drain well and transfer to a large bowl. Pour the sauce over the freshly cooked pasta, toss well, and serve.

4 to 6 portions

FRESH FROM
ITALY

Pasta Y Fagioli
. . .
Chopped Tomatoes
with Basic Vinaigrette
. . .
Chocolate-Hazelnut
Biscotti
. . .
Stuffed Strawberries

PASTA AND SHRIMP NAGSHEAD

Plump and succulent, shrimp are considered the jewels of the shellfish world. In this simple sauté, they share the limelight with red and yellow peppers, artichoke hearts, and feta cheese, set atop a bed of spinach fettuccine. It's a feast for the eyes as well as the palate!

8 ounces spinach fettuccine or linguine
4 tablespoons extra-virgin olive oil
1 medium-size red pepper, cut into ¹/₂-inch wide strips
1 medium-size yellow pepper, cut into ¹/₂-inch wide strips
1 large clove garlic, minced
1¹/₂ pounds raw extra-large shrimp, shelled
14-ounce can artichoke hearts, drained and quartered
1 tablespoon lemon juice
salt and freshly ground pepper to taste
1 cup crumbled feta cheese
paprika for garnish

1. Cook the pasta according to the package directions. Drain well and transfer to a large bowl or platter.

2. Heat the oil in a large skillet. Add the peppers and sauté over high heat until tender-crisp, about 2 to 3 minutes. Add the garlic and cook for 30 seconds.

3. Add the shrimp, artichokes, lemon juice, salt and pepper. Stir-fry for 3 to 4 minutes until the shrimp are cooked.

4. Sprinkle with the feta, remove from the heat, and spoon over the pasta. Sprinkle with paprika and serve.

4 portions

LINGUINE WITH GARLIC CRUMBS

Thin strands of pasta are heady with a garlic-infused oil and garnished with toasted bread crumbs and pine nuts for a simple, yet delicious meal. To extend the flavors, try adding a dusting of Parmesan to top off the dish.

12 ounces linguine
4 tablespoons extra-virgin olive oil
2 tablespoons butter
2 to 3 large cloves garlic, minced
1/2 teaspoon salt
freshly ground pepper to taste
1/2 cup French bread crumbs, toasted
3 tablespoons chopped fresh parsley
1/4 cup pine nuts, toasted

1. Cook the pasta according to the package directions. Drain well and transfer to a large bowl.

2. Heat the oil and butter in a small saucepan. Add the garlic and cook for 1 minute over medium heat to soften the garlic and release its essence.

3. Pour the garlic oil over the freshly cooked pasta. Add the salt, pepper, bread crumbs, parsley, and nuts, toss well, and serve warm or at room temperature.

4 portions

PASTA ROGERE

Pure, distinct flavors abound in this colorful pasta presentation. Bow ties are lavished with shrimp, arugula, and Parmesan and dressed in a simple balsamic vinaigrette. This elegant dish is quick to prepare and always receives accolades.

salt and freshly ground pepper to taste
1¹/₂ tablespoons balsamic vinegar
¹/₄ cup extra-virgin olive oil
12 ounces farfalle
1 pound poached or grilled shrimp
4 cups coarsely chopped, lightly packed arugula
¹/₂ cup coarsely grated Parmigiano-Reggiano cheese

1. In a small bowl, whisk together the salt, pepper, balsamic, and olive oil.

2. Cook the pasta according to the package directions. Drain well and transfer to a large bowl.

3. Add the shrimp, arugula, and Parmesan. Pour the vinaigrette over the pasta, toss well, and serve warm or at room temperature.

6 portions

PENNE WITH ROASTED TOMATOES AND HERBED GOAT CHEESE

Roasting tomatoes lends a rich, concentrated flavor to the fruit. Coupled with an herb-infused goat cheese, this topping transforms pasta into a lavish dish.

Roasted Tomatoes:
1 pound cherry tomatoes, halved
2 tablespoons extra-virgin olive oil
salt and freshly ground pepper to taste

Herbed Goat Cheese:
6 ounces goat cheese, crumbled
1 teaspoon dried basil
$1/2$ teaspoon dried thyme
$1/2$ teaspoon dried marjoram
$1/4$ teaspoon dried rosemary
2 tablespoons chopped fresh parsley
salt to taste
$1/4$ teaspoon freshly ground pepper
1 tablespoon balsamic vinegar
6 tablespoons extra-virgin olive oil

12 ounces penne

1. Preheat the oven to 400°. Grease a baking sheet.

2. Place the cherry tomatoes, cut side up, on the baking sheet. Drizzle with the 2 tablespoons olive oil and season with salt and pepper.

3. Roast for 20 to 25 minutes until carmelized on the bottom.

4. Prepare the Herbed Goat Cheese. In a bowl, combine the goat cheese, herbs, salt, pepper, balsamic, and olive oil. Mix well until evenly blended.

5. Cook the pasta according to the package directions. Drain well and transfer to a large bowl.

6. Add the roasted tomatoes and Herbed Goat Cheese to the freshly cooked pasta, toss gently until evenly coated, and serve.

6 or more side portions; 4 main-course portions

PASTA, PEAS, AND BACON

ONE-DISH LUNCH

Pasta, Peas, and Bacon
· · ·
Watermelon

O recchiette provides a background for this hearty salad featuring peas, bacon, waterchestnuts, and toasted pine nuts. This makes great luncheon fare and totes well to picnics.

12 ounces orecchiette (little ears)
2 cups (fresh or frozen) peas, cooked until tender-crisp
4 slices bacon, cooked and coarsely chopped
8-ounce can waterchestnuts, drained and sliced
$^1\!/_4$ cup pine nuts, toasted
$^1\!/_2$ cup thinly sliced scallions
salt and freshly ground pepper to taste
$^1\!/_2$ cup mayonnaise

1. Cook the pasta according to the package directions. Drain well and transfer to a large bowl.

2. Add the peas, bacon, waterchestnuts, pine nuts, and scallions. Season with salt and pepper and toss well.

3. Mix in the mayonnaise until evenly blended. Serve warm or at room temperature.

6 to 8 portions

FARFALLE WITH TOMATOES, CORN, AND BLUE CHEESE

Garden tomatoes and corn are dazzling vegetables of summer. Set over pasta and dressed in a blue cheese sauce, this makes a mouth-watering dish fit for a king!

1 cup sour cream
1/2 cup buttermilk
1/2 cup crumbled blue cheese
salt and freshly ground pepper to taste
12 ounces farfalle
1 bunch watercress, heavy stems removed
2 cups chopped tomatoes
1 1/2 cups corn kernels (fresh or frozen), blanched

1. In a small bowl, combine the sour cream, buttermilk, blue cheese, salt, and pepper and mix well.

2. Cook the pasta according to the package directions. Drain well and transfer to a large bowl.

3. Add the watercress, tomatoes, and corn.

4. Pour the blue cheese sauce over all, toss gently, and serve.

4 to 6 portions

A BIT OF AMERICANA

Grilled Chicken
Marinated in
Basic Vinaigrette
. . .
Farfalle with
Tomatoes, Corn, and
Blue Cheese
. . .
Dilled Onion Crostini
. . .
Strawberry-Rhubarb
Cobbler

ORZO PRIMAVERA

Orzo is the tiny, rice-shaped pasta. It makes an ideal base for this colorful medley of diced vegetables that's scented with a mint and cilantro vinaigrette. It tastes as good as it looks and is one of those all-occasion dishes that fits the theme, whether casual or fancy, intimate or grand.

1 pound orzo
1 cup frozen peas, thawed
2 large stalks celery, diced
1 medium-size red pepper, diced
1 medium-size yellow pepper, diced
1 medium-size zucchini, diced
1 cup thinly sliced scallions
2 large carrots, diced

Mint-Cilantro Vinaigrette:
1 teaspoon salt (or more to taste)
freshly ground pepper to taste
2 tablespoons finely chopped fresh mint
3 tablespoons finely chopped fresh cilantro
3 tablespoons lemon juice
3/4 cup extra-virgin olive oil

1. Cook the orzo according to the package directions. Drain well and transfer to a large bowl.

2. While the pasta is cooking, prepare the vinaigrette. In a small bowl, whisk together the salt, pepper, mint, cilantro, lemon juice, and olive oil.

3. Add all of the vegetables to the pasta and mix well.

4. Pour the vinaigrette over the warm pasta and stir until evenly coated. Serve warm or at room temperature.

10 or more portions

MIDDLE EASTERN FARFALLE

A symphony of Middle Eastern flavors shines in this pasta dish. Reminiscent of tabbouli, farfalle are coated with a garlic, mint, parsley, and lemon vinaigrette and adorned with tomatoes and chickpeas. Colorful and nutritious, it's absolutely addictive.

MIDDLE EASTERN PLEASURES

Red Pepper Hummus
with Crudités
. . .
Middle Eastern
Farfalle
. . .
Grilled Lamb Chops
. . .
Grilled Zucchini

1/2 cup thinly sliced scallions
1 1/2 cups finely chopped fresh parsley
3 tablespoons finely chopped fresh mint
1 large clove garlic, minced
salt and freshly ground pepper to taste
1/4 cup lemon juice
6 tablespoons extra-virgin olive oil
12 ounces farfalle
19-ounce can chickpeas, rinsed and drained
1 1/2 cups halved cherry tomatoes

1. In a medium-size bowl, combine the scallions, parsley, mint, garlic, salt, pepper, lemon juice, and olive oil.

2. Cook the pasta according to the package directions. Drain well and transfer to a large bowl.

3. Add the chickpeas and tomatoes. Pour the vinaigrette over the pasta and toss well until evenly mixed. Serve warm or at room temperature.

6 portions

PENNE WITH POTATOES AND GREEN BEANS GENOVESE

This lip-smacking pasta experience showcases red-skinned potatoes, green beans, and sun-dried tomatoes tossed with penne, and drizzled with a pesto cream sauce.

1 pound penne
1 pound new or red-skinned potatoes, cut into $3/4$-inch cubes, and cooked until tender
$1/2$ pound green beans, snapped in half, and poached until tender
1 cup coarsely chopped sun-dried tomatoes, rehydrated in hot water
$1/2$ cup chopped scallions
$1^1/4$ cups pesto (see page 12)
$1/2$ cup light cream

1. Cook the pasta according to the package directions. Drain well and transfer to a large bowl.

2. Add the potatoes, green beans, sun-dried tomatoes, and scallions to the freshly cooked pasta.

3. In a separate bowl, combine the pesto and cream, stirring until evenly mixed.

4. Pour the pesto sauce over the pasta, toss until evenly combined, and serve.

8 or more side portions; 5 to 6 main-course portions

PASTA AND GRILLED CHICKEN PUTTANESCA

Puttanesca is a spicy, exciting sauce. Its lively taste is attributed to the blending of its Niçoise ingredients—tomatoes, garlic, capers, anchovies, black olives, and red pepper flakes. This glorious dish features grilled chicken atop pasta napped in a fresh Puttanesca Sauce.

Puttanesca Sauce:
1 pound plum tomatoes, chopped
1/2 cup pitted Kalamata olives, coarsely chopped (see page 5)
2 tablespoons capers, rinsed
6 anchovy filets, rinsed, drained, and finely chopped
1 large clove garlic, minced
1/2 cup coarsely chopped Italian parsley
1/2 teaspoon crushed red pepper flakes
1/4 cup extra-virgin olive oil

2 boneless, skinless chicken breasts, split in half
2 tablespoons extra-virgin olive oil
salt and freshly ground pepper to taste
8 ounces fusilli

1. Make the Puttanesca Sauce. In a bowl, combine the tomatoes, olives, capers, anchovies, garlic, parsley, red pepper flakes, and olive oil. Let marinate at room temperature for 1 to 2 hours for the flavors to blend.

2. Brush the chicken with the 2 tablespoons olive oil. Season with salt and pepper. Grill over hot coals, 4-inches from the heat source, 4 to 5 minutes per side. Transfer to a plate and let cool slightly; then slice into 1/2-inch wide strips. Cover to keep warm.

3. Cook the pasta according to the package directions. Drain well and transfer to a large platter. Top the pasta with the chicken. Ladle the sauce over all and serve.

4 portions

ORECCHIETTE NIÇOISE

Dominated by the flavors of the Mediterranean, this pasta dish is enhanced by tuna, anchovies, hard-boiled eggs, and tomatoes and finished with a Basil Oil. Team it up with a mixed green salad to complete the meal.

Basil Oil:
1 cup lightly packed fresh basil
1 medium-size clove garlic, crushed
salt and freshly ground pepper to taste
6 tablespoons extra-virgin olive oil

12 ounces orecchiette (little ears)
6-ounce can tuna, drained
2-ounce can anchovies, rinsed, drained, and chopped
2 hard-boiled eggs, chopped
2 medium-size tomatoes, chopped

1. Prepare the Basil Oil. Put the basil, garlic, salt, and pepper in the bowl of a food processor and purée. With the motor running, add the oil in a slow, steady stream until completely incorporated and smooth.

2. Cook the pasta according to the package directions. Drain well and transfer to a large bowl.

3. Add the tuna, anchovies, eggs, and tomatoes. Drizzle with the Basil Oil and mix gently until evenly coated. Serve warm or at room temperature.

4 to 6 portions

RICOTTA GNOCCHI

Gnocchi are the small Italian dumplings Americans have come
to appreciate. Although not really pasta, they take the place of the
favored carbohydrate. Classically they are boiled and then served with
a sauce. Toppings are numerous as the gnocchi provides a versatile
base for saucing.

2 eggs
1 cup whole milk ricotta
1/4 cup grated Parmigiano-Reggiano cheese
1 cup all-purpose flour
salt and freshly ground pepper to taste
1/4 cup additional flour for coating gnocchi

Butter Sauce:
3 tablespoons butter, melted
1/4 cup grated Parmigiano-Reggiano cheese

1. In a large bowl, combine the eggs, ricotta, Parmesan, 1 cup flour,
salt, and pepper and mix well.

2. Using a tablespoon, scoop spoonfuls of dough into 1/4 cup additional flour. Coat each gnocchi lightly, gently rolling it into an oval. Do
not press firmly on the dough—you want the gnocchi to be soft and
fluffy. (Up to this point may be made several hours in advance and
placed on a wax paper-lined baking sheet and refrigerated until cooking time.)

3. Drop the gnocchi into boiling salted water in small batches. Cook
until the gnocchi rise to the top. This will only take a few minutes.
Remove the cooked gnocchi with a slotted spoon to a bowl. Drizzle
with the melted butter and sprinkle with the Parmesan. Serve at once.

5 to 6 side portions; 3 to 4 main-course portions

ITALIAN FEAST

Tomato Bruschetta
. . .
Veal Chops Tapenade
. . .
Ricotta Gnocchi
. . .
Mixed Greens with
Basic Vinaigrette
. . .
Chocolate-Hazelnut
Biscotti

TOPPINGS FOR GNOCCHI

Try any one of these sauces for a comforting, homestyle meal:

- Pesto
- Marinara sauce and mozzarella cheese
- Artichoke hearts, black olives, and sun-dried tomatoes with olive oil
- Roasted peppers with balsamic vinegar and olive oil
- Chopped tomatoes, Kalamata olives, and feta cheese with lemon juice and olive oil
- Prosciutto and shaved Parmesan cheese with olive oil
- Grilled or roasted vegetables—eggplant, peppers, mushrooms, and zucchini
- Olivada
- Sun-dried tomatoes, basil, and goat cheese
- Bacon and cheddar cheese
- Ratatouille
- Sausages and roasted peppers
- Arugula, tomatoes, and Romano cheese
- Lemon, butter, and capers
- Sautéed sage leaves with butter
- Sautéed onion, rosemary, and Parmesan cheese
- Sautéed assorted mushrooms

THE SALAD BOWL

For me, a dinner without a salad is like a heart without the soul. It's my favorite part of the meal, whether a simple green or main-dish variety. I love the interesting combinations of tastes, textures, and colors.

Salad creation is an art. Salads should look wonderful and taste delicious. The best salad utilizes only the freshest ingredients—an array of greens and vegetables, fruits and nuts, beans and grains, seafood, meats, and chicken—and are sauced with a complementary dressing.

I never expected to create so many new and different salads for this book. They just seemed to evolve. The ingredients danced together in interesting and simple ways, creating complex layers of flavor. I think you'll find these combinations tempting and tantalizing.

Celebrate the day with a fabulous salad!

GREEN SALADS

ASPARAGUS AND CHERRY TOMATOES

Piquant, colorful, and savory best describe this stylish salad of poached asparagus, chopped tomatoes, and capers dressed in a sherry vinaigrette.

2 pounds mature asparagus stalks, peeled and poached until tender-crisp
3/4 pound cherry tomatoes, halved
2 tablespoons capers

Sherry Vinaigrette:
salt and freshly ground pepper to taste
1 teaspoon Dijon mustard
1 1/2 tablespoons sherry vinegar
1/3 cup extra-virgin olive oil

1. Arrange the asparagus spears in a single layer in a serving dish. Scatter the tomatoes and capers over the spears.

2. In a small bowl, whisk together the salt, pepper, Dijon, vinegar, and olive oil.

3. Pour the vinaigrette over the vegetables, mix until evenly coated, and serve at room temperature. This may be left to marinate for 1 hour before serving.

6 portions

BLT SALAD WITH BLUE CHEESE DRESSING

The infamous sandwich combination of bacon, lettuce, and tomato is a natural salad winner when paired with a blue cheese topping.

1 head iceberg lettuce, cut into 4 to 6 wedges
2 large tomatoes, chopped
6 slices bacon, cooked and coarsely chopped
1/2 cup chopped scallions

Blue Cheese Dressing:
salt and freshly ground pepper to taste
1/4 cup mayonnaise
1/2 cup sour cream
3 tablespoons red wine vinegar
1/2 cup crumbled blue cheese

1. Place the lettuce on individual plates. Adorn each portion with equal amounts of tomato, bacon, and scallion.

2. In a small bowl, whisk together the salt, pepper, mayonnaise, sour cream, and vinegar. Stir in the blue cheese.

3. Spoon dollops of the dressing over each portion and serve at once.

4 to 6 portions

LIGHT SUMMER DINNER

Deviled Crab Cakes
· · ·
BLT Salad with Blue Cheese Dressing
· · ·
French Bread
· · ·
Mixed Berry Galette

CARLOS SALAD

HOMESTYLE
MEAL

Carlos Salad
. . .
Chicken Parmigiana
. . .
Pasta
. . .
Garlic Bread
. . .
Fresh Fruit

This typical Italian salad offers mixed greens with a symphony of vegetables, dressed in a simple, yet mouth-watering, red wine vinaigrette.

10 cups coarsely chopped mixed greens (green leaf and romaine)
2 cups coarsely chopped radicchio
2 cups frisée
1 large tomato, thinly sliced into wedges
1 large rib celery, thinly sliced
1 carrot, cut into thin rounds
$^1/_2$ cup thinly sliced Vidalia (or other sweet) onion
$^1/_2$ cup ripe black olives

Red Wine Vinaigrette:
1 teaspoon salt
freshly ground pepper to taste
3 tablespoons red wine vinegar
4 tablespoons extra-virgin olive oil
3 tablespoons olive oil (not extra-virgin)

1. Heap the lettuces in a large bowl. Add the tomato, celery, carrot, onion, and black olives.

2. In a separate small bowl, whisk together the salt, pepper, vinegar, and oils.

3. Pour the vinaigrette over the salad, toss well, and serve at once.

6 portions

SOUTHWESTERN CAESAR WITH GRILLED ROMAINE

This fiery, gutsy rendition of Caesar salad has robust flavors. Hearts of romaine are grilled, then napped in a zesty chili dressing, and topped off with cayenne-spiced croutons. This is sure to get your taste buds dancing!

Chili Mayonnaise:
salt and freshly ground pepper to taste
1 clove garlic, smashed
1/4 teaspoon Worcestershire sauce
1/2 teaspoon chili powder
1/8 teaspoon cayenne pepper
3 tablespoons mayonnaise

2 slices thin white sandwich bread, cut in half on the diagonal
2 tablespoons plus 1 teaspoon extra-virgin olive oil
cayenne pepper
2 hearts romaine, sliced in half lengthwise
2 tablespoons freshly grated imported Parmesan cheese

1. In a small bowl, whisk together the salt, pepper, garlic, Worcestershire, chili powder, cayenne, and mayonnaise.

2. Preheat the oven to 400°.

3. Brush the tops of the bread triangles with 1 teaspoon olive oil. Sprinkle with cayenne— the amount is to your discretion, depending on how spicy you want them.

4. Bake the croutons for 10 minutes until golden and crunchy.

5. Brush the hearts of romaine with 2 tablespoons olive oil. Grill over hot coals until lightly charred, about 2 minutes per side.

6. When ready to serve, remove the garlic from the dressing. Arrange half a romaine heart on each plate. Dab the hearts with dollops of the chili mayonnaise. Sprinkle with the Parmesan, garnish with a crouton point, and serve at once.

4 portions

A TASTE OF THE
SOUTHWEST

Black Bean Chili
· · ·
Cornbread
· · ·
Southwestern Caesar
with Grilled Romaine
(and Grilled Chicken)
· · ·
Orange Wedges

MESCLUN SALAD WITH TOASTED GOAT CHEESE

This salad is gourmet comfort food at its best! Warm rounds of herbed goat cheese adorn baby lettuces which are lightly dressed in a delicate balsamic vinaigrette.

14 cups mesclun
12 ounces chèvre, sliced into 12 rounds
3 tablespoons extra-virgin olive oil
1¹/₂ teaspoons herbs de Provence
1 cup fine French bread crumbs, toasted

Balsamic Vinaigrette:
salt and freshly ground pepper to taste
¹/₂ teaspoon stone ground mustard
1¹/₂ tablespoons balsamic vinegar
¹/₄ cup extra-virgin olive oil

1. Heap the mesclun in a large bowl and refrigerate.

2. Put the goat cheese slices on a plate and drizzle with the olive oil, coating all surfaces. Sprinkle with the herbs.

3. Coat the cheese rounds with the crumbs, covering completely. Place on a baking sheet and refrigerate for at least 1 hour and as much as overnight.

4. Preheat the oven to 400°.

5. Remove the cheese from the refrigerator and return to room temperature. Bake the rounds for 7 to 8 minutes until the centers are warm.

6. While the cheese is baking, prepare the vinaigrette. In a small bowl, whisk together the salt, pepper, mustard, balsamic, and olive oil. Pour the vinaigrette over the mesclun and toss well until evenly mixed.

7. Arrange the greens on individual plates, garnish each portion with 2 warm toasted cheese rounds, and serve at once.

6 portions

GREEN BEANS AND TOMATOES WITH GREEN OLIVE VINAIGRETTE

The chopped green olive and shallot vinaigrette adds piquancy to red leaf lettuce, poached green beans, and chopped tomatoes, making this a most savory salad.

1 large head red leaf lettuce, broken into bite-size pieces
2 large tomatoes, coarsely chopped
1/2 pound green beans, poached until tender-crisp

Green Olive Vinaigrette:
salt to taste
lots of freshly ground pepper
1 large shallot, thinly sliced
1/4 cup coarsely chopped pimiento-stuffed green olives
1 1/2 tablespoons red wine vinegar
1/3 cup extra-virgin olive oil

1. Heap the lettuce in a large bowl. Add the tomatoes and green beans.

2. In a separate small bowl, whisk together the salt, pepper, shallot, olives, vinegar, and oil.

3. Pour the vinaigrette over the salad, toss well, and serve at once.

4 to 6 portions

LUNCH FOR 6

Green Beans and
Tomatoes with Green
Olive Vinaigrette
· · ·
Assorted Rolls
· · ·
Potato and Goat
Cheese Frittata
· · ·
Ginger Crisps
· · ·
Lemon Sorbet

BABY SPINACH AND SHIITAKE MUSHROOMS

Tender leaves of baby spinach are coupled with warm, sautéed Oriental mushrooms. Dotted with toasted pine nuts, splashed with a balsamic vinaigrette, and garnished with the tangy flavor of chèvre, this is indeed a heady experience.

10 ounces baby spinach
1/4 cup pine nuts, toasted
2 tablespoons extra-virgin olive oil
1 large clove garlic, minced
1/2 pound shiitake mushrooms (stems trimmed), sliced
salt to taste
3 to 4 ounces goat cheese, crumbled

Balsamic Vinaigrette:
salt and freshly ground pepper to taste
1 teaspoon sugar
2 tablespoons balsamic vinegar
1/4 cup extra-virgin olive oil

1. Heap the spinach in a large bowl. Add the pine nuts.

2. Prepare the vinaigrette. In a small bowl, whisk together the salt, pepper, sugar, balsamic, and olive oil. Set aside.

3. Heat the 2 tablespoons olive oil in a large non-stick skillet. Add the garlic and mushrooms and season with salt. Cover and cook over medium-low heat until soft, about 10 minutes, stirring occasionally. Uncover and sauté until lightly golden. Remove from the heat and add to the spinach.

4. Pour the vinaigrette over the salad and toss well. Divide into portions, garnish each with some crumbled goat cheese, and serve at once.

4 to 6 portions

HARVEST BEET SALAD

Beets and blue cheese—just the mention of this combination arouses my taste buds. Earthy, ruby red beets and toasted walnuts are set on hearts of romaine and are cloaked in a creamy blue cheese dressing.

1 pound young beets, scrubbed
2 hearts romaine, split in half lengthwise
1/2 cup chopped walnuts, toasted
1/2 small red onion, thinly sliced into rings

Blue Cheese Dressing:
salt and freshly ground pepper to taste
1/3 cup mayonnaise
1 tablespoon light cream
1 tablespoon lemon juice
1/3 cup crumbled blue cheese (I prefer Saga Blue, but you may use Roquefort if you prefer.)

1. Put the beets in a saucepan and add cold water to cover. Bring to a boil, reduce the heat, cover, and simmer for 35 to 45 minutes, just until the beets are tender. Drain and let cool. When cool, slip off the skins and cut the beets into quarters.

2. Place half of a romaine heart on each plate and surround with beets. Sprinkle with the walnuts and garnish with onion rings.

3. In a separate bowl, whisk together the salt, pepper, mayonnaise, cream, and lemon juice. Stir in the blue cheese.

4. Put dollops of the dressing atop each portion and serve at once.

4 portions

HARVEST DINNER

Harvest Beet Salad
. . .
Roast Pork
. . .
Mashed Root
Vegetables
. . .
Caramel Apple Cake

SALAD ROMANO

ITALIAN IMPORT

Salad Romano
. . .
Osso Buco
. . .
Baked Risotto
. . .
Gelato

This Italian-inspired salad is a mélange of complementary flavors and textures. Tender, leafy spinach is embellished with the characteristic salty taste of thinly sliced prosciutto, the smoky taste of toasted pine nuts, the sweetness of golden raisins, and is garnished with the sharp flavor of lacy Parmesan Crisps. To sample it is to love it.

10 ounces fresh spinach, stems removed
1/8 pound thinly sliced imported prosciutto
1/4 cup yellow or golden raisins
3 tablespoons pine nuts, toasted
Parmesan Crisps (recipe follows)

Vinaigrette:
salt and freshly ground pepper to taste
1 clove garlic, smashed
*1 teaspoon Hot Mustard (see page 9, **The Uncommon Gourmet**)*
2 tablespoons balsamic vinegar
1/3 cup extra-virgin olive oil

1. Heap the spinach in a large bowl. Add the prosciutto, raisins, and pine nuts.

2. In a separate small bowl, whisk together the salt, pepper, garlic, mustard, vinegar, and olive oil.

3. When ready to serve the salad, remove the garlic from the vinaigrette. Pour the dressing over the salad and toss well. Garnish each salad with 2 Parmesan Crisps and serve at once.

4 to 6 portions

Parmesan Crisps:
1 1/2 cups freshly grated Parmigiano-Reggiano cheese

1. Preheat the oven to 350°. Line a baking sheet with parchment paper.

2. For each crisp, spread 2 tablespoons of grated cheese on the paper to form a 2-inch round.

3. Bake until the cheese is pale golden, about 10 minutes. Cool for 1 minute on the baking sheet; then remove the crisps to a rack to cool completely. Store in an air-tight container.

12 crisps

SALAD CORNUCOPIA

The dynamic trio of corn, tomatoes, and avocado basks in this salad lavished with a balsamic vinaigrette and dotted with toasted pine nuts.

1 head or 2 hearts romaine, cut into 1/2-inch wide strips
1 cup corn kernels (fresh or frozen), poached
12 cherry tomatoes, halved
1 ripe Haas avocado, peeled, pitted, and diced
3 tablespoons pine nuts, toasted

Balsamic Vinaigrette:
salt and freshly ground pepper to taste
1 teaspoon Dijon mustard
2 tablespoons balsamic vinegar
1/3 cup extra-virgin olive oil

1. Heap the romaine in a large bowl. Add the corn, tomatoes, avocado, and pine nuts.

2. In a separate small bowl, whisk together the salt, pepper, Dijon, balsamic, and olive oil until thick and creamy.

3. Pour the dressing over the salad, toss gently, and serve at once.

4 to 6 portions

4TH OF JULY CELEBRATION

Grilled Mussels
Green Goddess
. . .
Salad Cornucopia
. . .
Sweet Soy-Glazed Salmon
. . .
Basic Couscous**
. . .
Strawberry Shortcake

5-STAR CHOPPED SALAD

This is an offspring of the Chopped Tuna Salad that appears in this book, sporting a similar dressing. This recipe is lighter, with only four key ingredients, all chopped—mixed greens, tomatoes, mushrooms, and roasted red pepper—enabling you to sample all of the flavors in one biteful. Guaranteed you'll keep coming back for more!

12 to 14 cups chopped mixed greens (Boston lettuce and radicchio)
12 cherry tomatoes, quartered
6 ounces mushrooms, chopped
1 large roasted red pepper, chopped

Vinaigrette:
salt and freshly ground pepper to taste
1 large clove garlic, smashed
1 teaspoon Dijon mustard
1 teaspoon dried basil
2 tablespoons chopped Italian parsley
3 tablespoons red wine vinegar
9 tablespoons (1/2 cup plus 1 tablespoon) extra-virgin olive oil

   1. Heap the greens in a large bowl. Add the tomatoes, mushrooms, and roasted pepper.
   2. In a separate small bowl, whisk together the salt, pepper, garlic, Dijon, basil, parsley, vinegar, and olive oil until thick.
   3. When ready to serve, remove the garlic from the dressing. Pour the vinaigrette over the salad, toss well, and serve at once.

4 to 6 portions

SALAD MEZZALUNA

This summertime salad features ripe, garden tomatoes and grilled Vidalia onions atop mixed greens, complemented by a mouth-watering maple-balsamic vinaigrette.

1 large Vidalia (or other sweet) onion, cut into ¹/₂-inch
    thick slices
1 tablespoon olive oil
1 teaspoon sugar
salt and freshly ground pepper to taste
12 to 14 cups mixed greens (romaine and radicchio), broken into
    bite-size pieces
3 medium-size ripe tomatoes, chopped

Maple-Balsamic Vinaigrette:
salt and freshly ground pepper to taste
1 large clove garlic, smashed
2 tablespoons pure maple syrup
2 tablespoons balsamic vinegar
¹/₃ cup olive oil (not extra-virgin)

1. Brush the onion slices with the 1 tablespoon of oil. Sprinkle with the sugar and season with salt and pepper.

2. Grill or broil the onion slices until charred on both sides. Separate into individual rings and let cool.

3. Heap the greenery in a large bowl. Add the tomatoes and grilled onion rings.

4. In a separate small bowl, whisk together the salt, pepper, garlic, maple syrup, balsamic vinegar, and oil until completely blended.

5. When ready to serve, remove the garlic from the dressing. Pour the vinaigrette over the salad, toss well, and present at once.

4 to 6 portions

BUFFET DINNER
FOR 8

Assorted Melons
with Prosciutto
· · ·
Salad Mezzaluna
· · ·
Five Spice-Roasted
Salmon
· · ·
Fruited Rice Salad
· · ·
Coffee Gingersnap
Icebox Cake

MIXED GREENS WITH PEARS AND BRIE

LADIES
LUNCHEON

Corn Cakes with Sour
Cream and Caviar
. . .
Cream of Celery Soup
. . .
Mixed Greens with
Pears and Brie
. . .
Sourdough Bread
. . .
Lemon Coolers
. . .
Raspberry Sorbet

Sweet, succulent pears and creamy, buttery Brie cheese have a natural affinity. When set atop mixed greens, garnished with pecans, and dressed with a delicate lemon-balsamic vinaigrette, this combination is sure to garner praise.

12 cups mixed greens (Boston lettuce, endive, radicchio, and arugula),
   broken into bite-size pieces
1/2 cup toasted pecans, coarsely chopped
2 ripe pears, peeled, cored, and halved
1/2 pound Brie cheese, sliced into 8 pieces

Lemon-Balsamic Vinaigrette:
salt and freshly ground pepper to taste
1 large shallot, thinly sliced
1 tablespoon lemon juice
1 tablespoon balsamic vinegar
1/3 cup extra-virgin olive oil

1. Heap the greenery in a large bowl. Garnish with the pecans.

2. Slice the pear halves into 8 pieces.

3. In a separate bowl, whisk together the salt, pepper, shallot, lemon juice, vinegar, and oil.

4. Pour the vinaigrette over the salad and toss well. Arrange the greens on individual plates. Garnish each with the equivalent of half a pear and 2 slices of Brie. Serve at once.

4 portions

BOSTON LETTUCE, MUSHROOM, AND FENNEL SALAD

Shredded Boston lettuce is crowned with sliced white mushrooms and aromatic fennel. The creamy Dijon vinaigrette is a most complementary dressing, making this a dynamic combination.

> 1 large or 2 small heads Boston lettuce, cut into $1/2$-inch wide strips
> $1/2$ large fennel bulb (fronds removed), thinly sliced
> $1/2$ pound mushrooms, sliced
>
> *Dijon Vinaigrette:*
> salt and freshly ground pepper to taste
> 1 large clove garlic, smashed
> $1^1/2$ tablespoons Dijon mustard
> 2 tablespoons red wine vinegar
> 6 tablespoons extra-virgin olive oil

1. Heap the lettuce in a large bowl. Add the fennel and mushrooms.

2. In a separate small bowl, mix the salt, pepper, garlic, Dijon, and vinegar. Add the olive oil in a slow, steady stream, whisking until completely incorporated and the dressing is thick and creamy.

3. When ready to serve, remove the garlic from the dressing. Pour the vinaigrette over the salad, toss well until evenly mixed, and serve at once.

4 to 6 portions

ELEGANT
EVENING

Prosciutto-
Wrapped Figs
. . .
Salmon with
Pesto Crumbs
. . .
Boston Lettuce,
Mushroom, and
Fennel Salad
. . .
Coffee Mascarpone-
Raspberry Tart

SPINACH, BACON, AND FIG SALAD

Delicate leaves of baby spinach form the base of this interesting salad of contrasting tastes and textures. Sweet, dried figs, salty, hickory-flavored bacon, and crunchy, toasted walnuts are cloaked in a maple-mustard seed vinaigrette.

10 ounces baby spinach
12 Black Mission figs, stems removed
$1/4$ pound bacon, cooked and coarsely chopped
$1/2$ cup walnuts, toasted and coarsely chopped

Maple-Mustard Seed Vinaigrette:
salt and freshly ground pepper to taste
1 teaspoon mustard seeds
2 tablespoons pure maple syrup
2 tablespoons balsamic vinegar
$1/3$ cup olive oil (not extra-virgin)

1. Heap the spinach in a large bowl. Add the figs, bacon, and walnuts.

2. In a separate small bowl, whisk together the salt, pepper, mustard seeds, maple syrup, balsamic, and olive oil.

3. Pour the dressing over the salad, toss well, and serve at once.

4 to 6 portions

WARM CABBAGE, APPLE, AND GOAT CHEESE SALAD

Sautéed cabbage, onion, and apple have a magnetic attraction. When topped with goat cheese, these ingredients sparkle in this most savory, lustrous warm salad. Accompany it with some crusty peasant bread to complete the meal.

AUTUMN NITE
SUP

Warm Cabbage,
Apple, and Goat
Cheese Salad
. . .
French Bread
. .
Butterscotch
Pudding Cake

3 tablespoons cider vinegar
1¹/₂ teaspoons sugar
1 teaspoon salt
¹/₂ teaspoon freshly ground black pepper
¹/₄ cup extra-virgin olive oil
1 large Vidalia (or small Spanish) onion, thinly sliced
1 large clove garlic, minced
8 cups thinly sliced cabbage
2 Granny Smith apples, peeled, coarsely grated, and sprinkled with
    lemon juice
4 to 5 ounces goat cheese, crumbled

1. In a small bowl, combine the vinegar, sugar, salt, and pepper. Mix well and set aside.

2. Heat the oil in a large skillet. Add the onion and garlic and sauté over medium heat for 2 minutes.

3. Add the cabbage and sauté for about 5 minutes, stirring constantly, until the cabbage begins to wilt.

4. Pour the vinegar mixture over the cabbage and mix well. Remove from the heat.

5. Add the apples and goat cheese, mix well, and serve at once.

4 to 6 portions

SALAD MARLY

This could be one of my very favorite salad creations. A colorful array of bitter, peppery greenery—escarole, chicory, and radicchio—is enhanced by a mouth-watering, three-way vinaigrette featuring red wine, balsamic, and raspberry vinegars. It's both visually exciting and delicious!

ROMANTIC
DINNER FOR
TWO

Salad Marly
. . .
Curry-Mustard
Rack of Lamb
. . .
Roasted Sweet
Potatoes
. . .
Raspberry Torte

14 cups escarole, chicory, and radicchio, broken into bite-size pieces
1 large carrot, coarsely grated

Three-Way Vinaigrette:
salt and freshly ground pepper to taste
1 teaspoon Dijon mustard
1 tablespoon red wine vinegar
1 tablespoon balsamic vinegar
1 tablespoon raspberry vinegar
9 tablespoons (1/2 cup plus 1 tablespoon) extra-virgin olive oil

1. Heap the greenery in a large bowl. Garnish with the grated carrot.

2. In a separate bowl, whisk together the salt, pepper, Dijon, vinegars, and olive oil.

3. Pour the vinaigrette over the salad, toss gently, and serve at once.

6 portions

GADO GADO

Gado gado is the glorious Indonesian salad resplendent with vegetables, blanketed in a chili-infused peanut sauce, and garnished with hard-boiled eggs. I've taken the liberty of adding a watercress base to complement the vegetables. If you want to make this a hearty salad, try adding cooked shrimp or poached, shredded chicken to it.

> 1 bunch watercress, heavy stems removed
> 2 cups beansprouts
> 1/2 pound green beans, cut into 2-inch lengths and poached until
>   tender-crisp
> 1 cucumber, cut into 1/8 x 1/8 x 3-inch long matchstick pieces
> 2 hard-boiled eggs, sliced for garnish

> **Peanut Sauce:**
> 1 tablespoon smooth peanut butter
> 3 tablespoons ketchup
> 2 tablespoons light brown sugar
> 1 tablespoon soy sauce
> 1 tablespoon lemon juice
> salt to taste
> 1/2 teaspoon chili paste (available in Oriental grocers)
> 2 tablespoons vegetable oil
> 1/3 cup unsalted roasted peanuts, coarsely chopped

1. Heap the watercress on four plates. Top each with mounds of the beansprouts, green beans, and cucumber. Garnish each with slices of hard-boiled egg.

2. In a separate small bowl, whisk together the peanut butter, ketchup, sugar, soy sauce, lemon juice, salt, chili paste, and oil until evenly combined. Stir in the peanuts.

3. Spoon dollops of the dressing over each salad and serve at once.

4 portions

INDONESIAN FARE

Gado Gado
· · ·
Shrimp Curry
· · ·
Basmati Rice
· · ·
Fresh Pineapple
Chunks

GREEN GARDEN SALAD

The title is telling—all of the ingredients in this salad are green. The symphony of vegetables and the snappy sherry vinaigrette offer many levels of flavorful surprises—from the delicate anise taste of the fennel bulb, to the oniony aroma of scallions, the piquancy of green olives, the slight peppery quality of parsley, the sweetness of bell pepper, and the pungency of capers. This is definitely an all-occasion salad.

1/2 head green leaf lettuce, cut into 1/2-inch wide strips
1/2 cup Italian parsley leaves, stems removed
1/2 large fennel bulb (fronds removed), very thinly sliced
1/2 cup sliced scallions
2 large stalks celery, thinly sliced
1 cucumber, halved lengthwise and sliced
1/2 large green pepper, thinly sliced
1/2 cup pimiento-stuffed green olives, halved
2 hard-boiled eggs, whites finely chopped (reserve yolks)

Sherry Vinaigrette:
salt and freshly ground pepper to taste
1 large clove garlic, smashed
1 tablespoon Dijon mustard
2 tablespoons capers
2 tablespoons sherry vinegar
1/2 cup extra-virgin olive oil

1. Heap the lettuce in a large bowl. Add the parsley, fennel, scallions, celery, cucumber, green pepper, olives, and egg whites.

2. In a separate small bowl, whisk together the salt, pepper, garlic, Dijon, capers, and vinegar. Add the oil in a slow, steady stream, mixing until it is completely incorporated and the vinaigrette is thick and creamy.

3. When ready to serve, remove the garlic from the dressing. Pour the vinaigrette over the salad, toss well, and present.

6 portions

SALAD CHRISTINE

Vibrant and colorful, this salad features mandarin oranges and sweet, magenta-hued beets set against a leafy spinach background. Sprinkled with the salty, tangy flavor of feta cheese and blanketed in a creamy raspberry vinaigrette, this salad offers layers of flavors.

10 ounces spinach, heavy stems removed
1/2 pound beets, cooked, peeled, and chopped
11-ounce can mandarin oranges, drained
1/4 cup diced red onion
1/2 cup crumbled feta cheese

Raspberry Vinaigrette:
salt and freshly ground pepper to taste
1 large clove garlic, smashed
1/2 teaspoon dry mustard
1 1/2 tablespoons mayonnaise
2 tablespoons raspberry vinegar
1/3 cup extra-virgin olive oil

1. Heap the spinach in a large bowl. Add the beets, mandarin oranges, red onion, and feta.

2. In a separate small bowl, whisk together the salt, pepper, garlic, mustard, and mayonnaise. Add the vinegar and oil and stir until smooth and creamy.

3. When ready to serve, remove the garlic from the vinaigrette. Pour the dressing over the salad, toss well, and serve at once.

6 portions

AUTUMN REPAST

Salad Christine

Grilled Shrimps
and Scallops
. . .
Couscous and Peas
. . .
Baked Bananas Praline

GREENS WITH WALNUT VINAIGRETTE

This is a spruced-up version of an already savory salad from *The All-Occasion Cookbook*. I think you'll agree that it has style.

14 cups mixed greens (Boston lettuce, arugula, radicchio, and endive),
    separated into large pieces
$^1/_2$ cup walnuts, toasted and coarsely chopped
$^1/_3$ cup dried cherries
$^1/_3$ cup shaved Parmigiano-Reggiano cheese

Walnut Vinaigrette:
salt and freshly ground pepper to taste
$1^1/_2$ teaspoons Dijon mustard
2 tablespoons lemon juice
$^1/_4$ cup walnut oil
2 tablespoons olive oil (not extra-virgin)

1. Heap the lettuces in a large bowl. Add the walnuts and cherries.

2. In a separate small bowl, whisk together the salt, pepper, Dijon, lemon juice, walnut and olive oils.

3. Pour the dressing over the salad and toss well until evenly mixed. Garnish with the shaved cheese and serve at once.

4 to 6 portions

SALAD CAMPAGNA

Simple in design, but rich in flavor, this green leaf lettuce salad is blanketed in a savory roasted red pepper vinaigrette. Garnished with the mild, soft-textured specialty cheese, buffalo mozzarella, it is a flavor-rich experience.

> 12 to 14 cups green leaf lettuce, broken into bite-size pieces
> 1/2 pound buffalo mozzarella, cut into 6 slices
>
> **Roasted Pepper Vinaigrette:**
> salt and freshly ground pepper to taste
> 1 large clove garlic, smashed
> 1/4 cup puréed roasted red pepper
> 2 tablespoons balsamic vinegar
> 1/3 cup extra-virgin olive oil

1. Heap the lettuce in a large bowl.
2. In a separate small bowl, whisk together the salt, pepper, garlic, roasted pepper, balsamic, and olive oil.
3. When ready to serve, remove the garlic from the vinaigrette. Pour the dressing over the salad and toss well. Garnish each portion with a slice of fresh mozzarella and serve at once.

6 portions

BEST OF
CHOWDER

Salad Campagna
. . .
Salmon Chowder
. . .
Buttermilk-Scallion
Scones
. . .
Lemon Icebox Cookies

THE 47 HOUSE SALAD

This is my family's favorite stand-by green salad. It struts simple ingredients—shredded romaine with chopped tomato, cucumber, and red pepper—bathed in a lip-smacking, cheesy dressing. Once sampled, it's always favored!

1 large head (or 2 hearts) romaine, cut into $1/4$-inch wide strips
12 cherry tomatoes, quartered
1 pickling cucumber, diced into $1/2$-inch pieces
$1/2$ cup diced red pepper

Parmesan Vinaigrette:
salt and freshly ground pepper to taste
1 clove garlic, smashed
1 teaspoon Dijon mustard
1 teaspoon sugar
$1/4$ cup grated Parmigiano-Reggiano cheese
2 tablespoons red wine vinegar
6 tablespoons extra-virgin olive oil

1. Heap the romaine in a large bowl. Add the tomatoes, cucumber, and red pepper.

2. In a separate small bowl, whisk together the salt, pepper, garlic, mustard, sugar, Parmesan, and vinegar. Add the oil in a slow, steady stream, mixing until completely incorporated.

3. When ready to serve, remove the garlic from the dressing. Pour the vinaigrette over the salad, toss well, and serve at once.

4 to 6 portions

MESCLUN SALAD WITH SHERRY VINAIGRETTE

I love to add fruits and nuts to salads. In this dish, mesclun, the delicate mix of baby lettuces, is garnished with toasted pecans and red grapes, and coated with a light sherry vinaigrette. This elegant salad is perfect for a special luncheon or dinner party.

> *14 to 16 cups mesclun*
> *1 cup red grapes*
> *$1/2$ cup toasted pecans, coarsely chopped*
>
> **Sherry Vinaigrette:**
> *salt and freshly ground pepper to taste*
> *1 tablespoon whole grain mustard*
> *1 teaspoon sugar*
> *$1^1/2$ tablespoons sherry vinegar*
> *$1/2$ cup extra-virgin olive oil*

1. Heap the greens in a large bowl. Garnish with the grapes and pecans.

2. In a separate bowl, whisk together the salt, pepper, mustard, sugar, vinegar, and oil.

3. Pour the vinaigrette over the salad, toss gently, and serve at once.

6 portions

ROMAINE WITH TOMATO RELISH

Strips of romaine are lush with Mediterranean flavors—juicy, ripe tomatoes, rich roasted pepper, piquant capers, nutty-tasting Parmigiano-Reggiano cheese, and fruity olive oil.

Tomato Relish:
4 ripe plum tomatoes, coarsely chopped
1 roasted yellow pepper, chopped
1/3 cup chopped Vidalia (or other sweet) onion
1 tablespoon capers
salt and freshly ground pepper to taste
2 tablespoons balsamic vinegar
1/3 cup extra-virgin olive oil

2 hearts or 1 head romaine, cut into 1-inch wide strips
1/3 cup shaved Parmigiano-Reggiano cheese

1. In a bowl, combine the tomatoes, roasted pepper, onion, capers, salt, pepper, balsamic, and olive oil. Mix well and let marinate at room temperature for at least 30 minutes, and preferably for 2 to 3 hours.

2. Heap the romaine in a large bowl. Pour the relish over the greens, along with any accumulated juices. Toss well and divide the salad among individual plates. Garnish each with freshly shaved cheese and serve at once.

4 to 6 portions

SPINACH, BRIE, AND SUN-DRIED TOMATOES

T his spinach-based salad offers a wonderful balance of colors—
green, red, cream, and black—and flavors—the ripe, buttery richness
of Brie, the intense taste of sun-dried tomatoes, and the salty tang of
Kalamata olives.

10 ounces baby spinach
$^1/_4$ pound Brie cheese, cut into bite-size pieces
$^3/_4$ cup sun-dried tomatoes (rehydrated in hot water), coarsely chopped
$^1/_3$ cup Kalamata olives

Sherry Vinaigrette:
salt and freshly ground pepper to taste
pinch of sugar
$1^1/_2$ tablespoons sherry vinegar
$^1/_3$ cup extra-virgin olive oil

1. Heap the spinach in a large bowl. Add the Brie, sun-dried
tomatoes, and olives.

2. In a separate small bowl, whisk together the salt, pepper, sugar,
vinegar, and olive oil.

3. Pour the dressing over the salad, toss until evenly mixed, and
serve at once.

6 portions

VALENTINE'S
DINNER

Vegetable Pancakes
. . .
Spinach, Brie, and
Sun-Dried Tomatoes
. . .
Herbed Rack
of Lamb*
. . .
German Sweet
Chocolate Pie

SUMMER BEAN SALAD

Delicate mesclun, tender garden green beans, and toasted walnuts strut a savory whole grain mustard vinaigrette for a fresh taste of summer.

12 cups mesclun
1/2 pound green beans, poached until tender-crisp
1/2 cup coarsely chopped walnuts, toasted

Mustard Vinaigrette:
salt and freshly ground pepper to taste
1 tablespoon whole grain mustard
1 shallot, thinly sliced
1 1/2 tablespoons white wine vinegar
5 tablespoons extra-virgin olive oil

1. Heap the mesclun in a large bowl. Add the green beans and walnuts.

2. In a separate small bowl, whisk together the salt, pepper, mustard, shallot, vinegar, and oil.

3. Pour the vinaigrette over the salad, toss well, and serve at once.

4 portions

GOI SALAD

This Vietnamese-style salad showcases a shredded cabbage base nestled with carrot, red pepper, beansprouts, and onion, fragrant with fresh basil and mint, dotted with roasted peanuts, and dressed in a sweet and sour sauce. For a main-course salad, add cooked shrimp or poached, shredded chicken.

ASIAN IN DESIGN

Goi Salad
· · ·
Grilled Chicken with Peanut Sauce
· · ·
Sesame Noodles*

8 cups thinly sliced or shredded cabbage
2 carrots, coarsely grated
$1/2$ red pepper, cut into paper-thin slices
$1^1/2$ cups beansprouts
1 small onion, cut into paper-thin slices
3 tablespoons julienned fresh mint (cut into $1/4$-inch wide strips)
$1/4$ cup julienned fresh basil (cut into $1/4$-inch wide strips)
$1/4$ cup finely chopped roasted peanuts

Dressing:
5 tablespoons lime juice
3 tablespoons fish sauce (available in Oriental markets)
2 tablespoons water
$2^1/2$ tablespoons sugar
freshly ground pepper to taste
$1/2$ teaspoon crushed red pepper flakes (optional)

1. Heap the cabbage in a large bowl. Add the carrots, red pepper, beansprouts, onion, mint, and basil.

2. In a separate small bowl, whisk together the lime juice, fish sauce, water, sugar, pepper, and crushed red pepper flakes until the sugar dissolves.

3. Pour the dressing over the salad and toss well until evenly coated. Sprinkle with the chopped peanuts and serve at once.

4 to 6 portions

CARAMELIZED CORN, TOMATO, AND BASIL SALAD

Celebrate the fresh flavors of summer in this sparkling salad. Garden tomatoes, corn, and basil are drizzled with a light balsamic-red wine vinaigrette, highlighting the sweetness of this dynamic trio.

2 tablespoons extra-virgin olive oil
4 cups (fresh or frozen) corn kernels
3 cups halved cherry tomatoes
1/2 cup chopped Vidalia (or other sweet) onion
1/2 cup loosely packed, thinly sliced fresh basil

Red Wine-Balsamic Vinaigrette:
salt and freshly ground pepper to taste
1 tablespoon red wine vinegar
1 tablespoon balsamic vinegar
3 tablespoons extra-virgin olive oil

1. Heat the 2 tablespoons olive oil in a large skillet. Add the corn and cook over medium-high heat for 7 to 8 minutes, stirring often, until browned and caramelized. Remove from the heat and transfer to a large bowl and let cool.

2. Add the tomatoes, onion, and basil.

3. In a separate small bowl, whisk together the salt, pepper, red wine and balsamic vinegars, and olive oil.

4. Pour the vinaigrette over the salad and toss until evenly coated. Serve at room temperature.

4 to 6 portions

THREE BEAN SALAD

A mélange of beans—green, wax, and lima beans—share the limelight with sugar snap peas in this cilantro-laced salad. It's a sophisticated version of the typical bean salad, giving new definition to this popular picnic food.

1/2 pound green beans, poached for 5 minutes until tender-crisp
1/2 pound wax or yellow beans, poached for 5 minutes until tender-crisp
2 cups frozen baby lima beans, poached until tender-crisp
1/2 pound sugar snap peas, poached for 1 minute

Cilantro Vinaigrette:
1 teaspoon salt
freshly ground pepper to taste
1 medium-size clove garlic, crushed
1 1/2 teaspoons Dijon mustard
3 tablespoons finely diced red onion
1/2 teaspoon dried mint
2 tablespoons finely chopped fresh cilantro
2 tablespoons lemon juice
6 tablespoons extra-virgin olive oil

1. Heap all of the beans and sugar snap peas in a large bowl.
2. In a separate small bowl, whisk together the salt, pepper, garlic, Dijon, red onion, mint, cilantro, and lemon juice. Add the oil in a slow, steady stream until completely incorporated.
3. Pour the vinaigrette over the beans, toss well until evenly mixed, and let marinate for 1 to 2 hours. Serve at room temperature.

6 to 8 portions

PICNIC IN
THE PARK

Cold Roasted Chicken
. . .
Three Bean Salad
. . .
Corn and Barley Salad
. . .
Carrot Cake Muffins

MANGO SALAD

The exotically sweet, tart, and juicy flesh of the illustrious mango is set atop mesclun and napped with a fragrant mango purée.

12 cups mesclun
1 mango, peeled, pitted, and cut into bite-size chunks (set $1/4$ cup aside for the purée)
$1/3$ cup toasted pecans, coarsely chopped

Mango Dressing:
salt and freshly ground pepper to taste
1 tablespoon snipped chives
$1^1/2$ tablespoons mango purée
$1^1/2$ tablespoons white wine vinegar
$1/4$ cup extra-virgin olive oil

1. Heap the mesclun in a large bowl. Add the mango chunks and pecans.

2. Put the reserved $1/4$ cup mango in the bowl of a food processor and purée.

3. In a separate small bowl, whisk together the salt, pepper, mango purée, vinegar, and olive oil. Pour the dressing over the salad, toss gently until evenly coated, and serve at once.

4 portions

GREEN BEANS AND JICAMA

A gusty cilantro-lime vinaigrette is the perfect counterpoint to stalks of snappy green beans and to the sweet, nutty flavor and crunchy flesh of jicama.

1 pound green beans, poached until tender-crisp
1 pound jicama, peeled and cut into $^1/_4$ x $^1/_4$ x 3-inch matchstick pieces
$^1/_2$ small red onion, thinly sliced

Cilantro-Lime Vinaigrette:
1 teaspoon salt
freshly ground pepper to taste
1 large clove garlic, minced
1 teaspoon honey
$^1/_4$ cup coarsely chopped fresh cilantro
2 tablespoons lime juice
$^1/_3$ cup extra-virgin olive oil

1. Heap the green beans, jicama, and red onion in a large bowl.

2. In a separate small bowl, whisk together the salt, pepper, garlic, honey, cilantro, lime juice, and olive oil.

3. Pour the vinaigrette over the salad, toss well, and serve. This may be made ahead and left to marinate for 1 hour.

6 portions

GARDEN MEAL

Bruschetta with Dried
Fruit Mascarpone
. . .
Roasted Portobellos
with Tomato Relish
. . .
Israeli Couscous
. . .
Green Beans
and Jicama

MOROCCAN SALAD

The Moroccan palette encompasses a variety of savory ingredients including tomatoes, bell peppers, garlic, cilantro, and paprika. Tomatoes and peppers are a classic combination and make a most tantalizing marinated salad.

5 to 6 large, ripe tomatoes, coarsely chopped
*2 large roasted red peppers, coarsely chopped (see page 243, **The Uncommon Gourmet**)*
2 large roasted green peppers, coarsely chopped

Dressing:
salt and freshly ground pepper to taste
1 clove garlic, minced
1/2 teaspoon paprika
1 tablespoon finely chopped fresh cilantro
3 tablespoons lemon juice
1/2 cup extra-virgin olive oil

1. Put the tomatoes and roasted peppers in a large bowl.

2. In a separate small bowl, whisk together the salt, pepper, garlic, paprika, cilantro, lemon juice, and olive oil.

3. Pour the dressing over the vegetables and let marinate at room temperature for 1 to 2 hours before serving.

6 portions

SHREDDED ROMAINE WITH APRICOTS AND CUMIN DRESSING

Shredded romaine basks in the glory of Moroccan influences. Apricots, almonds, and cumin reflect the rich flavors of the cuisine, creating a seductive salad.

2 hearts of romaine, cut into $1/2$-inch wide strips
$1/2$ cup dried apricots, sliced in half
$1/4$ cup slivered almonds, toasted

Cumin Dressing:
salt and freshly ground pepper to taste
1 large clove garlic, smashed
1 teaspoon Dijon mustard
$1/2$ teaspoon Worcestershire sauce
$1/2$ teaspoon ground cumin
$1/4$ cup mayonnaise
2 tablespoons white vinegar
2 tablespoons olive oil (not extra-virgin)

1. Heap the lettuce in a large bowl. Add the apricots and almonds.

2. In a separate small bowl, mix the salt, pepper, garlic, Dijon, Worcestershire, cumin, and mayonnaise. Stir in the vinegar and mix until evenly combined. Whisk in the olive oil.

3. When ready to serve, remove the garlic from the dressing. Pour the dressing over the salad, toss well until evenly mixed, and serve at once.

4 to 6 portions

CHOPPED VEGETABLE SALAD

This colorful, chopped vegetable salad of Middle Eastern origin is addictive—one spoonful just won't suffice! It makes a welcome addition to barbecues and totes well to picnics.

3 large tomatoes, diced into 1/2-inch pieces
2 large pickling cucumbers, diced into 1/2-inch pieces
1 green pepper, diced into 1/2-inch pieces
2 stalks celery, diced into 1/2-inch pieces
2 scallions, sliced into 1/4-inch rounds
1 cup diced radishes
2/3 cup diced red onion

Mint Vinaigrette:
1 to 1 1/4 teaspoons salt
freshly ground pepper to taste
1 1/2 teaspoons dried mint
1 1/2 tablespoons lemon juice
1 tablespoon red wine vinegar
6 tablespoons olive oil (not extra-virgin)

1. Combine all of the vegetables in a large bowl.

2. In a separate small bowl, whisk together the salt, pepper, mint, lemon juice, vinegar, and oil.

3. Pour the dressing over the vegetables and toss well. Let marinate at room temperature for 1 to 2 hours (and as much as 4 hours), stirring occasionally. Taste the salad and adjust the seasoning if necessary and serve.

4 to 6 portions

WATERMELON, CUCUMBER, AND JICAMA SALAD

This colorful, light, crunchy, and refreshing salad featuring the bulbous root, jicama, and kissing cousins, watermelon and cucumber, is fragrant with lime and cilantro.

4 cups seedless watermelon, cut into $^1/_2$-inch cubes
1 cucumber, peeled, and cut into $^1/_2$-inch cubes
1 jicama, peeled and cut into $^1/_2$-inch cubes
$^1/_3$ cup thinly sliced scallions

Lime-Cilantro Vinaigrette:
$^1/_2$ teaspoon salt
freshly ground pepper to taste
$^1/_8$ teaspoon cayenne pepper
$^1/_2$ cup loosely packed, coarsely chopped fresh cilantro
2 tablespoons lime juice
2 tablespoons extra-virgin olive oil

1. Heap the watermelon, cucumber, jicama, and scallions in a large bowl.

2. In a separate small bowl, whisk together the salt, pepper, cayenne, cilantro, lime juice, and olive oil.

3. Pour the vinaigrette over the salad, toss well, and serve at room temperature.

4 portions

ALL-AMERICAN
BACKYARD
BARBECUE

Grilled Burgers
. . .
All-American
Potato Salad
. . .
Sweet Pickled Vidalias
. . .
Watermelon,
Cucumber, and
Jicama Salad
. . .
Peanut Butter
Swirl Brownies
. . .
Orange Creamsicle
Smoothies

GREEK SALAD ATHENA

Feta is the classic Greek cheese that gives this salad its identity. It has a rich, tangy flavor and adds zest to this lettuce, tomato, cucumber, red onion, and olive composition. The salad is delicious topped with grilled chicken for a heartier meal and is also great stuffed into pita pockets.

1 head iceberg lettuce, broken into bite-size pieces
2 medium-size tomatoes, chopped
1 pickling cucumber, sliced into rounds
$1/2$ large green pepper, sliced
1 small red onion, thinly sliced into rings
12 Kalamata olives
$2/3$ cup crumbled feta cheese

Dressing:
salt and freshly ground pepper to taste
$1/4$ teaspoon sugar
$3/4$ teaspoon dried oregano
$1/4$ cup mayonnaise
2 tablespoons red wine vinegar
2 tablespoons olive oil (not extra-virgin)

1. Heap the lettuce in a large bowl. Add the tomatoes, cucumber, green pepper, red onion, and olives. Sprinkle with the feta cheese.

2. In a separate bowl, whisk together the salt, pepper, sugar, oregano, and mayonnaise. Stir in the vinegar, mixing until well combined. Whisk in the oil.

3. Pour the dressing over the salad, toss well until evenly mixed, and serve at once.

6 portions

CUCUMBER SALAD

Delicately pickled in rice vinegar, dotted with chopped red pepper and red onion, and flavored with dill, these cucumber rounds are light, refreshing, and fat free! They're absolutely addictive!

2 cucumbers, thinly sliced
1/2 cup diced red pepper
1/4 cup diced red onion

Vinaigrette:
3/4 cup rice vinegar
3 tablespoons sugar
1/2 teaspoon salt
freshly ground pepper to taste
2 tablespoons finely chopped fresh dill

1. Put the cucumber rounds in a large bowl. Add the diced pepper and onion.

2. In a separate small bowl, combine the vinegar, sugar, salt, pepper, and dill and mix well.

3. Pour the dressing over the cucumber mixture, toss until evenly coated, and let marinate at room temperature for at least 1 to 2 hours (or 6 to 8 hours in the refrigerator) before serving.

4 to 6 portions

BEST OF ASIAN

Thai Hot and Sour
Shrimp Soup
· · ·
Grilled Tuna with
Wasabi Mayonnaise
· · ·
Cucumber Salad
· · ·
Ginger Ice Cream

ONION SLAW

Onions shouldn't only be for cooking. They make a spectacular, creamy, marinated salad that's an excellent companion to grilled steak, chicken, burgers, and fish.

2 large Spanish (or other sweet) onions, cut into $^1/_4$-inch thick rings

Creamy Dressing:
$1^1/_2$ cups sour cream
salt and freshly ground pepper to taste
1 teaspoon dried dill
$^1/_4$ cup sugar
3 tablespoons white vinegar

1. Separate the onion slices into individual rings. Soak in warm water for 30 minutes; then drain well and pat dry. Transfer the onions to a large bowl.

2. In a separate bowl, mix the sour cream, salt, pepper, dill, sugar, and vinegar until evenly combined.

3. Pour the sour cream dressing over the onions and stir well. Let marinate overnight in the refrigerator. When ready to serve, mix thoroughly and present.

6 portions

GREEN BEAN AND POTATO SALAD

Potatoes and green beans have a natural affinity. In this rendition they are accented by toasted walnuts, sweet onion, and the robust taste of a garlicky blue cheese dressing.

1 pound red-skinned potatoes, cut into 1-inch pieces
1/2 pound green beans, snapped in half, and poached until tender-crisp
1/2 cup chopped Vidalia (or other sweet) onion
1/4 cup coarsely chopped walnuts, toasted

Blue Cheese Dressing:
1 teaspoon salt
freshly ground pepper to taste
1 large clove garlic, crushed
1/4 cup mayonnaise
2 tablespoons sour cream
2 tablespoons buttermilk
1 1/2 teaspoons red wine vinegar
1/2 cup crumbled blue cheese

1. Boil the potatoes in salted water until fork tender, about 10 to 15 minutes. Drain well and transfer to a large bowl.

2. While the potatoes are cooking, whisk together the salt, pepper, garlic, mayonnaise, sour cream, buttermilk, and vinegar. Stir in the blue cheese.

3. Add the green beans, onion, and walnuts to the warm potatoes.

4. Pour the dressing over the potato salad. Toss gently until evenly coated and serve warm or at room temperature.

4 to 6 portions

FIRE UP THE GRILL

Grilled Chicken, Mushrooms, and Tomatoes Marinated in Basic Vinaigrette
. . .
Green Bean and Potato Salad
. . .
Watermelon
. . .
Double Fudge Brownies

COLESLAW

This homespun recipe of shredded cabbage and carrots sporting a creamy, caraway-scented dressing continues to be an all-American favorite. It's particularly good with barbecued chicken, burgers, ribs, and fish.

1 small head cabbage, coarsely shredded
2 large carrots, coarsely grated

Dressing:
1 teaspoon salt
freshly ground pepper to taste
5 tablespoons sugar
1 cup mayonnaise
1¹/₂ teaspoons caraway seeds
¹/₄ cup white vinegar

1. Heap the cabbage and carrots in a large bowl.

2. In a separate bowl, mix the salt, pepper, sugar, mayonnaise, and caraway seeds until evenly blended. Whisk in the vinegar.

3. Pour the dressing over the slaw, tossing until evenly coated. Let marinate in the refrigerator for at least 3 to 4 hours for cabbage to soften.

4. When ready to serve, bring the coleslaw to room temperature, mix well, and present.

6 to 8 portions

ALL-AMERICAN POTATO SALAD

This classic comfort food takes on a modern day turn with red pepper and cornichons, elevating it to new, zesty heights. Cornichons are the gourmet of pickles—they're crisp, tart, and gherkin-size.

2 pounds red-skinned potatoes, cut into 1-inch chunks with their skin
3/4 cup mayonnaise
2 tablespoons red wine vinegar
1/4 cup minced fresh parsley
salt and freshly ground pepper to taste
1 cup chopped celery
1 cup chopped scallions
1 medium-size red pepper, chopped
1/4 cup chopped cornichons

1. Cook the potatoes in boiling salted water to cover until fork tender, about 10 to 15 minutes. Drain well and transfer to a large bowl.

2. While the potatoes are cooking, combine the mayonnaise, vinegar, parsley, salt, and pepper and mix well.

3. Add the celery, scallions, red pepper, and cornichons to the warm potatoes.

4. Pour the flavored mayonnaise over the salad, toss gently until evenly combined, and serve warm or at room temperature.

6 to 8 portions

ALL-AMERICAN BACKYARD BARBECUE

Grilled Burgers
. . .
All-American Potato Salad
. . .
Sweet Pickled Vidalias
. . .
Watermelon, Cucumber, and Jicama Salad
. . .
Peanut Butter Swirl Brownies
. . .
Orange Creamsicle Smoothies

VEGETABLES NIÇOISE

I have redefined the classic Niçoise salad and given it a new personality. The basic components—tomatoes, potatoes, green beans, artichokes, and olives—are cloaked in a creamy, basil-scented tuna sauce, creating a lush and hearty dish.

1 pint cherry tomatoes
1 pound red-skinned potatoes, cut into bite-size chunks and cooked until
  tender
$^2/_3$ pound green beans, poached until tender-crisp
14-ounce can artichoke hearts, drained and cut into quarters
1 yellow pepper, thinly sliced
1 cup large pitted black olives

Tuna Sauce:
$3^1/_2$-ounce can tuna, drained
salt and freshly ground pepper to taste
1 medium-size clove garlic, crushed
1 tablespoon Dijon mustard
1 teaspoon dried basil
1 tablespoon capers
2 tablespoons balsamic vinegar
$^1/_4$ cup dry white wine
$^1/_2$ cup extra-virgin olive oil

1. Put the tomatoes, potatoes, green beans, artichoke hearts, pepper, and olives in a large bowl.

2. Put the tuna, salt, pepper, garlic, mustard, basil, capers, vinegar, and wine in the bowl of a food processor and purée. Add the oil in a slow, steady stream until it is completely incorporated.

3. Pour the tuna purée over the vegetables, mix well, and serve.

6 portions

GRAIN AND LEGUME SALADS

TABBOULEH

This cracked wheat salad, blushing with chopped parsley, mint, and tomatoes, is heralded as one of the great Mediterranean dishes. It's important to finely chop all of the ingredients as small as possible for peak results.

MIDDLE EASTERN TASTES

Pizzetta with
Onion and Feta
. . .
Tabbouleh
. . .
Tsaziki
. . .
Turkish Lamb Burgers
. . .
Baklava*

1 cup bulgur
boiling water
2¹/2 cups finely chopped fresh curly parsley
¹/2 cup finely chopped fresh mint
3 large tomatoes, seeded and finely chopped
1 large or 2 small pickling cucumbers, finely chopped
1 cup finely chopped scallions

Lemon Vinaigrette:
salt and freshly ground pepper to taste
¹/2 cup lemon juice
¹/2 cup extra-virgin olive oil

1. Place the bulgur in a 2-quart mixing bowl and add enough boiling water to come 2 inches above the bulgur. Allow to stand for 1 hour, or until the bulgur is light and fluffy. Toss with a fork and squeeze out any excess water.

2. Add the parsley, mint, tomatoes, cucumbers, and scallions to the bulgur.

3. In a separate small bowl, whisk together the salt, pepper, lemon juice, and olive oil. Pour the vinaigrette over the salad, tossing until evenly distributed. Serve atop leaves of Boston lettuce.

6 portions

FRUITED BULGUR SALAD

Cracked wheat forms the base of this salad that's enlivened with
toasted almonds and a trio of dried fruits—apricots, figs, and raisins.
The dried fruits have more concentrated sweetness and flavor than
fresh, lending a rich taste to the bulgur. This makes a wonderful
companion to roast chicken or pork.

1 cup bulgur
1 cup boiling water
1/2 cup chopped dried figs
1/2 cup chopped dried apricots
1/3 cup raisins
1/3 cup slivered almonds, toasted and coarsely chopped
1/2 cup loosely packed fresh mint, chopped
3 tablespoons snipped chives

Balsamic Vinaigrette:
salt and freshly ground pepper to taste
3 tablespoons balsamic vinegar
1/4 cup extra-virgin olive oil

1. Place the bulgur in a large bowl. Add the boiling water, mix well,
cover, and let stand for 30 minutes. Fluff with a fork.

2. Add the figs, apricots, raisins, almonds, mint, and chives.

3. In a separate small bowl, whisk together the salt, pepper,
balsamic, and olive oil. Pour the vinaigrette over the salad, toss well
until evenly coated, and serve. This may be made 2 hours in advance
and left to marinate at room temperature.

6 portions

TOO BUSY TO
COOK

Roast Pork
. . .
Fruited Bulgur Salad
. . .
Honeyed
Butternut Squash
. . .
Pears

FEZ'S CRACKED WHEAT SALAD

This perky bulgur salad is embellished with the lush ingredients of Greek cuisine—tomatoes, Kalamata olives, feta cheese, mint, lemon juice, and olive oil.

1 cup bulgur
boiling water
2^1/2 cups grape tomatoes
^{1}/2 pound green beans, cut into 1-inch lengths and poached until
    tender-crisp
^{1}/2 cup pitted Kalamata olives (see page 5)
^{1}/2 cup chopped Vidalia (or other sweet) onion
6 ounces feta cheese, crumbled

Mint Vinaigrette:
salt and freshly ground pepper to taste
2 tablespoons chopped fresh mint
^{1}/4 cup lemon juice
6 tablespoons extra-virgin olive oil

1. Place the bulgur in a 2-quart mixing bowl and add enough boiling water to come 2 inches above the bulgur. Allow to stand for 1 hour, or until the bulgur is light and fluffy. Toss with a fork and squeeze out any excess water.

2. Add the tomatoes, green beans, olives, onion, and feta to the bulgur and mix well.

3. In a separate small bowl, whisk together the salt, pepper, mint, lemon juice, and olive oil. Pour the vinaigrette over the salad, toss until evenly mixed, and serve. (This may be made 6 to 8 hours in advance and refrigerated; return to room temperature to serve.)

6 to 8 portions

CORN AND BARLEY SALAD

This hearty double-grain salad offers double the pleasure. Corn and barley team up in this dazzling dish that's laced with a sherry vinaigrette. The more you sample, the more you'll want! I especially like to serve this salad at summertime buffets and backyard barbecues.

Sherry Vinaigrette:
salt and freshly ground pepper to taste
1 large clove garlic, smashed
5 drops of Tabasco sauce (or more to taste)
3 tablespoons sherry vinegar
1/2 cup extra-virgin olive oil

1 cup pearl barley
4 cups water
1 teaspoon salt
2 1/2 cups corn kernels (fresh or frozen)
1/2 cup thinly sliced scallions
1/4 cup finely chopped Italian parsley

1. In a small bowl, whisk together the salt, pepper, garlic, Tabasco, vinegar, and oil. Set aside.

2. Put the barley, water, and salt in a large saucepan. Bring to a boil, cover, lower the heat, and simmer for 35 to 40 minutes until tender. Drain off any excess water and transfer the barley to a large bowl.

3. Add the corn, scallions, and parsley and mix well.

4. Remove the garlic from the vinaigrette, pour the dressing over the warm salad and toss well until evenly mixed. Serve warm or at room temperature.

8 portions

TAIL-GATING
PARTY

Cold Roasted Chicken
. . .
Corn and Barley Salad
. . .
Moroccan Salad
. . .
Spiced Chocolate
Chip Cake

FRUITED RICE SALAD

BUFFET DINNER FOR 8

Assorted Melons
with Prosciutto
. . .
Salad Mezzaluna
. . .
Five Spice-Roasted
Salmon
. . .
Fruited Rice Salad
. . .
Coffee Gingersnap
Icebox Cake

Basmati and wild rice are punctuated with a potpourri of dried fruits and nuts—apricots, cranberries, orange peel, candied ginger, and pistachio nuts—and cloaked with a honey-orange vinaigrette, giving rise to an intriguing marriage of flavors.

1/2 cup raw wild rice
31/2 cups water
salt to taste
1 cup basmati rice
1/2 cup chopped dried apricots
1/3 cup dried cranberries or craisins
1/2 cup shelled pistachio nuts
1 tablespoon finely grated orange peel
11/2 tablespoons minced crystallized candied ginger

Orange Dressing:
salt and freshly ground pepper to taste
2 tablespoons honey
1/4 cup finely chopped fresh parsley
1/3 cup orange juice
3 tablespoons extra-virgin olive oil

1. Put the wild rice in a fine mesh colander and rinse well under cold water. In a small saucepan, bring 1½ cups water and salt to a boil. Add the wild rice, cover, lower the heat, and simmer gently for 35 to 40 minutes. Drain well and transfer the rice to a large bowl.

2. While the wild rice is cooking, prepare the basmati rice. Put the basmati rice in a fine mesh colander and rinse under cold water until the water runs clear. In a medium-size saucepan, bring 2 cups water and salt to a boil. Add the rice, cover, lower the heat, and simmer for 17 minutes. Fluff with a fork and transfer the rice to the large bowl.

3. Add the apricots, cranberries, pistachio nuts, orange peel, and candied ginger to the rice and mix well.

4. In a separate small bowl, whisk together the salt, pepper, honey, parsley, orange juice, and olive oil. Pour the dressing over the salad and toss well until evenly combined. Serve at room temperature.

6 to 8 portions

CHICKPEA SALAD

Chock full of ingredients popular to the Mediterranean—chickpeas, roasted peppers, and olives—this salad is both colorful and toothsome. Serve it as a light luncheon dish or as part of an antipasto.

2 (19-ounce) cans chickpeas, rinsed and drained
1 large roasted red pepper, chopped
$^1/_2$ cup pitted Kalamata olives (see page 5)
$^1/_2$ cup small pimiento-stuffed green olives
$^1/_2$ cup diced red onion

Mint Vinaigrette:
salt and freshly ground pepper to taste
$^1/_3$ cup finely chopped fresh mint
2 tablespoons red wine vinegar
$^1/_3$ cup extra-virgin olive oil

1. In a large bowl, combine the chickpeas, roasted pepper, olives, and onion.

2. In a separate small bowl, whisk together the salt, pepper, mint, vinegar, and oil.

3. Pour the vinaigrette over the salad, mixing until evenly coated. Serve at room temperature. (This may be made 4 to 6 hours in advance and left to marinate in the refrigerator. Return to room temperature to serve.)

6 portions

MIDDLE EASTERN
FLAVORS

Baba Ghanoush
. . .
Pita Bread
. . .
Tabbouleh-Crusted
Haddock
. . .
Chickpea Salad

COUSCOUS AND CHICKPEA SALAD

Move over tabbouleh, you've met your match! This couscous and chickpea salad rivals any cracked wheat version. The semolina grain and garbanzo beans are mixed with chopped tomatoes and scallions, and are perfumed with mint, cilantro, and basil. This makes great warm weather fare.

> 2 cups water
> $3/4$ teaspoon salt
> $1^1/2$ cups instant couscous
> $1^1/2$ cups canned chickpeas, rinsed and drained
> $1^1/2$ cups seeded and diced tomatoes
> $1/2$ cup thinly sliced scallions

> *Lemon Vinaigrette:*
> salt and freshly ground pepper to taste
> $1/3$ cup finely chopped fresh mint
> $1/3$ cup finely chopped fresh basil
> $1/3$ cup finely chopped fresh cilantro
> $1/3$ cup lemon juice
> $1/3$ cup extra-virgin olive oil

1. Put the water and salt in a 3-quart saucepan. Bring to a boil and stir in the couscous. Cover, turn off the heat, and let steam for 5 minutes. Fluff with a fork and transfer to a large bowl.

2. Add the chickpeas, tomatoes, and scallions and mix well.

3. In a separate bowl, whisk together the salt, pepper, herbs, lemon juice, and olive oil. Pour the vinaigrette over the salad, toss well until evenly combined, and serve at room temperature. (This may be made 2 to 3 hours in advance and left to marinate.)

6 to 8 portions

BLACK BEAN-CORN SALAD

This colorful, Mexican-style, diced vegetable salad sparkles with
vibrant flavors. Corn, black beans, tomatoes, red onion, and avocado
are spiked with a cumin and cilantro-flavored vinaigrette, making it
akin to a salsa. Enjoy it at backyard barbecues and picnics. You may
choose to use canned black beans, but be sure to rinse them well first.

MEXICAN
MADNESS

Black Bean-Corn Salad
· · ·
Chicken with
Cilantro Cream
· · ·
White Rice
· · ·
Orange Wedges

3 cups cooked black beans
2 cups corn kernels (fresh or frozen), cooked until tender-crisp
1^1/2 cups quartered cherry tomatoes
1 small red onion, diced
1 large Haas avocado, peeled, pitted, and diced

Cumin Vinaigrette:
1 teaspoon salt
freshly ground pepper to taste
1 small clove garlic, minced
1 teaspoon ground cumin
^{1}/8 teaspoon cayenne pepper
^{1}/4 cup finely chopped fresh cilantro
2 tablespoons lime juice
^{1}/3 cup extra-virgin olive oil

1. Combine the beans, corn, tomatoes, red onion, and avocado in a
large bowl.

2. In a separate small bowl, whisk together the salt, pepper, garlic,
cumin, cayenne, cilantro, lime juice, and olive oil.

3. Pour the vinaigrette over the salad and toss well. Serve at room
temperature.

6 to 8 portions

CORN SALSA SALAD

**EASY
WEEKNIGHT
DINNER**

Black Bean Dip
with Crudités
· · ·
Grilled Salmon
· · ·
Corn Salsa Salad
· · ·
Rice
· · ·
Orange Wedges

Is it a salsa or a salad? Actually it doubles as both. The salad boasts the integral ingredients of fresh salsa—corn, tomatoes, peppers, and red onion—liberally seasoned with garlic, cilantro, and lime juice. If you want to spice it up, add diced jalapeño pepper. It makes burgers, steak, and chicken sparkle, and takes on a new personality as a dip with tortilla chips.

4 cups corn kernels (fresh or frozen), blanched
4 ripe plum tomatoes, chopped
1 medium-size green pepper, diced
1 medium-size red pepper, diced
$2/3$ cup diced red onion

Cilantro Dressing:
salt and lots of freshly ground pepper to taste
2 large cloves garlic, minced
$1/2$ teaspoon ground cumin
$1/3$ cup finely chopped fresh cilantro
3 tablespoons lime juice
$1/4$ cup extra-virgin olive oil

1. Put the corn, tomatoes, peppers, and red onion in a large bowl.

2. In a separate small bowl, whisk together the salt, pepper, garlic, cumin, cilantro, lime juice, and olive oil.

3. Pour the dressing over the vegetables, toss well, and serve. This may be made up to 2 hours in advance and left to marinate at room temperature.

6 portions

MEXICAN-STYLE SALAD

This stylish South-of-the-Border salad will command your attention with its presentation. Shredded romaine, black beans, corn, olives, and Jack cheese are spiked with a tomato salsa and cradled in baked tortilla shells.

6 (10-inch) fresh tortillas or bag of restaurant-style tortilla chips
cooking oil spray

Salsa:
4 ripe plum tomatoes, diced
1/4 cup diced red onion
salt and freshly ground pepper to taste
1 large clove garlic, minced
1 jalapeño pepper, seeded and minced
1/4 cup finely chopped fresh cilantro
2 tablespoons red wine vinegar
6 tablespoons extra-virgin olive oil

9 cups shredded romaine
15-ounce can black beans, rinsed and drained
1 1/2 cups corn kernels (fresh or frozen), blanched
1/2 cup ripe black olives
1 1/2 cups grated Monterey Jack cheese

1. Preheat the oven to 350°. Grease a 7-inch wide ovenproof bowl (Pyrex or stainless).

2. Place a tortilla inside the bowl, pressing gently so that the tortilla conforms to the shape of the bowl with some pleating. Coat the tortilla with cooking spray. Bake for 18 to 20 minutes until golden and crisp. Remove the shell from the bowl to a rack to cool. Repeat with the remaining tortillas. (The shells may be make a day in advance and stored in an airtight container.)

3. In a bowl, combine the tomatoes, onion, salt, pepper, garlic, jalapeño, cilantro, vinegar, and olive oil. Let marinate at room temperature for at least 30 minutes and as much as 4 hours for the flavors to blend.

4. To serve, place a tortilla shell (or a layer of tortilla chips) on each plate. Place shredded romaine in each basket. Sprinkle each with black beans, corn, olives, and cheese. Spoon the salsa over each portion and present.

6 portions

LENTIL SALAD

Easy to prepare and a favorite at picnics, this lentil salad is ablaze with flavor. The tiny lens-shaped legume is embellished with chopped parsley, mint, onion, and scallion and finished with lemon juice and fruity olive oil. The flavors are reminiscent of the much prized tabbouleh.

1 cup brown lentils
salt
1 cup finely chopped fresh parsley
3 tablespoons finely chopped fresh mint
1/2 cup thinly sliced scallions
1/2 cup diced red onion

Lemon Vinaigrette:
1 teaspoon salt
freshly ground pepper to taste
1/4 cup lemon juice
6 tablespoons extra-virgin olive oil

1. Bring a saucepan of salted water to a boil. Add the lentils, lower the heat, and simmer for 20 to 25 minutes until the lentils are tender-crisp. Drain well and transfer to a large bowl.

2. Add the parsley, mint, scallions, and onion.

3. In a separate small bowl, whisk together the salt, pepper, lemon juice, and olive oil. Pour the dressing over the salad, mix well until evenly combined, and serve at room temperature.

4 portions

ARUGULA, TOMATOES, AND WHITE BEANS

Italian in design, this salad combination is not only fragrant, but is also visually exciting. The green, peppery-flavored leaves of arugula provide the background for red, juicy tomatoes and tender, white cannellini beans; all is drizzled with a simple balsamic vinaigrette.

1 pound arugula, heavy stems removed
1 1/2 cups canned cannellini beans, rinsed and drained
2 large ripe tomatoes, chopped

Balsamic Vinaigrette:
salt and freshly ground pepper to taste
1 large clove garlic, smashed
2 tablespoons balsamic vinegar
1/4 cup extra-virgin olive oil

1. Heap the arugula in a large bowl. Add the beans and tomatoes.

2. In a separate small bowl, whisk together the salt, pepper, garlic, balsamic, and oil.

3. When ready to serve, remove the garlic from the vinaigrette. Pour the dressing over the salad, toss well, and serve at once.

6 portions

SPRING-SUMMER
LUNCHEON

Parmesan Bites
. . .
Arugula, Tomatoes,
and White Beans

Deviled Salmon Cakes
. . .
Dessert Cups with
Assorted Berries and
Whipped Cream

TUNA AND WHITE BEANS

This classic combination hailed from Tuscany offers simple comfort. Lush with extra-virgin olive oil and sage, it gives new definition to canned tuna!

4 cups canned cannellini beans, rinsed and drained
12 to 13-ounce can tuna, drained and broken up into chunks
1/2 cup diced red onion

Sage Dressing:
1 teaspoon salt
lots of freshly ground pepper
1 teaspoon dried sage
3 tablespoons lemon juice
1/2 cup extra-virgin olive oil

1. Put the beans, tuna, and red onion in a large bowl.

2. In a separate small bowl, whisk together the salt, pepper, sage, lemon juice, and olive oil.

3. Pour the dressing over the salad, toss gently, and serve. This may be made in advance and stored in the refrigerator; return to room temperature to present.

4 to 6 portions

SALAD DAZE

Pasta with Yellow
Pepper Relish
. . .
Tuna and
White Beans
. . .
French Bread
. . .
Red Grapes

HEARTY SALADS

APRICOT CHICKEN SALAD

Feast on this summertime chicken salad lush with Moroccan flavors— dried apricots, raisins, lemon, and cilantro.

2 large boneless, skinless chicken breasts, trimmed
salt to taste
1 cup coarsely chopped dried apricots
$1/3$ cup golden raisins
$1/2$ cup finely diced celery
$1/4$ cup diced red onion

Apricot Dressing:
$3/4$ cup Hellmann's mayonnaise
salt to taste
$1/4$ teaspoon cayenne pepper
$1/3$ cup finely chopped fresh cilantro
3 tablespoons lemon juice
$1/2$ cup apricot preserves

1. Preheat the oven to 400°.

2. Place the chicken breasts in a single layer on silver foil. Season with salt and wrap securely. Place the packet on a baking sheet. Bake for 20 minutes. Remove the packet from the pan to a board to cool. Once cool, cut the chicken into $3/4$-inch chunks.

3. Heap the chicken in a large bowl. Add the dried apricots, raisins, celery, and onion and mix well.

4. In a separate bowl, mix the mayonnaise, salt, cayenne, cilantro, lemon juice, and apricot preserves until evenly blended.

5. Add the dressing to the chicken, toss well until evenly coated, and serve. You may refrigerate the salad until needed; return to room temperature to serve.

6 portions

ROMAINE, CHICKEN, AND TOMATOES WITH AVOCADO RANCH DRESSING

TEX-MEX MENU

Black Bean Dip
with Tortillas
. . .
Romaine, Chicken,
and Tomatoes
with Avocado
Ranch Dressing
. . .
Grilled Pineapple

This hearty salad features a romaine base topped with grilled chicken, chopped tomatoes, and sieved hard-boiled eggs. The avocado-infused ranch dressing is a perfect accent to the composition.

1 large head romaine, broken into bite-size pieces
1 pound chicken tenders, grilled and cut into 1-inch chunks
2 ripe tomatoes, chopped
2 hard-boiled eggs, sieved

Avocado Ranch Dressing:
1/2 cup sour cream
1/4 cup mayonnaise
1 ripe Haas avocado, peeled, pitted, and puréed
salt and freshly ground pepper to taste
1/2 teaspoon garlic powder
1/2 teaspoon onion powder
2 tablespoons lime juice

1. Arrange the lettuce on individual plates. Top with equal portions of chicken and tomato. Garnish with the sieved eggs.

2. In a separate bowl, combine the sour cream, mayonnaise, avocado, salt, pepper, garlic powder, onion powder, and lime juice, stirring until evenly blended.

3. Spoon generous dollops of dressing atop each salad and serve. Any leftover dressing may be used as a dip for chips and crudités, or as a topping for grilled chicken or fish.

4 to 6 portions

LOBSTER CAESAR SALAD

This is the ultimate Caesar salad. The classic is embellished with chopped tomatoes, hard-boiled eggs, and chunks of lobster meat, elevating it to new gastronomic heights. This makes an elegant luncheon dish or light dinner for al fresco dining.

1 medium-size head romaine, broken into bite-size pieces
1 pound lobster meat, cut into 3/4-inch chunks
2 hard-boiled eggs, coarsely chopped
2 medium-size tomatoes, chopped
1/4 cup freshly grated Parmigiano-Reggiano cheese

Dressing:
salt and freshly ground pepper to taste
1 large clove garlic, smashed
1 teaspoon Dijon mustard
1/2 teaspoon Worcestershire sauce
1 1/2 tablespoons capers
1/4 cup mayonnaise
3 tablespoons red wine vinegar
1/4 cup extra-virgin olive oil

1. Heap the romaine in a large bowl. Add the lobster, eggs, tomatoes, and cheese.

2. In a separate bowl, whisk together the salt, pepper, garlic, Dijon, Worcestershire, capers, and mayonnaise. Add the vinegar and stir until evenly blended. Whisk in the olive oil.

3. When ready to serve, remove the garlic from the dressing. Pour the dressing over the salad, toss gently, and serve at once.

4 main-course portions; 6 to 8 side portions

POTATO AND MUSSEL SALAD

Treasures from the sea and tubers from the earth sparkle with a creamy Dijon vinaigrette. This makes a lovely luncheon salad.

Dijon Vinaigrette:
salt and freshly ground pepper to taste
1 large clove garlic, minced
2 tablespoons Dijon mustard
1/4 cup chopped fresh parsley
2 tablespoons balsamic vinegar
6 tablespoons extra-virgin olive oil

1 1/2 pounds red-skinned potatoes, cut into 1-inch chunks with their skin
salt
2 pounds mussels, scrubbed and debearded
1 cup water
1/2 cup thinly sliced scallions

1. In a small bowl, mix the salt, pepper, garlic, Dijon, parsley, and balsamic. Add the olive oil in a slow, steady stream, whisking until completely incorporated and the dressing is creamy.

2. Cook the potatoes in boiling salted water to cover until fork tender, about 10 to 15 minutes. Drain well and transfer to a large bowl.

3. While the potatoes are cooking, prepare the mussels. Heap the mussels and 1 cup water in a large pot. Cover and cook over medium-high heat just until the mussels open, about 5 minutes. Drain well. Discard any unopened ones. When the mussels are cool enough to handle, remove the shells.

4. Add the warm mussels and scallions to the warm potatoes.

5. Pour the vinaigrette over the salad, toss gently until evenly combined, and serve warm or at room temperature on a bed of greens.

4 main-course portions; 6 salad portions

AL FRESCO
DINNER

Cold Cucumber Soup
. . .
Potato and
Mussel Salad
. . .
Sourdough Bread
. . .
Orange Tea Cakes
. . .
Assorted Berries

SALMON, TOMATOES, AND BLACK BEANS

Poached salmon, chopped tomatoes, and black beans are liberally seasoned with bold Mexican flavors for a zesty and hearty luncheon salad.

1 pound salmon, poached and broken up into chunks
4 plum tomatoes, chopped
2 (19-ounce) cans black beans, rinsed and drained
1/2 cup minced scallions
1/2 cup minced celery

Zesty Vinaigrette:
salt and freshly ground pepper to taste
2 large cloves garlic, minced
2 teaspoons ground cumin
1/2 teaspoon crushed red pepper flakes
1/2 teaspoon cayenne pepper
1/4 cup chopped fresh cilantro
1 teaspoon finely grated lime peel
1/2 cup lime juice
1/4 cup extra-virgin olive oil

1. In a large bowl, combine the salmon, tomatoes, black beans, scallions, and celery.

2. In a separate small bowl, whisk together the salt, pepper, garlic, cumin, red pepper flakes, cayenne, cilantro, lime peel, lime juice, and olive oil.

3. Pour the dressing over the salad and toss gently until evenly mixed. Mound the salad atop shredded red or green leaf lettuce and serve at room temperature.

6 portions

GRAPEFRUIT, AVOCADO, AND SHRIMP SALAD

This composed salad is blushing with shrimp, buttery avocados, and ruby red grapefruit. Refreshing and light, it is offset by a cilantro-lime vinaigrette.

MEXICAN LIMELIGHT

Sangriá
. . .
Salsa Fresca
. . .
Baked Tortillas
. . .
Grapefruit, Avocado, and Shrimp Salad

1 large head Boston lettuce
2 dozen extra-large shrimp, shelled and poached
2 Haas avocados, peeled, pitted, and cut into 1/2-inch wide wedges
2 ruby red grapefruits, peeled, sectioned, and membranes removed
1/2 cup thinly sliced scallions

Cilantro-Lime Vinaigrette:
salt and freshly ground pepper to taste
1 tablespoon honey
2 tablespoons finely chopped fresh cilantro
3 tablespoons lime juice
1/2 cup extra-virgin olive oil

1. Arrange the lettuce on a large platter. Mound the shrimp in the center of the lettuce. Surround the shellfish with alternating wedges of avocado and grapefruit, forming spokes of a wheel. Sprinkle with the scallions.

2. In a small bowl, whisk together the salt, pepper, honey, cilantro, lime juice, and olive oil. Drizzle the dressing over the salad and serve at once.

4 luncheon portions; 6 salad portions

CURRIED TUNA SALAD

Tuna is enlivened with cream cheese, curry, mango chutney, and toasted almonds. This Indian-inspired dish is sweet, spicy, fruity, and absolutely addictive!

12 to 13-ounce can tuna, drained and broken up into chunks
4 ounces cream cheese, at room temperature
1/4 cup mayonnaise
1 teaspoon curry powder
*1/2 cup mango chutney (see page 211, **The All-Occasion Cookbook**)*
1/4 cup sliced almonds, toasted

1. Put the tuna in a mixing bowl. Add the cream cheese and mayonnaise and mix until evenly combined.

2. Stir in the curry powder and chutney. Mound on a bed of lettuce and sprinkle with the toasted almonds. Serve at room temperature.

3 to 4 portions

CHOPPED TUNA SALAD

Chopped salads are extremely stylish and fun to eat. This hearty, yet light composition features tuna surrounded by a myriad of chopped ingredients—Boston lettuce, hard-boiled eggs, celery, red onion, roasted red pepper, cherry tomatoes, and Kalamata olives. The layers of complex Niçoise flavors transform tuna into an epicurean treat.

SUMMER
SOLSTICE

Borscht
. . .
Chopped Tuna Salad
. . .
French Bread
. . .
Assorted Melons

12 cups chopped mixed greens (Boston lettuce and radicchio)
13-ounce can tuna, drained and coarsely flaked
4 hard-boiled eggs, chopped
2 large stalks celery, diced
1/4 cup diced red onion
1 roasted red pepper, chopped
12 cherry tomatoes, quartered
1/3 cup pitted Kalamata olives (see page 5)

Basil Vinaigrette:
salt and freshly ground pepper to taste
1 large clove garlic, smashed
1 teaspoon Dijon mustard
1 teaspoon dried basil
3 tablespoons chopped Italian parsley
2 tablespoons capers
3 tablespoons red wine vinegar
9 tablespoons (1/2 cup plus 1 tablespoon) extra-virgin olive oil

1. Heap the lettuces in a large bowl. Add the tuna, eggs, celery, onion, roasted pepper, tomatoes, and olives.

2. In a separate smaller bowl, whisk together the salt, pepper, garlic, Dijon, basil, parsley, capers, vinegar, and olive oil until thick. Pour the vinaigrette over the salad, toss well until evenly coated, and serve at once.

4 to 6 portions

MEMORABLE MAINSTAYS

The main course is what distinguishes the meal. It's the portion of the repast that's hearty, wholesome, savory, and brimming with panache. Whether steeped in tradition or an innovative combination of contemporary cuisine, the main course offers comfort.

I've learned that sometimes less is more—that the simplest preparation is often the best. When you start with top quality meats, chicken, and seafood, little needs to be done to ensure flavor-packed results. Mere seasoning with salt, pepper, and herbs, a coating of butter or oil, and grilling or sautéing will provide a succulent meal. You'll taste the pure, fresh flavor of the food. Of course, a simple sauce, relish, or dressing will most certainly enhance the food and add pizzazz to the dish.

Make it fresh, keep it simple, and let the flavors do their magic!

SUMPTUOUS MEATS

MEATLOAF

This blue plate special is packed with old-fashioned goodness. Beef, pork, and veal are the meats of choice, adding extra flavor and succulence to this homestyle recipe. Mashed potatoes makes a sumptuous accompaniment.

1 tablespoon olive oil (not extra-virgin)
1 medium yellow onion, finely diced
1 large stalk celery, finely diced
1/2 medium-size red pepper, finely diced
3 cloves garlic, minced
1 pound ground beef
1/2 pound ground veal
1/2 pound ground pork
2 eggs, lightly beaten
1 teaspoon salt
1/2 teaspoon freshly ground pepper
1 teaspoon dried thyme
1 tablespoon Worcestershire sauce
1/4 cup chopped fresh parsley
1/2 cup milk
1 1/4 cups fresh bread crumbs

1. Preheat the oven to 350°.

2. Heat the oil in a skillet. Add the onion, celery, and red pepper and sauté over medium heat until soft. Add the garlic and sauté for 1 minute more. Remove from heat and let cool.

3. In a large bowl, mix the beef, veal, and pork. Add the eggs, salt, pepper, thyme, Worcestershire sauce, parsley, milk, and bread. Mix until evenly combined.

4. Add the cooled, sautéed vegetables and mix well. Transfer the mixture to a baking pan and form the meat into a loaf, 11 inches long.

5. Bake for 1 hour. Let rest for 10 minutes; then slice and serve with any accumulated pan juices.

6 to 8 portions

LONDON BROIL

Fire up the grill! This London broil is a great choice for outdoor barbecues or summer get-togethers. Thick cut, boneless shell sirloin is the preferred meat for this marinated, gustatory dish, redolent with garlic, Dijon, and Port wine.

salt and freshly ground pepper to taste
2 large cloves garlic, crushed
1 tablespoon Dijon mustard
1 teaspoon mustard seeds
$^{1}/_{4}$ cup Ruby Port wine
2 tablespoons balsamic vinegar
2 tablespoons extra-virgin olive oil
2 pounds boneless shell sirloin, $1^{1}/_{2}$-inches thick, trimmed of heavy fat

1. In a bowl, combine the salt, pepper, garlic, Dijon, mustard seeds, Port wine, balsamic vinegar, and olive oil. Pour the sauce over the meat and let marinate for 1 to 2 hours and as much as overnight in the refrigerator. Return to room temperature before grilling.

2. Grill the meat over hot coals, 4 inches from the heat source, 5 to 6 minutes per side for rare to medium-rare, basting with the reserved marinade. Let the meat rest for 5 minutes; then carve into thin slices and serve.

4 to 6 portions

BACKYARD
GET-TOGETHER

The 47 House Salad
. . .
London Broil
. . .
Roasted Corn
. . .
Double Fudge
Brownies

POT ROAST

Americans have been preparing pot roast for centuries. Pot roast is actually beef that is first browned, then braised very slowly with liquid to produce fork-tender meat. What distinguishes this homestyle recipe is the addition of root vegetables, prunes, and Port wine producing a slightly sweet, heavenly, rich-flavored sauce.

3 to 3$^{1}/_{2}$ pound chuck roast, trimmed of heavy fat
salt and freshly ground pepper to taste
flour for dredging
2 tablespoons olive oil (not extra-virgin)
1 large clove garlic, minced
1 teaspoon Dijon mustard
1 large sweet onion, chopped
10 large pitted prunes
2 cups Ruby Port wine
$^{1}/_{2}$ pound carrots, peeled and cut into 2-inch lengths (Do not use peeled baby carrots.)
$^{1}/_{2}$ pound parsnips, peeled and cut into 2-inch lengths
1 pound red-skinned potatoes, cut into 1$^{1}/_{2}$-inch chunks

1. Preheat the oven to 350°.

2. Season the meat with salt and pepper and dredge in flour.

3. Heat the oil over high in a large Dutch oven or casserole. Add the meat and quickly brown the roast on all sides. Season the meat with garlic and Dijon. Add the onion, prunes, and wine.

4. Cover tightly and roast in the oven for 1$^{1}/_{2}$ hours; then add the carrots, parsnips, and potatoes. Cover and continue cooking for 1$^{1}/_{2}$ hours longer until the meat and vegetables are very tender.

5. Remove the meat to a platter and carve into slices. Surround with the vegetables. Transfer the prunes, half of the chopped onions, and some of the pan juices to a food processor and purée. Whisk the purée into the remaining pan juices and serve the sauce alongside the roast.

6 to 8 portions

STUFFED FLANK STEAK

This glorious stuffed flank steak boasts a filling with rich tastes and contrasting textures. Spinach, goat cheese, raisins, Parmigiano-Reggiano cheese, prosciutto, and roasted peppers are all tucked inside the rolled meat. Roasted to a turn and oozing with flavor, this dish makes a grand statement.

10-ounce package frozen spinach, thawed and squeezed of excess liquid
4 ounces goat cheese
3 tablespoons raisins
$1/4$ cup grated Parmigiano-Reggiano cheese
$2^1/2$ tablespoons extra-virgin olive oil
1 large clove garlic, crushed
$1/4$ teaspoon freshly ground pepper
$1^1/2$ pound flank steak
$1/4$ pound thinly sliced imported prosciutto
3 roasted red peppers, sliced in half
coarse salt to taste

1. Preheat the oven to 350°.

2. In a bowl, combine the spinach, goat cheese, raisins, and Parmesan cheese and mix well.

3. In a separate bowl, mix 2 tablespoons olive oil, garlic, and pepper.

4. Butterfly the meat by slicing it horizontally through the middle, as if you were slicing a bagel in half. Stop $1/2$-inch before reaching the opposite side, creating a hinge. Open the meat flat on the work surface.

5. Place the prosciutto in a single layer on the meat. Brush the prosciutto with the seasoned olive oil. Arrange a layer of roasted peppers on top. Spread with the spinach mixture.

6. Starting with the long side, roll the steak up jelly-roll fashion. Tie tightly with string at 2-inch intervals. Place seam side down in a roasting pan. Brush with the remaining $1/2$ tablespoon oil and season with salt.

7. Roast for 35 to 40 minutes for rare to medium-rare. Let the meat rest for 10 minutes; then slice into 1-inch thick pieces and serve.

4 to 6 portions

FATHER'S DAY
DINNER

Bruschetta with
Black Olive Pesto
. . .
Stuffed Flank Steak
. . .
Smashed Potatoes
. . .
Chocolate Swirl
Poundcake

CARNE ASADA

Get ready to grill this Mexican favorite that showcases barbecued skirt steak served with Pico de Gallo. Pico de Gallo is also known as salsa fresca and is the universal table condiment of Northern Mexico. It's zip turns ordinary food into memorable occasions.

2 pounds skirt steak, cut crosswise into 4 to 6 portions (if unavailable,
substitute a 2 pound flank steak)
kosher salt to taste
$1/4$ teaspoon freshly ground pepper
6 tablespoons lime juice
2 tablespoons olive oil (not extra-virgin)
Pico de Gallo (recipe follows)

1. Put the meat in a non-reactive baking dish.
2. In a bowl, combine the salt, pepper, lime juice, and olive oil. Pour the mixture over the meat and let marinate for 1 to 2 hours.
3. Grill over hot coals, 4 inches from the heat source, 3 to 4 minutes per side for medium-rare. Slice and serve topped with spoonfuls of Pico de Gallo. To slice skirt steak, cut the meat against the grain into slices. To slice flank steak, cut the meat thinly on the diagonal.

4 to 6 portions

Pico de Gallo:
28-ounce can diced tomatoes, drained
$1/2$ small yellow onion, finely chopped
1 jalapeño pepper, stemmed and some seeds removed
salt and freshly ground pepper to taste
1 large clove garlic, minced
$1/4$ cup finely chopped fresh cilantro
1 tablespoon lime juice

Combine all of the ingredients and let sit at room temperature for 1 hour before serving. Do not refrigerate, as the flavor of the tomatoes dissipates.

GRILLED SESAME BEEF

Sirloin tip strips are daubed with a snappy Oriental-flavored sauce of soy, sesame, ginger, and scallions. Juicy and tender, the barbecued meat is lip-smacking good. This marinade is equally fabulous over pork tenderloins, tuna steaks, chicken breasts, and salmon steaks. Try serving a mixed grill—it's interesting and fun!

> 2 pounds sirloin tip strip steak, trimmed of heavy fat
> 3 tablespoons dark brown sugar
> 2 tablespoons grated gingerroot
> $^1/_4$ cup soy sauce
> 1 tablespoon Oriental sesame oil
> 3 tablespoons vegetable oil
> 1 tablespoon sesame seeds, toasted
> 3 tablespoons thinly sliced scallions

1. Put the meat in a roasting pan.

2. In a bowl, whisk together the brown sugar, ginger, soy, sesame oil, vegetable oil, sesame seeds, and scallions. Pour the marinade over the meat and let marinate for 1 hour and as much as overnight in the refrigerator. Return to room temperature before grilling.

3. Grill over hot coals, 4 inches from the heat source, 4 to 5 minutes per side for medium-rare, basting with any reserved marinade. Let rest for 5 minutes; then slice and serve.

6 portions

ORIENT EXPRESS

Scallion Pancakes
. . .
Grilled Sesame Beef
. . .
White Rice
. . .
Date Wontons

MALAYSIAN BEEF AND PINEAPPLE

This simple stir-fry combines steak with sweet onion and juicy pineapple. The velvety coconut milk sauce fragrant with garlic and ginger is the magical ingredient that makes this curry-style dish sizzle with flavor.

salt and freshly ground pepper to taste
$1/2$ cup well-stirred unsweetened coconut milk
2 tablespoons soy sauce
2 tablespoons dark brown sugar
3 tablespoons vegetable oil
1 medium-large size sweet onion, thinly sliced
2 tablespoons grated gingerroot
3 large cloves garlic, minced
1 pound sirloin tip strip, thinly sliced
cornstarch for dredging
2 cups pineapple chunks, cut into $3/4$-inch cubes
$1/2$ cup sweetened, shredded coconut, toasted

1. Prepare the coconut sauce. In a bowl, combine the salt, pepper, coconut milk, soy sauce, and brown sugar.

2. Heat 1 tablespoon oil in a wok or large skillet. Add the onion and stir-fry for 2 minutes over high heat. Add the ginger and garlic and stir-fry for 1 minute more.

3. Add the coconut sauce, lower the heat, and simmer for 8 minutes, stirring occasionally, until the sauce thickens. Remove the sauce to a bowl.

4. Season the meat with salt and pepper and dredge in cornstarch.

5. Heat the remaining 2 tablespoons oil in the wok. Add the meat and stir-fry over high heat until browned. Add the pineapple and mix well. Add the reserved sauce and stir-fry for 1 to 2 minutes until the sauce glazes the meat. Transfer to a platter, sprinkle with the toasted coconut, and serve at once with basmati rice.

4 portions

GLAZED CORNED BEEF

Corned beef and cabbage is a classic boiled dinner. Fork tender and ablush with a Maple-Dijon Glaze, this corned beef recipe goes one step beyond the traditional. Surrounded by a host of boiled vegetables and an assortment of mustards, it's a complete meal.

IRISH-STYLE
MENU

Glazed Corned Beef
. . .
Irish Soda Bread
. . .
Indian Pudding

4 to 4¹/2 pound corned beef
freshly ground pepper to taste
1 teaspoon mustard seeds
1 bay leaf
¹/4-inch thick slice gingerroot
4 whole cloves
2 tablespoons dark brown sugar
1 green cabbage (about 3 pounds), cut into 6 wedges
3 medium-size sweet onions, cut in half
6 carrots, cut into 2-inch lengths (Do not use peeled baby carrots.)
6 parsnips, cut into 2-inch lengths
6 medium-size red potatoes, cut in half
Maple-Dijon Glaze (recipe follows)

1. Place the meat, pepper, mustard seeds, bay leaf, ginger, cloves, and brown sugar in a large stockpot. Fill with enough cold water so that the meat is covered by 4 inches. Bring to a boil, skimming off any surface scum. Reduce the heat, cover, and simmer until the meat is fork tender, about 3 hours. Remove the meat to a roasting pan, fat side up.

2. Preheat the oven to 450°.

3. Add the cabbage, onions, carrots, parsnips, and potatoes to the broth. Bring to a boil, reduce the heat, cover, and simmer until the vegetables are tender, about 20 to 25 minutes.

4. Brush the Maple-Dijon Glaze over the meat, coating all exposed surfaces generously.

5. Roast for 20 minutes until browned. Slice and serve at once surrounded by the boiled vegetables.

6 to 8 portions

Maple-Dijon Glaze:
2 tablespoons dark brown sugar
2 tablespoons pure maple syrup
2 tablespoons Dijon mustard

Combine all of the glaze ingredients and mix well.

TURKISH LAMB BURGERS

These big, juicy burgers sizzle with Turkish influences. Mixed with onion, spices, and pine nuts and dressed with a yogurt sauce, these lamb patties win the best of barbecue.

1¹/2 pounds ground lamb
salt and freshly ground pepper to taste
¹/2 teaspoon cinnamon
¹/2 teaspoon allspice
2 tablespoons finely chopped fresh parsley
3 tablespoons diced sweet onion
2 tablespoons pine nuts, toasted
Yogurt Sauce (recipe follows)

1. In a bowl, combine the lamb, salt, pepper, cinnamon, allspice, parsley, onion, and pine nuts and mix well.

2. Form the meat into 4 patties, ³/4-inch thick.

3. Grill or broil the burgers, 4 inches from the heat source, 3 to 4 minutes per side for rare to medium-rare—or longer according to taste. Serve with dollops of Yogurt Sauce.

4 portions

Yogurt Sauce:
¹/2 cup plain yogurt
salt and freshly ground pepper to taste
¹/4 teaspoon ground cumin
¹/4 teaspoon paprika

Combine all of the ingredients and mix well. Refrigerate until needed.

CURRY-MUSTARD RACK OF LAMB

ROMANTIC
DINNER
FOR TWO

Salad Marly
· · ·
Curry-Mustard
Rack of Lamb
· · ·
Roasted Sweet
Potatoes
· · ·
Raspberry Torte

Curry powder, the celebrated Indian seasoning, is actually a fragrant blend of 20 herbs and spices. When combined with sharp-flavored Dijon mustard and the sweetness of honey, it makes a gustatory glaze for rack of lamb. This is an easy, elegant, and most savory dish!

  2 racks of lamb, cut in half
  $^1/_4$ cup Dijon mustard
  $1^1/_2$ teaspoons curry powder
  2 tablespoons honey
  1 large clove garlic, crushed
  salt and freshly ground pepper to taste

1. Preheat the oven to 400°.

2. Place the racks of lamb in a roasting pan.

3. In a bowl, combine the mustard, curry, honey, garlic, salt, and pepper and mix well. Paint all the surfaces of the lamb with the sauce.

4. Roast for 25 minutes for rare to medium-rare. Slice into individual chops and serve.

4 to 6 portions

GRILLED HERBED LEG OF LAMB

Barbecued leg of lamb is a splendid company dish. This lamb is encrusted with a potpourri of herbs, lending a marvelous fragrant, grilled flavor to the meat.

5 pound boned leg of lamb (weight after boned), trimmed of heavy fat

Herb Marinade:
1 large clove garlic, crushed
salt to taste
1 teaspoon coarsely ground pepper
1 teaspoon dried thyme
1 teaspoon dried marjoram
1 teaspoon dried rosemary
1 teaspoon sweet paprika
1/4 cup red wine vinegar
3 tablespoons olive oil

1. Combine all of the marinade ingredients. Paint all surfaces of the lamb with the marinade. Cover and let marinate overnight in the refrigerator. Return to room temperature before grilling.

2. Grill the lamb over hot coals, 4 inches from the heat source, 10 to 12 minutes per side for medium-rare. Serve hot off the grill, carving the meat into thin slices.

10 to 12 portions

STUFFED LEG OF LAMB

This is an elegant and impressive way to serve lamb. The savory filling lends an Italian flair to this glorious dish. Each slice of meat oozes with stuffing rich with spinach, bread crumbs, pine nuts, raisins, and Parmigiano-Reggiano cheese.

Stuffing:
10-ounce package frozen chopped spinach, thawed and squeezed of
    excess liquid
1 cup fresh French bread crumbs
1/3 cup grated Parmigiano-Reggiano cheese
1/4 cup raisins
2 tablespoons pine nuts
salt and pepper to taste
2 large cloves garlic, minced
2 tablespoons extra-virgin olive oil

5 pound boned, butterflied leg of lamb (weight after boning)
1 tablespoon extra-virgin olive oil
salt and freshly ground pepper to taste
1 teaspoon dried thyme
1 teaspoon dried rosemary

1. Preheat the oven to 400°.

2. Make the stuffing. In a bowl, combine all of the stuffing ingredients and mix well.

3. Lay the lamb flat on a board. Spread the stuffing mixture evenly over the butterflied surface of the meat. Starting at the long side, roll the lamb up jelly-roll fashion. Tie the roast at 2-inch intervals with string. Place seam side down in a roasting pan.

4. Rub the meat with olive oil and season with salt, pepper, thyme, and rosemary.

5. Roast for 50 to 60 minutes for rare to medium-rare. Remove from the oven, cover loosely with foil, and let the roast rest for 10 minutes before carving. Cut into 3/4-inch thick slices and serve.

8 to 10 portions

GRADUATION
DINNER

Honey-Mustard Dip
with Crudités
. . .
Stuffed Leg of Lamb
. . .
Garlic Mashed
Potato Cakes
. . .
Roasted Asparagus**
. . .
Spice Poundcake

LAMB WITH SCALLIONS

Hoisin sauce is the notable Oriental bean sauce rich with soybeans, garlic, and spices. It adds a sweet and spicy note to this celebrated classic stir-fry. Present it on a bed of white rice.

1 tablespoon soy sauce
1 tablespoon dry sherry
1 tablespoon cornstarch
freshly ground pepper to taste
1 pound lean boneless lamb loin, cut into 2-inch long x ¹/₂-inch
    wide pieces
3 tablespoons vegetable oil
1 large clove garlic, minced
3 thin slices gingerroot
1 bunch scallions, cut into 2-inch lengths
Hoisin Sauce (recipe follows)

1. In a medium-size bowl, combine the soy, sherry, cornstarch, and pepper. Add the lamb and mix well. Let marinate for 15 to 20 minutes.

2. Heat the oil in a wok or large skillet. Add the garlic and ginger and stir-fry over high heat for 30 seconds.

3. Add the lamb and any marinade and stir-fry for 2 minutes until the lamb is browned on both sides. Add the scallions and Hoisin Sauce and stir-fry for 1 to 2 minutes. Serve at once.

3 to 4 portions

Hoisin Sauce:
2 tablespoons hoisin sauce
1 teaspoon sugar

Combine the hoisin and sugar and mix well. Set aside until needed. (The sauce may be prepared a day in advance and refrigerated.)

OSSO BUCO

Claiming Italian ancestry, this prized dish from Milan is made with meaty veal shanks that are braised with garlic and diced vegetables in a light tomato sauce. Traditionally it is garnished with gremolata and served with a side of risotto.

ITALIAN IMPORT

Salad Romano
. . .
Osso Buco
. . .
Baked Risotto
. . .
Gelato

> 5 pounds veal shanks, cut 1^1/$_2$-inches thick, trimmed of fat
> salt and freshly ground pepper to taste
> flour for dredging
> ^{1}/$_4$ cup plus 1 tablespoon extra-virgin olive oil
> 1 large yellow onion, diced
> 2 large carrots, diced
> 2 large stalks celery, diced
> 3 large cloves garlic, minced
> ^{1}/$_2$ teaspoon dried basil
> ^{1}/$_2$ teaspoon dried rosemary
> 28-ounce can diced tomatoes, drained
> 1 cup dry white wine
> 1 cup beef broth
> Gremolata (recipe follows)

1. Season the shanks with salt and pepper and dredge in flour.

2. Heat ^{1}/$_4$ cup oil in a large Dutch oven or casserole. Add the veal and brown on all sides over medium-high heat. Remove to a plate when browned. (You may have to do this in batches, so as not to crowd the meat.)

3. Preheat the oven to 350°.

4. Add the remaining 1 tablespoon oil to the pan. Add the onion, carrots, celery, garlic, basil, and rosemary. Lower the heat to medium and cook for 10 minutes until the vegetables are tender. Add the tomatoes, wine, and broth and season with salt and pepper.

5. Return the browned veal and any accumulated juices to the casserole, being careful to stand the bones upright to preserve the marrow in the bones. Cover and bake for 2 hours until the veal is fork tender.

6. To serve, sprinkle the shanks with the Gremolata and present with risotto.

4 to 6 portions

Gremolata:
$1/2$ cup finely chopped fresh parsley
1 tablespoon finely grated lemon zest
1 large clove garlic, minced

Combine all of the ingredients and mix well.

BALSAMIC-GLAZED VEAL CHOPS

ITALIAN SUPPER

Olive Biscotti
. . .
Balsamic-Glazed
Veal Chops
. . .
Pasta with Roasted
Peppers and Potatoes
. . .
Sliced Tomatoes and
Buffalo Mozzarella
. . .
Italian Ices

Balsamic vinegar is more than just vinegar. It's sweet-tart flavor makes it distinctive. When reduced, it turns into an exquisite, syrupy sauce that's divine over grilled veal chops. The sauce is also fabulous over grilled steak, duck breast, chicken, and salmon.

Balsamic Glaze:
1/2 cup balsamic vinegar
2 tablespoons orange juice

4 veal chops, 1 to 1 1/4-inches thick
extra-virgin olive oil
salt and freshly ground pepper to taste
1 teaspoon dried rosemary

1. Make the Balsamic Glaze. Combine the vinegar and orange juice in a small saucepan. Bring to a boil over medium-high heat and boil for 3 to 4 minutes until reduced by half its volume and becomes thick and syrupy. Remove from the heat.

2. Rub the veal with olive oil. Season with salt, pepper, and rosemary.

3. Grill or broil the chops, 4 inches from the heat source, 4 minutes per side for medium-rare. Drizzle each chop with a spoonful of glaze and serve.

4 portions

VEAL CHOPS TAPENADE

Grilled veal chops take on a new personality when topped with tapenade, the rich olive paste hailed from France. Lush with olives, capers, anchovies, and garlic, the tapenade lends a Provencal flavor to the veal.

Tapenade:
1/2 cup pitted Kalamata olives (see page 5)
1 medium-size clove garlic, crushed
1 1/2 teaspoons capers
1/2 teaspoon anchovy paste
freshly ground pepper to taste
2 tablespoons extra-virgin olive oil

4 to 6 loin or rib veal chops, 1-inch thick
extra-virgin olive oil
salt and freshly ground pepper to taste

1. Prepare the Tapenade. Put all of the Tapenade ingredients in the bowl of a food processor and purée. Transfer the mixture to a bowl and set aside. (This may be prepared 1 day in advance and refrigerated; return to room temperature to serve.)

2. Brush the veal chops with olive oil. Season with salt and pepper. Grill or broil the chops, 4 inches from the heat source, 4 minutes per side for medium-rare.

3. Top each chop with a dollop of Tapenade and serve.

4 to 6 portions

FIVE SPICE-RUBBED RIBS

Ribs are hallowed as the essence of barbecue. These baby back pork ribs are dry rubbed with an aromatic spice mixture and roasted to perfection, giving rise to culinary magic and moist, tender meat. For a traditional feast, serve the ribs with baked beans, coleslaw, and cornbread.

Spice Rub:
2 teaspoons five spice powder (It generally consists of cinnamon, fennel, star anise, cloves, and Szechuan pepper.)
1 teaspoon salt
1 teaspoon garlic powder
1 teaspoon ground ginger
1/4 cup dark brown sugar

3 pounds baby back ribs

1. Preheat the oven to 350°.
2. In a small bowl, combine the ingredients of the spice mix. Rub both sides of the rack of ribs generously with the spices, pressing the seasonings into the meat. Place on a baking sheet.
3. Roast for 1 hour. Slice into individual ribs and serve.

4 to 6 portions

SOUTHWESTERN BASH

Five Spice-Rubbed Ribs
. . .
Smokey Mashed Sweet Potatoes

Onion Slaw
. . .
Congo Bars

PORK TENDERLOIN CUBANO

Latino is the new wave in food. Indulge in the flavors of Cuban cuisine—garlic, orange juice, lime juice, rum, and oregano—that dominate these marinated pork tenderloins.

2 (12 to 14 ounce) pork tenderloins
salt and freshly ground pepper to taste
2 large cloves garlic, crushed
1 small yellow onion, diced
1 teaspoon dried oregano
2 tablespoons unsulfered molasses
1/4 cup orange juice
2 tablespoons lime juice
2 tablespoons dark rum

1. Place the pork in a roasting pan.

2. In a bowl, whisk together the salt, pepper, garlic, onion, oregano, molasses, orange juice, lime juice, and rum. Pour the marinade over the pork, coating all surfaces. Cover and refrigerate for 2 hours and as much as overnight. Return to room temperature before grilling.

3. Grill the tenderloins over hot coals, 4 inches from the heat source, about 5 minutes per side for medium-rare, basting with the reserved marinade. (If the weather is inclement, you may choose to roast the pork in a 400° oven for 20 to 25 minutes.) Let the meat rest for 5 minutes; then slice into 3/4-inch thick rounds and serve.

4 portions

SPICY PORK AND GREEN BEANS

This Oriental recipe combines pork and green beans in a simple stir-fry, enhanced by a zippy, spicy sauce. The beans are twice-cooked—first poached, then stir-fried with the meat and seasonings.

1/2 pound lean pork, cut into julienne pieces, 2-inches long x 1/4-inch wide
cornstarch for dredging
2 tablespoons vegetable oil
2 large cloves garlic, minced
1 tablespoon grated gingerroot
1 pound green beans, cut into 2-inch lengths and poached 3 minutes until
tender-crisp
Spicy Sauce (recipe follows)

1. Dredge the pork lightly in cornstarch.

2. Heat the oil in a wok or large skillet. Add the garlic and ginger and stir-fry over high heat for 30 seconds.

3. Add the pork and stir-fry for 2 minutes until the pork loses its pink color. Add the green beans and stir-fry for 1 minute. Add the Spicy Sauce and stir-fry for 2 minutes more until the sauce cooks down and glazes the meat. Serve at once accompanied by white rice.

4 portions

Spicy Sauce:
2 tablespoons mirin (available in Oriental markets)
3 tablespoons soy sauce
1 teaspoon Oriental sesame oil
1 teaspoon sugar
1 teaspoon crushed red pepper flakes

Combine all of the sauce ingredients and mix well. Set aside until needed.

SAUSAGE, PEPPERS, AND POTATOES

Italian in design, this rustic, hearty, and wholesome dish is sheer comfort food. It's the perfect dinner on a cold winter's night.

2 large Idaho potatoes, cut into 1¹/₄-inch chunks
1 large red pepper, cut into 1¹/₄-inch chunks
1 large green pepper, cut into 1¹/₄-inch chunks
6 large cloves garlic, coarsely chopped
salt and freshly ground pepper to taste
¹/₂ teaspoon dried oregano
2 tablespoons red wine vinegar
¹/₄ cup extra-virgin olive oil
1 pound sweet Italian sausages, cut into 1¹/₄-inch thick rounds (If you like it spicy, you may substitute hot Italian sausages, or a mixture of sweet and hot.)

1. Preheat the oven to 400°. Grease a 9 x 13-inch pan.

2. Put the potatoes, peppers, and garlic in the prepared pan.

3. In a small bowl, whisk together the salt, pepper, oregano, vinegar, and oil. Drizzle the vinaigrette over the potato mixture.

4. Roast for 25 minutes, stirring after 15 minutes. Add the sausages and mix well. Roast for 20 minutes more until the sausages are cooked and the peppers and potatoes are browned, stirring once. Serve at once.

4 portions

CURRANT-GLAZED HAM

Ham is definite party fare. It dazzles with a glistening currant glaze and serves a crowd when thinly sliced.

8 to 9 pound fully cooked spiral-sliced boneless or semi-boneless ham
3/4 cup currant jelly
1/2 cup packed dark brown sugar

1. Preheat the oven to 350°.
2. Set the ham in a large roasting pan, flat end down.
3. Combine the currant jelly and brown sugar and mix well. Pour the glaze over the ham, coating the entire surface.
4. Bake for 1¼ to 1½ hours, basting every 15 minutes until browned and crisp. Slice and serve warm or at room temperature with the pan juices.

10 to 12 portions

EASTER DINNER

Currant-Glazed Ham
. . .
Corn Pudding
. . .
Greens with
Walnut Vinaigrette
. . .
Layered Sponge Cake

BEST OF
BIRD

CHICKEN POT PIE

Hailed as an old-fashioned favorite, pot pies have made a comeback and now hold a place of importance in diners, restaurants, and home kitchens. This simplified version is chock full of chicken chunks paired with a host of vegetables, laced with a creamy sauce, and crowned with puff pastry.

$1/2$ pound puff pastry, thawed
$1/2$ cup mayonnaise
$1/4$ cup light cream
4 tablespoons butter
1 cup diagonally sliced carrots ($1/4$-inch thick rounds)
1 cup diagonally sliced parsnips ($1/4$-inch thick rounds)
1 large yellow onion, chopped
$1/4$ pound shiitake mushrooms, sliced
salt and freshly ground pepper to taste
$3/4$ teaspoon dried thyme
3 cups cooked chicken (or turkey), cut into 1-inch x 2-inch pieces
$1/2$ cup frozen peas, thawed
1 egg, beaten

1. Unroll the puff pastry onto a board and allow to rest for 30 minutes.

2. Preheat the oven to 425°. Grease a 2-quart casserole.

3. In a small bowl, combine the mayonnaise and cream, mixing until smooth. Set aside.

4. Heat the butter in a large skillet. Add the carrots, parsnips, onion, and mushrooms. Season with salt, pepper, and thyme and sauté over medium-high heat until the vegetables are tender-crisp and golden, about 10 minutes, stirring often. Remove from the heat.

5. In a large bowl, combine the chicken, peas, and sautéed vegetables and mix well. Add the mayonnaise mixture, stirring until evenly coated. Turn the filling into the prepared baking dish.

6. Top the mixture with the puff pastry, draping the pastry over the sides of the casserole. Press the edges to seal. Trim the overhanging dough, making a neat edge. Brush the pastry with the beaten egg.

7. Bake for 20 minutes until the top is puffed and golden. Serve at once.

4 to 6 portions

ROASTED CHICKEN WITH WINTER VEGETABLES

Hearty and homespun, this recipe stars a perfect roast chicken surrounded by an array of winter vegetables. As the chicken cooks, the juices from the bird baste the vegetables, infusing them with a marvelous flavor. Don't be alarmed by the long list of ingredients— it's a complete meal in a dish!

Winter Vegetables:
1 large red onion, cut into 8 wedges
2 large carrots, halved lengthwise and cut into 2-inch pieces (Do not use
*   peeled baby carrots.)*
2 large parsnips, halved lengthwise and cut into 2-inch pieces
2 medium-size red-skinned potatoes, each cut into 8 pieces
6 Brussel sprouts, cut in half through the core
2 large stalks celery, cut into 2-inch pieces
1/2 pound butternut squash, peeled and cut into 1-inch chunks
1 head garlic, separated into individual cloves

1/4 cup plus 1 tablespoon olive oil
1/2 cup chicken broth
salt and freshly ground pepper to taste
2 teaspoons dried thyme
3 1/2 to 4 pound whole chicken
2 large cloves garlic, crushed
1 teaspoon ground sage
paprika

1. Preheat the oven to 400°. Grease a large roasting pan.

2. Put all of the winter vegetables in the pan. Drizzle with 1/4 cup olive oil and the chicken broth. Season with salt, pepper, and 1 teaspoon thyme and mix well.

3. Season the interior cavity of the chicken with salt and pepper. Separate the skin from the breast and insert the crushed garlic under the skin. Rub the exterior of the bird with 1 tablespoon olive oil. Season with salt, pepper, 1 teaspoon dried thyme, and sage. Place the bird, breast side up, on top of the bed of vegetables. Dust the chicken and vegetables with a generous coating of paprika.

4. Roast for 40 minutes. Stir the vegetables. Make a foil tent to cover only the breast meat of the bird. Return to the oven and roast for 20 minutes more.

5. Remove the chicken from the oven and let rest for 10 minutes before carving. Serve the chicken and vegetables with the pan juices spooned over all.

4 to 6 portions

CHICKEN BIANCO

This stylish dish will capture your attention with its vibrancy. Sautéed breasts are lavished with tomatoes, artichokes, and capers, and finished with dry sherry for a simple, yet flavor-packed dish. It's sure to become a family favorite.

TRIP TO ITALY

Roasted Mushrooms
. . .
Chicken Bianco
. . .
Baked Polenta
. . .
Lemon Ricotta Cake

14-ounce can diced tomatoes, drained
14-ounce can artichoke hearts, drained and cut in half
1^1/$_2$ tablespoons capers
2 tablespoons chopped Italian parsley
^{1}/$_2$ cup dry sherry
2 boneless, skinless chicken breasts, split in half and pounded to ^{1}/$_2$-inch thickness
salt and freshly ground pepper to taste
flour for dredging
2 tablespoons butter

1. In a bowl, combine the tomatoes, artichokes, capers, parsley, and sherry.

2. Season the chicken with salt and pepper and dredge in flour.

3. Heat the butter in a large skillet. When hot, add the chicken and sauté over medium-high heat, 3 to 4 minutes per side until browned. Add the tomato mixture and simmer for 2 to 3 minutes more until the sauce thickens, spooning the glaze over the chicken as it cooks. Serve at once.

4 portions

CHICKEN WITH MUSHROOM RAGOUT

Sautéed breasts are surrounded by an earthy, wild mushroom ragout and finished with a splash of Verdicchio wine for an Italian touch. This is my standby recipe when having impromptu guests for dinner—everyone is always satisfied!

6 tablespoons extra-virgin olive oil
1 pound assorted mushrooms (shiitake, cremini, and oyster), sliced
salt and freshly ground pepper to taste
1/2 teaspoon dried thyme
1/2 teaspoon dried marjoram
1 large clove garlic, crushed
3 whole boneless, skinless chicken breasts, split in half and pounded to an
    even thickness
flour for dredging
1 cup sweet Verdicchio wine
1/4 cup chopped fresh parsley

1. Heat 3 tablespoons olive oil in a large skillet. Add the mushrooms, season with salt, pepper, thyme, and marjoram and sauté over medium heat until golden, stirring occasionally. Add the garlic and sauté for 1 minute more. Remove the mushrooms from the pan and set aside.

2. Season the chicken with salt and pepper and dredge in flour.

3. Heat the remaining 3 tablespoons olive oil in the skillet. Add the chicken and sauté over medium-high heat, 3 to 4 minutes per side until browned. Add the sautéed mushrooms, wine, and parsley. Turn the heat to high and cook for 2 to 3 minutes, until the sauce thickens and forms a glaze, basting the chicken with the sauce. Serve at once.

6 portions

CHICKEN WITH CILANTRO CREAM

MEXICAN MADNESS

Black Bean-Corn Salad
. . .
Chicken with Cilantro Cream
. . .
White Rice
. . .
Orange Wedges

Mexican influences dominate these succulent, sautéed breasts that are nestled with tomatoes, garlic, and cilantro and are bathed in a lime and tequila-flavored cream sauce. This yummy dish is great served over a bed of white rice.

2 tablespoons lime juice
$1/2$ cup tequila
$1/2$ cup light cream
3 boneless, skinless chicken breasts, split in half
salt and freshly ground pepper to taste
flour for dredging
3 tablespoons butter
1 large clove garlic, smashed
$14^1/2$-ounce can diced tomatoes
$1/4$ cup finely chopped fresh cilantro

1. In a bowl, combine the lime juice, tequila, and light cream and mix well. Set aside.

2. Season the chicken with salt and pepper and dredge in flour.

3. Heat the butter in a large skillet. Add the garlic and sauté over medium-high heat for 1 minute. Add the chicken and sauté for 4 to 5 minutes per side until browned.

4. Add the tomatoes, cilantro, and cream mixture and simmer for 3 to 4 minutes more until the cream thickens and glazes the chicken, basting occasionally. Serve over white rice.

6 portions

CHICKEN WITH ARUGULA RELISH

This trendy, vibrant dish showcases chicken breasts stacked with prosciutto, sautéed until golden, and topped with a lusty tomato and arugula relish. This makes an impressive presentation with layers of interesting flavors.

3 boneless, skinless chicken breasts, split in half and pounded to
    1/2-inch thickness
salt and freshly ground pepper to taste
6 slices imported prosciutto, each about 1/16-inch thick
3 tablespoons extra-virgin olive oil
Arugula Relish (recipe follows)

1. Season the chicken with salt and pepper. Place a slice of prosciutto on each breast, trimming any extra. With a meat tenderizer or mallet, pound the entire surface of the ham so that it adheres to the chicken. (This may be done in advance and refrigerated until needed; return to room temperature to cook.)

2. Heat 1 1/2 tablespoons olive oil in a large skillet. Add 3 pieces of chicken, prosciutto side down, and sauté over medium-high heat, 3 minutes per side until cooked and golden. Transfer to a platter, ham side up. Repeat with the remaining oil and chicken. Serve hot or at room temperature, topping each portion with spoonfuls of Arugula Relish.

6 portions

Arugula Relish:
6 cups lightly packed, coarsely chopped arugula
12 cherry tomatoes, quartered
3 tablespoons pine nuts, toasted
salt and freshly ground pepper to taste
2 tablespoons balsamic vinegar
3 tablespoons extra-virgin olive oil

1. Heap the arugula in a large bowl. Add the tomatoes and pine nuts.

2. In a small bowl, whisk together the salt, pepper, balsamic, and olive oil. Pour the dressing over the relish, toss well, and let sit for 30 minutes for the flavors to mellow.

CHICKEN MARCELLA

This is one of my absolute favorite chicken recipes. The inspiration for it was born from Chicken Lucia (*The Uncommon Gourmet*) and Chicken Rustica (*The All-Occasion Cookbook*), encompassing the best of both. It tastes every bit as good as it looks!

2 (14-ounce) cans artichoke hearts, drained and cut in half
$^3/_4$ cup coarsely chopped sun-dried tomatoes
$^1/_2$ cup pitted Kalamata olives (see page 5)
1 cup dry white wine
3 tablespoons lemon juice
3 whole boneless, skinless chicken breasts, cut into $1^1/_2$-inch chunks
salt and freshly ground pepper to taste
flour for dredging
3 tablespoons olive oil (not extra-virgin)
2 tablespoons butter
2 large cloves garlic, smashed
$1^1/_2$ teaspoons dried oregano

1. In a bowl, combine the artichokes, sun-dried tomatoes, olives, wine, and lemon juice and set aside.

2. Season the chicken with salt and pepper and dredge in flour.

3. Heat the oil and butter in a large skillet. Add the garlic and cook over medium-high heat for 1 minute. Add the chicken, sprinkle with the oregano, and sauté for 3 to 4 minutes per side until browned. Add the artichoke mixture and simmer for 3 to 4 minutes more until the sauce thickens and glazes the chicken, basting occasionally. Serve at once.

6 portions

ITALIAN REPAST

Tomato Bruschetta
. . .
Chicken Marcella
. . .
Israeli Couscous
. . .
Tiramisu**

PARMESAN-CRUSTED CHICKEN

Dipped in basil oil and dressed with a cheesy crumb crust, these chicken breasts are then baked to a crispy turn. The basil oil, akin to pesto, combines basil, garlic, and olive oil, lending a taste of Italy to this dish.

1 cup loosely packed fresh basil
salt and freshly ground pepper to taste
1 large clove garlic, crushed
1/4 cup extra-virgin olive oil
1/2 cup fresh bread crumbs
1/2 cup grated Parmigiano-Reggiano cheese
2 large boneless, skinless chicken breasts, split in half

1. Preheat the oven to 400°. Grease a baking sheet.

2. Put the basil, salt, pepper, garlic, and olive oil in the bowl of a food processor and purée. Transfer the purée to a bowl.

3. In a separate dish, combine the bread crumbs and cheese and mix well.

4. Dip both sides of the breasts in the basil oil and then roll each piece in the crumb mixture, coating generously. Place on the prepared pan.

5. Bake for 20 minutes until cooked and golden. Serve hot, warm, or at room temperature.

4 portions

CHICKEN MIRANDA

Chicken breasts share the limelight with sautéed mushrooms and green olives, seasoned with garlic and oregano, and splashed with lemon juice for simple pleasure. The dashing combination of flavors is sublime.

6 tablespoons olive oil (not extra-virgin)
$3/4$ pound white mushrooms, quartered
salt and freshly ground pepper to taste
3 boneless, skinless chicken breasts, cut into $1^1/2$-inch chunks
flour for dredging
2 large cloves garlic, smashed
1 teaspoon dried oregano
$3/4$ cup small pimiento-stuffed green olives
3 tablespoons lemon juice
$1/4$ cup finely chopped fresh parsley

1. Heat 2 tablespoons olive oil in a large skillet. Add the mushrooms, season with salt and pepper, and sauté over medium heat until golden, stirring occasionally. Remove the mushrooms from the pan and set aside.

2. Season the chicken with salt and pepper and dredge in flour.

3. Heat the remaining 4 tablespoons olive oil in the skillet. Add the chicken and garlic, season with oregano, and sauté over medium heat, 4 to 5 minutes per side until browned. Add the sautéed mushrooms, olives, lemon juice, and parsley and sauté for 1 to 2 minutes more. Serve at once.

6 portions

HONEY-GLAZED CHICKEN AND RED ONIONS

Sautéed chicken breasts are coupled with caramelized red onions and finished with a honey-balsamic glaze. The slight tartness of the vinegar complements the sweetness of the honey, resulting in a perfect balance of flavors.

1/4 cup honey
1/2 cup balsamic vinegar
2 tablespoons olive oil (not extra-virgin)
2 large red onions, thinly sliced
salt and freshly ground pepper to taste
1 large clove garlic, minced
3 whole boneless, skinless chicken breasts, split in half
flour for dredging
3 tablespoons butter

1. In a small bowl, combine the honey and balsamic vinegar and mix well. Set aside.

2. Heat the olive oil in a large skillet. Add the onions, season with salt and pepper and sauté over medium-high heat until lightly golden, about 15 to 20 minutes. Add the garlic and sauté for 1 minute more. Remove the mixture from the pan and set aside.

3. Season the chicken with salt and pepper and dredge in flour.

4. Heat the butter in the skillet. Add the chicken and sauté over medium-high heat, 4 to 5 minutes per side until browned. Return the onions to the pan. Pour the honey mixture over all and simmer for 1 to 2 minutes until the sauce thickens and glazes the chicken and onions, basting often. Serve at once, topping each piece of chicken with a portion of caramelized onions.

6 portions

CHICKEN WITH MARSALA CREAM

This delectable take-off on the classic Chicken Marsala gives a quick-to-fix meal with deep, rich flavor. Boneless breasts are sautéed until golden, adorned with bacon and garlic, and napped with a lush Marsala cream sauce. Note that the Marsala wine is dry and not the typical overly sweet variety.

²/₃ cup dry Marsala wine
²/₃ cup light cream
3 boneless, skinless breasts, split in half and pounded to ¹/₂-inch thickness
salt and freshly ground pepper to taste
flour for dredging
4 tablespoons butter
1 large clove garlic, minced
¹/₄ pound thick-sliced bacon, cooked until crisp and chopped

1. Combine the Marsala and cream and mix well. Set aside.

2. Season the chicken with salt and pepper and dredge in flour.

3. Heat the butter in a large non-stick skillet. Add the chicken and sauté over high heat, 2 to 3 minutes per side until browned. Add the garlic and sauté for 1 minute more.

4. Add the chopped bacon and cream mixture and simmer for 3 minutes more until the sauce thickens and glazes the chicken, basting occasionally. Serve at once.

6 portions

EATING IN WITH STYLE

Chicken with
Marsala Cream
. . .
Slow-Roasted
Tomatoes**
. . .
Baked Risotto
. . .
Lemon Ricotta Cake

OVEN-FRIED CHICKEN

Fried chicken is as all-American as the red, white, and blue. This low fat, homespun alternative to the classic is moist on the inside, crispy on the outside, and packed with zesty flavor. This blue ribbon winner is finger-licking good!

2 cups crushed cornflake crumbs[†]
2 to 3 tablespoons Old Bay Seasoning (depending on how zesty you
    like it)
1/2 cup buttermilk
1 (4 to 4 1/2 pound) chicken, cut into eighths (or the equivalent amount
    of chicken parts)

1. Preheat the oven to 400°. Grease a large baking sheet.
2. In a bowl, combine the cornflake crumbs and Old Bay and mix well.
3. Pour the buttermilk into a bowl.
4. Dip each piece of chicken in the buttermilk, then roll in the cornflake mixture, coating all surfaces of the chicken with the crumbs. Place skin side up on the prepared baking sheet. Mix the cornflakes and seasonings after dipping each piece of chicken to redistribute the Old Bay.
5. Bake for 40 to 45 minutes until browned and crisp. Serve hot, warm, or at room temperature.

4 to 6 portions

[†]To crush cornflake crumbs—Place the cornflakes in a plastic ziploc bag. Press out all the air and seal the bag. Using a rolling pin, roll over the crumbs to crush them to a medium-size flake. This is any easy, no mess method!

ORANGE-GLAZED CHICKEN TENDERS

Chicken tenders, the juicy, tender strips of the breast meat, are quickly sautéed and glazed with a cloying orange, currant jelly, and Port wine sauce, reminiscent of Cumberland Sauce.

2 pounds chicken tenders
salt and freshly ground pepper to taste
flour for dredging
4 tablespoons butter
1 large clove garlic, smashed
1 large shallot, thinly sliced
Orange-Currant Sauce (recipe follows)

1. Season the chicken with salt and pepper and dredge in flour.

2. Heat the butter in a large skillet. Add the garlic and shallot and sauté over high heat for 1 minute. Add the chicken and sauté for 2 minutes per side until golden.

3. Add the Orange-Currant Sauce and simmer for 2 to 3 minutes, basting the chicken with the sauce until it forms a glaze. Serve at once.

6 portions

Orange-Currant Sauce:
$1/2$ cup orange juice
$1/4$ cup currant jelly, melted
2 tablespoons Dijon mustard
$1/4$ cup Ruby Port wine

Combine all of the sauce ingredients and mix well.

SIMPLY SUPER SUPPER

Orange-Glazed Chicken Tenders
. . .
Wild Rice Pilaf
. . .
Spinach, Bacon, and Fig Salad
. . .
Lemon Sorbet and Raspberry Sorbet

CHICKEN CHIMICHURRI

Chimichurri is the traditional sauce of Argentina, equivalent in popularity to ketchup. Similar to a spicy parsley pesto, it's basic components consist of parsley, garlic, oil, and vinegar. Chimichurri sauce is also special over grilled steak and fish.

3 boneless, skinless chicken breasts, split in half
salt and pepper to taste
1 large clove garlic, crushed
2 tablespoons chopped fresh oregano
2 tablespoons lime juice
2 tablespoons extra-virgin olive oil
Chimichurri Sauce (recipe follows)

1. Put the chicken in a non-reactive dish.

2. In a bowl, combine the salt, pepper, garlic, oregano, lime juice, and olive oil and mix well. Brush the chicken with the marinade and let sit at room temperature for 30 minutes or in the refrigerator for 6 hours. (Return to room temperature to cook.)

3. Grill over hot coals, 4 inches from the heat source, 4 to 5 minutes per side. Serve topped with spoonfuls of the Chimichurri Sauce.

6 portions

Chimichurri Sauce:
1 cup packed Italian parsley
1/4 cup fresh oregano leaves
salt and freshly ground pepper to taste
3 large cloves garlic, crushed
1/4 teaspoon crushed red pepper flakes
2 tablespoons white vinegar
2 to 3 tablespoons lime juice
3 tablespoons olive oil (not extra-virgin)

Put the parsley, oregano, salt, pepper, garlic, red pepper flakes, vinegar, and lime juice in the bowl of a food processor and purée. With the motor running, add the oil in a slow, steady stream until completely incorporated and the sauce is smooth. Transfer to a container and store in the refrigerator until needed. Return to room temperature to serve.

CHICKEN PAOLO

Sautéed breasts are stacked with roasted peppers, prosciutto, and mozzarella cheese and run under the broiler until browned and bubbly. This heavenly dish with Italian influences makes great company fare.

CASUAL DINNER WITH FRIENDS

Mixed Greens with
Basic Vinaigrette
. . .
Chicken Paolo
. . .
Pasta with Pesto
. . .
Pear Crisp

3 large boneless, skinless chicken breasts, split in half and pounded to an even thickness
salt and freshly ground pepper to taste
flour for dredging
1/4 cup olive oil
2 large roasted red peppers, each cut into thirds
1/8 pound thinly sliced imported prosciutto
1/4 pound mozzarella cheese, sliced into 6 pieces

1. Season the chicken with salt and pepper and dredge in flour.

2. Heat the oil in a large skillet. Add the chicken and sauté over medium-high heat, 3 to 4 minutes per side until browned. Transfer the chicken to a baking sheet.

3. Place a piece of roasted pepper on each breast. Distribute the prosciutto evenly over the peppers. Cover with slices of mozzarella. (Up to this point may be prepared in advance and refrigerated; return to room temperature before proceeding.)

4. Run under the broiler for about 1 minute until the cheese is browned and bubbly. Serve at once.

6 portions

CHICKEN FRANCESCA

This dish is lip-smacking good. Chicken breasts are sautéed with shallots and capers and blanketed in a light tarragon-cream sauce. The delectable sauce is also wonderful over scallops or shrimp. This is definite party fare.

> 3 tablespoons lemon juice
> 3/4 cup white wine
> 3/4 cup light cream
> 3 boneless, skinless chicken breasts, split in half and pounded to
>   1/2-inch thickness
> salt and freshly ground pepper to taste
> flour for dredging
> 4 tablespoons butter
> 1 teaspoon dried tarragon
> 1/4 cup diced shallots
> 2 tablespoons capers
> 1/4 cup chopped fresh parsley

1. In a bowl, combine the lemon juice, wine, and cream and set aside.

2. Season the chicken with salt and pepper and dredge in flour.

3. Heat the butter in a large skillet. Add the chicken and sprinkle with the tarragon. Sauté over high heat, 2 to 3 minutes per side until browned and cooked. Add the shallots and capers and sauté for 1 minute more.

4. Reduce the heat to medium-high and add the cream mixture. Simmer for 1 to 2 minutes until the sauce thickens and glazes the chicken, basting occasionally. Sprinkle with the parsley and serve at once.

6 portions

CHICKEN CARLA

This Italian-style recipe is dazzling. Chunks of chicken are nestled with caramelized onion, roasted red peppers, and assorted wild mushrooms in this colorful and lusty sautéed medley. The combination of tastes and textures will romance your senses.

6 tablespoons extra-virgin olive oil
1 large Vidalia (or other sweet) onion, sliced
1/2 pound assorted wild mushrooms (shiitake and cremini), thickly sliced
salt and freshly ground pepper to taste
2 roasted red peppers, cut into 1/2-inch wide strips
2 large cloves garlic, minced
3 large boneless, skinless chicken breasts, cut into 1 1/2-inch chunks
flour for dredging
1/2 cup white wine
1/4 cup chopped Italian parsley

1. Heat 3 tablespoons olive oil in a large skillet. Add the onion and mushrooms and season with salt and pepper. Sauté over medium-high heat until browned, stirring occasionally. Add the roasted peppers and garlic and sauté for 1 minute more. Remove the mixture from the pan and set aside.

2. Season the chicken with salt and pepper and dredge in flour.

3. Heat the remaining 3 tablespoons olive oil in the skillet. Add the chicken and sauté over medium-high heat, 3 to 4 minutes per side until browned. Add the sautéed vegetables, wine, and parsley and simmer for 2 to 3 minutes more until the wine is slightly reduced and glazes the chicken, basting occasionally. Serve at once.

6 portions

DINNER ITALIAN-STYLE

Chicken Carla
. . .
Penne with Roasted Tomatoes and Goat Cheese
. . .
Salad Marly

CHICKEN PARMIGIANA

This Italian classic takes on homespun style in this stream-lined version. Sautéed boneless breasts are napped with a mouth-watering marinara sauce, topped with a duo of cheeses, and run under the broiler until browned and bubbly. I like to serve freshly cooked spaghetti alongside topped with some of the sauce.

3 boneless, skinless chicken breasts, split in half and pounded to
1/2-inch thickness
salt and freshly ground pepper to taste
flour for dredging
3 tablespoons extra-virgin olive oil
1 1/2 cups Marinara Sauce (see page 182)
6 ounces mozzarella, sliced into 6 pieces
3 tablespoons freshly grated Parmigiano-Reggiano cheese

1. Season the chicken with salt and pepper and dredge in flour.

2. Heat the oil in a large skillet. Add the chicken and sauté over medium-high heat, 3 to 4 minutes per side until browned. Remove the pan from the heat.

3. Spoon a generous portion of Marinara Sauce over each breast. Top each piece with a slice of mozzarella and sprinkle with Parmesan cheese.

4. Run the chicken under the broiler until browned and bubbly. Serve at once.

6 portions

CHICKEN ISABELLA

This sautéed medley features chicken breasts surrounded by
caramelized onions, dried figs, and prosciutto with a Madeira glaze.
The combination of the rich taste of the onions, the sweet dried fruit,
and the slightly salty ham is complex and lusty.

CIAO ITALIAN

Romaine with
Tomato Relish

. . .

Chicken Isabella

. . .

Linguine with
Garlic Crumbs

2 tablespoons extra-virgin olive oil
1 large yellow onion, thinly sliced
8 dried figs, stems removed and quartered
2 large cloves garlic, minced
2 tablespoons balsamic vinegar
3 boneless, skinless chicken breasts, split in half
salt and freshly ground pepper to taste
flour for dredging
4 tablespoons butter
1 teaspoon dried rosemary, crushed
$^1/_4$ pound imported prosciutto, sliced 1/8-inch thick, cut into
   $^1/_2$-inch squares
1 cup Madeira wine

1. Heat the oil in a large skillet. Add the onion and figs and sauté
over medium-high heat until the onion begins to turn golden, stirring
occasionally. Add the garlic and sauté for 1 minute. Add the balsamic
and cook for 1 minute more. Remove the mixture to a bowl and set
aside.

2. Season the chicken with salt and pepper and dredge in flour.

3. Heat the butter in the skillet. Add the chicken, season with the
rosemary and sauté over high heat, 4 to 5 minutes per side until
browned. Add the proscuitto, onion-fig mixture, and wine and simmer
for 2 to 3 minutes until the sauce thickens and glazes the chicken,
basting occasionally. Serve at once.

6 portions

GRILLED CHICKEN WITH SALSA VERDE

These grilled breasts are napped with salsa verde, the classic Italian parsley-laced sauce. Punctuated with garlic, capers, and anchovies, the green-hued sauce turns ordinary grilled chicken into an exquisite meal.

3 boneless, skinless chicken breasts, split in half
2 tablespoons extra-virgin olive oil
salt and freshly ground pepper to taste
Salsa Verde (recipe follows)

1. Brush the chicken with the olive oil. Season with salt and pepper.
2. Grill or broil the chicken, 4 inches from the heat source, 4 to 5 minutes per side. Serve hot off the grill or at room temperature with a dollop of Salsa Verde.

6 portions

Salsa Verde:
1 cup tightly packed Italian parsley
salt and freshly ground pepper to taste
1 large clove garlic, crushed
1 1/2 tablespoons capers, rinsed and drained
4 anchovies, rinsed
2 tablespoons red wine vinegar
1/3 cup extra-virgin olive oil

Put the parsley, salt, pepper, garlic, capers, anchovies, and vinegar in the bowl of a food processor and purée. With the motor running, add the oil in a slow, steady stream until completely incorporated. Transfer the sauce to a bowl. (This may be prepared a day in advance and refrigerated; return to room temperature to serve.)

CHICKEN SOFRITO

Sofrito is the savory Mediterranean-born sauce of sautéed onion, garlic, peppers, and herbs used to highlight various dishes. These chicken breasts are sautéed until crisp and browned and then napped with a sumptuous Sofrito. I like to serve this with a rice accompaniment and spoon the Sofrito over the rice as well.

> *2 boneless, skinless chicken breasts, split in half*
> *salt and freshly ground pepper to taste*
> *flour for dredging*
> *1/4 cup extra-virgin olive oil*
> *Sofrito (recipe follows)*

1. Season the chicken with salt and pepper and dredge in flour.
2. Heat the oil in a large skillet. Add the chicken and sauté over medium-high heat, 4 to 5 minutes per side until cooked and browned. Stir in the Sofrito, heat through, and serve at once with a rice accompaniment.

4 portions

> *Sofrito:*
> *1/4 cup extra-virgin olive oil*
> *1 Spanish onion, sliced*
> *1 large red pepper, sliced into 1/2-inch wide strips*
> *1 large green pepper, sliced into 1/2-inch wide strips*
> *2 large cloves garlic, crushed*
> *1/4 cup finely chopped fresh cilantro*
> *2 tablespoons chopped fresh parsley*
> *salt and freshly ground pepper to taste*

Heat the oil in a large skillet. Add the onion, peppers, garlic, cilantro, and parsley. Season with salt and pepper and sauté over medium-high heat, stirring occasionally, until the vegetables are tender and golden. Set aside. (This may be prepared several hours in advance and stored in the refrigerator until needed.)

MEDITERRANEAN
PLEASURES

Bruschetta with
Black Olive Pesto
. . .
Chicken Sofrito
. . .
White Rice
. . .
Green Beans and
Tomatoes with Green
Olive Vinaigrette

BASQUE-STYLE CHICKEN

Basque cooking is peasant-style feast at its best. Rooted in the Pyrenees of Spain, its cuisine is simple, using only fresh ingredients. Sautéed tomatoes, peppers, onion, and garlic comprise the heart and soul of some of the region's great dishes.

6 tablespoons olive oil
1 large yellow onion, chopped
1 large red pepper, chopped
2 large cloves garlic, crushed
14-ounce can diced tomatoes
salt and freshly ground pepper to taste
1 bay leaf
2 tablespoons chopped fresh parsley
$1/2$ teaspoon dried thyme
$1/8$ teaspoon sweet Spanish paprika
3 boneless, skinless chicken breasts, split in half
flour for dredging

1. Heat 2 tablespoons olive oil in a large saucepan. Add the onion and red pepper and sauté over medium-high heat until the onion is golden, about 10 minutes, stirring occasionally. Add the garlic and sauté for 1 minute more. Add the tomatoes, salt, pepper, bay leaf, parsley, thyme, and paprika. Bring to a boil, cover, lower the heat, and simmer for 10 minutes, stirring occasionally. Remove from the heat and set aside.

2. Season the chicken with salt and pepper and dredge in flour.

3. Heat the remaining 4 tablespoons olive oil in a large skillet. Add the chicken and sauté over high heat, 4 to 5 minutes per side until cooked and golden. Add the tomato sauce, lower the heat, and simmer for 3 to 4 minutes more. Serve with a rice accompaniment.

6 portions

SWEET CHILI-GLAZED CHICKEN

Barbecued chicken is an all-American backyard classic. These boneless breasts are lovingly enrobed in a sweet mint and tomato-based sauce and grilled until glazed. The sauce is also marvelous on grilled pork.

> 3 large boneless chicken breasts, split in half (either skinless or
>   with the skin)
> 2/3 cup chili sauce
> salt and freshly ground pepper to taste
> 2 teaspoons dried mint
> 2 tablespoons sugar
> 1/4 cup cider vinegar
> 2 tablespoons olive oil (not extra-virgin)

1. Put the chicken in a non-reactive baking dish.

2. In a bowl, combine the chili sauce, salt, pepper, mint, sugar, vinegar, and oil and mix well. (The sauce may be made up to 2 days in advance and stored in the refrigerator.) Pour the sauce over the chicken and let marinate for 30 minutes and as much as 6 hours in the refrigerator. Return to room temperature to cook.

3. Grill the chicken over hot coals, 4 inches from the heat source, 4 to 5 minutes per side, basting with the sauce. Serve hot off the grill or at room temperature.

4 to 6 portions

FEZ'S FEAST

Red Pepper Hummus
with Crudités
. . .
Sweet Chili-Glazed
Chicken
. . .
Fez's Cracked
Wheat Salad
. . .
Baklava*

CHICKEN PAPRIKASH

The infamous Hungarian dish takes on new style and definition, streamlining it for active lifestyles. Sautéed breasts are enveloped in a red-hued, tomato-based, sour cream sauce punctuated with paprika. It's absolutely divine.

4 tablespoons vegetable oil
1 large yellow onion, diced
1 tablespoon sweet paprika
14-ounce can diced tomatoes
1 large roasted red pepper, diced
1/2 cup white wine
salt and freshly ground pepper to taste
3 boneless, skinless chicken breasts, cut into 1 1/2-inch chunks
flour for dredging
1/2 cup sour cream

1. Heat 1 tablespoon oil in a large skillet. Add the onion and sauté over medium heat until soft and translucent. Add the paprika, tomatoes, roasted pepper, wine, salt, and pepper. Simmer for 2 to 3 minutes, then transfer to a bowl and set aside. (Up to this point may be done several hours in advance and refrigerated; return to room temperature before proceeding.)

2. Season the chicken with salt and pepper and dredge in flour.

3. Heat the remaining 3 tablespoons oil in the skillet. Add the chicken and sauté over high heat, 2 to 3 minutes per side until browned. Add the tomato sauce and simmer for 2 minutes until warm. Reduce the heat to low, add the sour cream, and heat gently. Do not let the sauce boil. When hot, serve at once over buttered noodles.

6 portions

MAPLE-GLAZED CHICKEN

Boneless breasts are enrobed in a marinade rich with garlic, ginger, lime, and maple syrup. Grilled until glazed and crusty, the fusion of flavors—zesty, sweet, and tart—provides a star-spangled experience. This is great at barbecues.

> 2 whole boneless, skinless chicken breasts, split in half
> salt to taste
> 1/4 teaspoon freshly ground pepper
> 2 large cloves garlic, crushed
> 1 tablespoon grated gingerroot
> 1 tablespoon Dijon mustard
> 3 tablespoons pure maple syrup
> 2 tablespoons lime juice
> 2 tablespoons olive oil (not extra-virgin)

1. Put the chicken in a glass or Pyrex baking dish.

2. In a bowl, combine the salt, pepper, garlic, ginger, Dijon, maple syrup, lime juice, and olive oil. Pour the marinade over the chicken and let sit for 1 to 2 hours in the refrigerator. Return to room temperature to cook.

3. Grill over hot coals, 4 inches from the heat source, 4 to 5 minutes per side until cooked and browned. Serve hot off the grill, warm, or at room temperature.

4 portions

UM UM GOOD!

Maple-Glazed Chicken
. . .
Smokey Mashed
Sweet Potatoes
. . .
Green Beans with
Toasted Hazelnuts
. . .
Blueberry-Cornmeal
Cake

CHICKEN COUNTRY CAPTAIN

Claiming Indian origin, this dish is now very much an American favorite. In my rendition, chicken tenders are simmered in a curry-infused tomato sauce rich with onion, green pepper, and currants and garnished with toasted almonds. It's slightly sweet, slightly hot, and very delicious.

5 tablespoons butter
1 large yellow onion, chopped
1 large green pepper, chopped
2 large cloves garlic, crushed
14-ounce can diced tomatoes
3 tablespoons currants
salt and freshly ground pepper to taste
1 tablespoon curry powder
1/2 teaspoon dried thyme
2 pounds chicken tenders, trimmed
flour for dredging
1/2 cup blanched almonds, toasted

1. Heat 2 tablespoons butter in a large skillet. Add the onion and green pepper and sauté over medium heat until the onion is soft and lightly brown, about 10 minutes. Add the garlic and sauté for 1 minute more. Add the tomatoes, currants, salt, pepper, curry, and thyme. Simmer for 5 minutes, stirring occasionally. Remove from the heat to a bowl and set aside.

2. Season the chicken with salt and pepper and dredge in flour.

3. Heat the remaining 3 tablespoons butter in the skillet. Add the chicken and sauté over medium-high heat, about 3 minutes per side until browned.

4. Add the reserved tomato sauce. Simmer for 2 to 3 minutes until heated through. Sprinkle with the toasted almonds and serve over basmati rice.

4 to 6 portions

CHICKEN TIKKA

This traditional Indian dish is lively and delicious. As is typical, the chicken is distinguished by an aromatic yogurt and spice marinade and grilled to a turn. Grilled onions, tomatoes, and peppers make a flavorful accompaniment.

3 large boneless, skinless chicken breasts, split in half
1 cup plain yogurt
3 tablespoons lemon juice
3 tablespoons vegetable oil
1 teaspoon salt
3 large cloves garlic, crushed
1 tablespoon grated gingerroot
1 teaspoon ground cumin
1 teaspoon ground coriander
1 teaspoon paprika
1 teaspoon turmeric
1/4 teaspoon (or more to taste) cayenne pepper

1. Put the chicken in a glass or Pyrex dish.

2. In a bowl, combine the yogurt, lemon juice, oil, salt, garlic, and spices and mix well. Pour the marinade over the chicken, turning to coat well. Cover and refrigerate for 4 to 6 hours.

3. Grill over hot coals, 4 inches from the heat source, 4 to 5 minutes per side, basting with the marinade. Serve hot off the grill with basmati rice.

4 to 6 portions

INDIAN-STYLE
FAVORITES

Chicken Tikka
. . .
Madras Rice
. . .
Grilled Assorted
Vegetables—Onions,
Peppers, and
Tomatoes
. . .
Grape Nuts Custard

MANGO CHICKEN

Mango adds a refreshing taste and sparkling twist to sautéed chunks of chicken. Accented with ginger, garlic, cilantro, and lime, it's lively, fruity, and seductively delicious.

1 tablespoon honey
2 tablespoons lime juice
2 pounds boneless, skinless chicken, cut into 1 1/2-inch chunks
salt and freshly ground pepper to taste
flour for dredging
6 tablespoons butter
1 large clove garlic, minced
1 tablespoon grated gingerroot
2 mangoes, peeled, pitted, and cut into 3/4-inch chunks
1/4 cup finely chopped fresh cilantro

1. Combine the honey and lime juice and mix well. Set aside.

2. Season the chicken with salt and pepper and dredge in flour.

3. Heat the butter in a large skillet. Add the garlic and ginger and sauté for 1 minute over medium-high heat. Add the chicken and sauté for 3 minutes per side. Add the mango, cilantro, and honey-lime mixture, and sauté for 1 to 2 minutes, stirring occasionally. Serve with basmati or jasmine rice.

6 portions

HERB-ROASTED CHICKEN ON PASTA NEST

Slathered with an aromatic, herbed mustard, this split bird is nestled atop angel hair pasta and roasted to a juicy turn. The pasta under the chicken remains soft while the pasta surrounding it is crunchy, lending an interesting contrast of textures.

> 12 ounces dry angel hair pasta
> 2 tablespoons extra-virgin olive oil
>
> **Herbed Mustard:**
> 1/3 cup Dijon mustard
> salt and freshly ground pepper to taste
> 1 large clove garlic, crushed
> 1 teaspoon dried sage
> 1 teaspoon dried rosemary
> 1 teaspoon dried thyme
> 1 teaspoon dried orange peel
> 1/4 cup chopped fresh parsley
> 1 tablespoon extra-virgin olive oil
> 4 pound whole chicken, split in half, trimmed of heavy fat

1. Preheat the oven to 450°. Grease a 9 x 13-inch pan.
2. Cook the angel hair in boiling water for 2 minutes and drain well. Transfer to the prepared pan. Drizzle with 2 tablespoons olive oil and toss well.
3. Prepare the Herbed Mustard. In a small bowl, combine all of the ingredients and mix well.
4. Slather the underside of the chicken with some of the mustard coating. Place the chicken, skin side up, on the pasta. Separate the skin from the breast and spread some mustard mixture on the chicken meat under the skin. Spread the remaining mustard coating on the thighs, legs, and wings.
5. Roast for 40 to 45 minutes. Cut the chicken into serving pieces and present with a portion of the pasta.

6 portions

POULTRY PLEASER

Harvest Beet Salad
. . .
Herb-Roasted Chicken
on Pasta Nest

Roasted Winter
Vegetables**
. . .
Buttermilk Poundcake

ROASTED CORNISH HENS

Butterflied Cornish hens are enlivened with a fragrant herbs de Provence rub. Simple, yet moist and succulent, these darling little hens win best of bird.

4 (1¼ to 1½ pound) Cornish hens
salt and freshly ground pepper to taste
2 cloves garlic, crushed
4 teaspoons herbs de Provence
2 tablespoons lemon juice
2 tablespoons extra-virgin olive oil

1. Preheat the oven to 450°.

2. Butterfly each hen by cutting along the side of the breast bone down the middle of the bird. Open the cavity as you would the pages of a book and spread out the hen, pressing to flatten it.

3. Season the hens with salt and pepper.

4. In a small bowl, combine the garlic, herbs de Provence, lemon juice, and olive oil. Rub the mixture evenly over the birds. Place skin side up in a large roasting pan.

5. Roast for 25 minutes until cooked and golden. Serve with the pan juices.

4 portions

PAN-ROASTED DUCK BREAST

The duck breast is the choicest part of the bird. Boneless breasts are similar to lean red meat and should be served rare to medium-rare for peak enjoyment. Blushing with a strawberry glaze, these breasts are a real showstopper. This easy and elegant entrée is sure to impress your guests.

2 boneless Muscovy duck breasts, each about 1 pound
salt and freshly ground pepper to taste

Strawberry Glaze:
1/4 cup balsamic vinegar
2 tablespoons strawberry preserves

1. Preheat the oven to 425°.

2. Score the skin of the duck breasts. Season the breasts with salt and pepper.

3. Place the breasts, skin side down in a large skillet and cook over medium heat until the skin is well-browned and crisp, about 5 to 6 minutes. Drain off the fat, turn the breasts over, and place in the oven for 5 minutes for rare; 6 to 7 minutes for medium. Remove from the oven and let rest for 5 minutes.

4. While the duck is resting, prepare the glaze. In a small saucepan, bring the balsamic vinegar to a boil over medium-high heat. Boil until slightly reduced and syrupy. Remove from the heat and stir in the preserves.

5. Slice the duck breasts and serve drizzled with the warm Strawberry Glaze.

4 portions

EASY
ENTERTAINING

Baby Spinach and
Shiitake Mushrooms
. . .
Pan-Roasted
Duck Breast
. . .
Wild Rice Pilaf
. . .
Almond Cream Cake

SEAFOOD
DELIGHTS

BAKED BLUEFISH WITH OLIVE CRUMBS

Mediterranean flavors dominate these bluefish filets that are peppered with crumbs, Kalamata olives, garlic, and capers. It's totally scrumptious!

2 pounds bluefish filets
salt and freshly ground pepper to taste
1 1/2 cups French bread crumbs
2/3 cup pitted Kalamata olives, chopped (see page 5)
1/4 cup chopped sweet onion
1 large clove garlic, minced
1 tablespoon capers
1/4 cup extra-virgin olive oil

1. Preheat the oven to 400°. Grease a large baking dish.

2. Place the bluefish in the prepared pan. Season with salt and pepper.

3. In a bowl, combine the crumbs, olives, onion, garlic, capers, and olive oil and mix well. Spread the crumb mixture evenly over the filets.

4. Bake for 25 to 30 minutes until golden. Serve at once.

4 to 6 portions

BLUE ON BLUE

The assertive flavor of bluefish is complemented by the sharp tang of blue cheese and the nuttiness of toasted walnuts in this delectable baked entrée.

2 pounds bluefish filets
salt and freshly ground pepper to taste
1 cup fresh bread crumbs
$^1/_2$ cup ground walnuts
$^1/_2$ cup crumbled Roquefort cheese
$^1/_4$ cup olive oil (not extra-virgin)

1. Preheat the oven to 400°. Grease a large baking dish.
2. Place the bluefish in the prepared pan. Season with salt and pepper.
3. In a bowl, combine the crumbs, walnuts, cheese, and oil and mix well. Spread the crumb mixture evenly over the fish.
4. Bake for 25 to 30 minutes until golden. Serve at once with the pan juices spooned over the fish.

6 portions

FLAVORS OF SUMMER

Bruschetta with
Olivada**
· · ·
Blue on Blue
· · ·
Caramelized Corn,
Tomato, and
Basil Salad
· · ·
Honeydew Melon
with Raspberry Sorbet

ROASTED COD CHARMOULA

FLAVORS OF NORTH AFRICA

Roasted Cod
Charmoula
. . .
Lentil Salad
. . .
Moroccan Salad

Charmoula is a very flavorful, zesty Moroccan fish marinade and sauce. It's classically made with cilantro, lemon, sweet paprika, garlic, and cumin, but each cook has her own version. It also makes a dashing sauce for grilled swordfish, tuna, salmon, and shrimp.

2 pounds cod filets

Charmoula:
1/4 cup coarsely chopped fresh cilantro
1/4 cup coarsely chopped Italian parsley
2 large cloves garlic, minced
1/2 teaspoon salt
1 teaspoon sweet paprika
1 teaspoon ground cumin
1/4 teaspoon cayenne pepper
3 tablespoons lemon juice
1/3 cup extra-virgin olive oil

1. Preheat the oven to 450°.
2. Place the cod in a large baking dish.
3. In a bowl, combine all of the ingredients of the Charmoula and mix well. Spread the paste evenly over the fish filets.
4. Roast for 12 to 15 minutes. Serve at once with the pan juices spooned over each portion.

4 to 6 portions

ROASTED COD WITH MANGO SALSA

I love to adorn fish with fruits as they lend a refreshing taste and add sparkle to the filets. The sweet and mild taste of cod is enlivened by a snappy mango salsa that's punctuated with jalapeño and cilantro. If you wish, you may substitute haddock or scrod.

2 pounds cod filets
2 tablespoons extra-virgin olive oil
salt and freshly ground pepper to taste
Mango Salsa (recipe follows)

1. Preheat the oven to 450°. Grease a large baking dish.

2. Place the cod filets in the prepared pan. Brush with the olive oil and season with salt and pepper.

3. Roast for 12 to 15 minutes just until the center turns from translucent to opaque. Serve at once with the Mango Salsa spooned over each portion.

4 portions

Mango Salsa:
2 cups peeled, diced mango
1 small red pepper, diced
1/4 cup snipped chives
1 jalapeño pepper, seeded and finely diced
1/4 cup coarsely chopped fresh cilantro
salt and freshly ground pepper to taste
1 tablespoon honey
2 tablespoons lime juice

Combine all of the salsa ingredients and let sit at room temperature for 1 to 2 hours for the flavors to blend. (This may be prepared 24 hours in advance and refrigerated; return to room temperature to serve.)

ENTERTAINING
WITH STYLE

Mesclun Salad with
Toasted Goat Cheese
. . .
Roasted Cod with
Mango Salsa
. . .
Basmati Rice Pilaf
. . .
Spice Poundcake

SOFT-SHELL CRAB REMOULADE

Soft-shell crabs are one of the glorious, eagerly anticipated tastes of summer. These succulent gems are simply sautéed until golden, then crowned with a zesty Remoulade Sauce, giving rise to a lofty presentation. The Remoulade Sauce is also great over pan-fried sole and catfish.

8 soft-shell crabs, cleaned
freshly ground pepper to taste
flour for dredging
1/2 cup olive oil (not extra-virgin)
Remoulade Sauce (recipe follows)

1. Season the crabs with pepper and dredge in flour.

2. Heat 1/4 cup oil in a large skillet. Add 4 crabs and sauté over medium-high heat, 2 to 3 minutes per side until golden. Remove to a baking sheet and keep warm in a low oven. Repeat with the remaining oil and crabs. Serve with dollops of Remoulade Sauce.

4 portions

Remoulade Sauce:
1/2 cup mayonnaise
salt to taste
1/4 teaspoon freshly ground pepper
pinch of cayenne pepper
1/2 teaspoon dried tarragon
1 tablespoon Dijon mustard
2 tablespoons finely chopped cornichons
1 tablespoon capers, chopped
1 tablespoon finely chopped fresh parsley
1 tablespoon tarragon vinegar

Combine all of the ingredients and mix well. Store in the refrigerator until needed. (This will keep for 4 to 5 days.)

TABBOULEH-CRUSTED HADDOCK

Tabbouleh is the classic Middle Eastern dish featuring bulgur or cracked wheat. It's highlighted by chopped parsley, tomatoes, scallions, and lemon. Haddock filets bask in the glory of a tabbouleh topping, elevating the mild, sweet fish to gastronomic heights.

Bulgur:
1/2 cup bulgur
1/2 cup boiling water
1 1/2 cups finely chopped fresh curly parsley
1 cup seeded, chopped plum tomatoes
1/4 cup thinly sliced scallions
3 tablespoons lemon juice
3 tablespoons extra-virgin olive oil
salt and freshly ground pepper to taste

2 pounds haddock filets

1. Put the bulgur in a large mixing bowl. Pour the boiling water over the cracked wheat, mix well, cover, and let sit for 30 minutes for bulgur to absorb the liquid. Fluff with a fork.

2. Add the parsley, tomatoes, scallions, lemon juice, and olive oil and mix well. Season with salt and pepper. Let sit at room temperature at least 30 minutes and up to 2 hours for the flavors to blend.

3. Preheat the oven to 400°.

4. Put the haddock in a large baking dish. Cover the filets with the tabbouleh, making a thick topping.

5. Bake for 15 minutes and serve.

6 portions

MIDDLE EASTERN FLAVORS

Baba Ghanoush
. . .
Pita Bread
. . .
Tabbouleh-Crusted Haddock
. . .
Chickpea Salad

GRILLED HALIBUT WITH RED PEPPER MAYONNAISE

The mild, sweet flavor of this white-fleshed fish is enhanced with a creamy roasted red pepper mayonnaise spiked with garlic, basil, and capers. The mayonnaise is also splendid over grilled salmon, scallops, shrimp, and chicken.

2 pounds halibut steaks, 1-inch thick
2 tablespoons extra-virgin olive oil
salt and freshly ground pepper to taste
Red Pepper Mayonnaise (recipe follows)

1. Brush the halibut with the olive oil and season with salt and pepper.

2. Grill over hot coals, 4 inches from the heat source, 4 to 5 minutes per side. Serve at once with dollops of Red Pepper Mayonnaise.

4 portions

Red Pepper Mayonnaise:
1 large roasted red pepper, puréed
1/4 cup mayonnaise
1 1/2 teaspoons capers
salt and freshly ground pepper to taste
1 small clove garlic, crushed
1 tablespoon finely chopped fresh basil

Combine all of the ingredients and mix well. Store in the refrigerator until needed. (This may be prepared 2 days in advance.)

GLAZED ORANGE ROUGHY

I recently had my first encounter with this New Zealand native and was immediately smitten with the mild, tasty white fish. Simply prepared with an orange-currant glaze, it could become a classic.

Orange Sauce:
$1/2$ cup orange juice
2 tablespoons soy sauce
$1/4$ cup currant jelly, melted

2 pounds orange roughy filets
salt and freshly ground pepper to taste
flour for dredging
$1/2$ cup butter

1. In a small bowl, combine the orange juice, soy, and currant jelly and mix well.

2. Season the filets with salt and pepper and dredge in flour.

3. Heat the butter in a large non-stick skillet. Add the filets and sauté over high heat for 2 to 3 minutes per side until browned.

4. Add the Orange Sauce and simmer for 1 to 2 minutes more, spooning the sauce over the fish until it thickens and glazes the fish. Be careful not to let the sauce burn. Serve at once with the glaze spooned over the filets.

4 to 6 portions

BEST KEPT
SECRETS

Glazed Orange
Roughy
. . .
Fruited Rice Salad
. . .
Asparagus and
Raspberries
. . .
Carrot Cake Muffins

DEVILED SALMON CAKES

These plump, moist cakes are rich with salmon and spiked with Worcestershire, Dijon, and cayenne, giving rise to zesty flavor. Coated with fresh bread crumbs and sautéed until golden, they're served with a piquant tartar sauce for deviled madness.

1 pound salmon, boned, skinned, and cut into 1-inch chunks
1/4 cup finely diced red onion
salt and freshly ground pepper to taste
1/2 to 1 teaspoon Worcestershire sauce
1 teaspoon dry mustard
generous pinch of cayenne pepper
2 cups French bread crumbs
2 tablespoons vegetable oil
2 tablespoons butter
Tartar Sauce (recipe follows)

1. Put the salmon in the bowl of a food processor and purée. Transfer the purée to a bowl.

2. Add the onion, salt, pepper, Worcestershire, mustard, cayenne, and 1 cup bread crumbs and mix well.

3. Form the mixture into 8 equal-sized cakes (2$\frac{1}{2}$ inches in diameter). Dip each cake in the remaining 1 cup bread crumbs, coating completely. Refrigerate for 1 to 2 hours.

4. Heat the oil and butter in a large skillet. Sauté the cakes over medium-high heat, 2 to 3 minutes per side, until cooked and golden. Serve with dollops of Tartar Sauce.

4 portions

Tartar Sauce:
3/4 cup mayonnaise
salt and freshly ground pepper to taste
1 teaspoon Worcestershire sauce
1 tablespoon capers
2 tablespoons finely chopped sweet onion
3 tablespoons finely chopped dill pickle
1/4 cup chopped fresh parsley

Combine all of the ingredients and mix well. Store in the refrigerator until needed. (This will keep for 1 week.)

SALMON WITH PESTO CRUMBS

Pesto, the lush Genovese sauce of ground basil, pine nuts, Parmesan and olive oil, gives salmon distinction. Filets are lavished with pesto, topped with crumbs, and baked until golden.

2 pounds salmon filets
salt and freshly ground pepper to taste
6 tablespoons pesto (see page 12)
3/4 to 1 cup coarse French bread crumbs

1. Preheat the oven to 400°. Grease a large baking dish.

2. Place the salmon in the prepared pan. Season with salt and pepper. Spread the pesto evenly over the filet. Sprinkle with the bread crumbs.

3. Roast for 20 minutes for medium-rare. Slice into portions and serve.

6 portions

ELEGANT
EVENING

Prosciutto-Wrapped
Figs
· · ·
Salmon with
Pesto Crumbs
· · ·
Boston Lettuce,
Mushroom, and
Fennel Salad

Coffee Mascarpone-
Raspberry Tart

SWEET SOY-GLAZED SALMON

This blue ribbon winner bears resemblance to teriyaki, yet is more delicate. Grilled salmon filets are radiant with a glaze of sweetened soy sauce that's divine.

1/2 cup soy sauce
1/2 cup mirin (sweetened rice wine)
1/4 cup dry sherry
2 tablespoons sugar
2 pounds salmon filets, cut into 4 to 6 pieces
2 scallions, thinly sliced on the diagonal

1. Combine the soy, mirin, sherry, and sugar in a small saucepan. Cook over medium heat, stirring until the sugar dissolves. Remove from the heat and let cool. (This may be done up to 24 hours in advance.)

2. Put the salmon in a large baking dish. Pour the soy mixture over the filets and let marinate for 10 to 15 minutes.

3. Grill or broil the fish, 4 inches from the heat source, 4 to 5 minutes per side, basting with the marinade so that it glazes the fish. Serve hot off the grill sprinkled with the scallions.

4 to 6 portions

FIVE SPICE-ROASTED SALMON

Salmon filets are encrusted with a potpourri of fragrant spices—-
Chinese five spice powder, orange peel, and ginger—and baked to
perfection. The combination of flavors is complex and wonderful.

2 pounds salmon filets
2 tablespoons olive oil (not extra-virgin)
salt and freshly ground pepper to taste
2 teaspoons five spice powder
1 teaspoon dried orange peel
1/2 teaspoon ground ginger
2 tablespoons firmly packed dark brown sugar

1. Preheat the oven to 400°. Grease a large baking dish.

2. Place the salmon in the prepared pan. Brush the filets with the oil
and season with salt and pepper.

3. In a small bowl, combine the five spice powder, orange peel,
ginger, and brown sugar and mix well. Sprinkle the mixture evenly
over the fish.

4. Roast for 20 to 25 minutes. Serve with the pan juices spooned
over the fish.

4 to 6 portions

BUFFET DINNER
FOR 8

Assorted Melons
with Prosciutto
. . .
Salad Mezzaluna
. . .
Five Spice-Roasted
Salmon
. . .
Fruited Rice Salad
. . .
Coffee Gingersnap
Icebox Cake

SCALLOPS WITH BACON CRUMBS

Scallops bask under a luscious crumb topping oozing with Monterey Jack cheese and punctuated with the hickory flavor of bacon.

2 pounds sea scallops
salt and freshly ground pepper to taste
1 cup French bread crumbs
4 tablespoons butter, melted
6 slices bacon, cooked and chopped
1 cup grated Monterey Jack cheese

1. Preheat the oven to 400°.

2. Spread the scallops out in a single layer in a large baking dish. Season with salt and pepper.

3. In a bowl, combine the bread crumbs and butter, stirring until evenly mixed. Add the bacon and cheese and mix well.

4. Spoon the crumb mixture evenly over the scallops.

5. Bake for 15 to 20 minutes until cooked and golden. Serve at once.

6 portions

GRILLED SCALLOPS WITH SMOKEY CORN SALSA

Scallops are grilled to a crusty turn and embellished with a seductive, slightly smokey-flavored fresh corn, red pepper, and cucumber salsa. I like to serve the scallops with Israeli couscous and spoon the salsa over both.

> *2 pounds sea scallops*
> *2 tablespoons olive oil (not extra-virgin)*
> *salt and freshly ground pepper to taste*
> *Smokey Corn Salsa (recipe follows)*

1. Skewer the scallops. Brush the shellfish with oil and season with salt and pepper.

2. Grill over hot coals, 4 inches from the heat source, 3 to 4 minutes per side until charred and cooked through. Serve the scallops topped with spoonfuls of the salsa.

4 to 6 portions

> ***Smokey Corn Salsa:***
> *1 cup corn kernels (fresh or frozen)*
> *1/4 teaspoon liquid smoke*
> *1/2 cup diced red pepper (cut into 1/4-inch dice)*
> *1/2 cup diced, peeled seedless cucumber (cut into 1/4-inch dice)*
> *1/4 cup diced Vidalia (or other sweet) onion (cut into 1/4-inch dice)*
> *2 tablespoons sour cream*
> *salt and freshly ground pepper to taste*
> *1 1/2 teaspoons honey*
> *1 tablespoon lime juice*

1. Blanch the corn and drain well. While it is still warm, add the liquid smoke and mix well. Let cool for 15 minutes; then add the red pepper, cucumber, and onion.

2. In a separate small bowl, whisk together the sour cream, salt, pepper, honey, and lime juice. Pour the dressing over the vegetables and mix well. Let sit for 20 to 30 minutes for the flavors to mellow.

DINNER ON THE PATIO

Grilled Scallops with Smokey Corn Salsa
. . .
Wild Rice Pilaf
. . .
Mesclun Salad with Sherry Vinaigrette
. . .
Strawberry Shortcake

SCALLOPS WITH SUN-DRIED TOMATO PESTO

Scallops are embraced with a lush pesto, redolent with the intense flavor of sun-dried tomatoes. The simplicity of the dish makes it extra special.

> 2 pounds sea scallops
> salt and freshly ground pepper to taste
> Sun-Dried Tomato Pesto (recipe follows)

1. Preheat the oven to 400°. Grease a large baking dish.

2. Place the scallops in a single layer in the prepared pan. Season with salt and pepper and cover with the Sun-Dried Tomato Pesto.

3. Bake for 15 to 20 minutes until cooked and browned. Serve at once.

6 portions

> **Sun-Dried Tomato Pesto:**
> $1/2$ cup well-packed sun-dried tomatoes, plumped in hot water for
>   30 seconds and drained
> $1/4$ cup well-packed fresh basil
> $1^{1}/2$ tablespoons pine nuts, toasted
> 2 tablespoons grated Parmigiano-Reggiano cheese
> 1 large clove garlic, crushed
> salt and freshly ground pepper to taste
> $1/3$ cup extra-virgin olive oil

1. Put the sun-dried tomatoes, basil, pine nuts, cheese, garlic, salt, and pepper in the bowl of a food processor. Pulse until the mixture forms a paste.

2. With the motor running, add the oil in a slow, steady stream until completely incorporated. Transfer the pesto to a container and store in the refrigerator for up to 1 week until needed.

LOBSTER ROLLS

Lobster is the prized meat used in this lavish seafood salad that's tucked inside a toasted roll. This old-time summer favorite still reigns supreme!

1 pound cooked lobster meat, cut into $^1/_2$-inch pieces
$^2/_3$ cup diced celery
1$^1/_2$ tablespoons capers
1 teaspoon dried tarragon
$^1/_2$ cup mayonnaise
4 grinder rolls (7 to 8 inches long), toasted or grilled

1. In a large bowl, combine the lobster, celery, capers, tarragon, and mayonnaise and mix well.

2. Pile the lobster filling into the rolls and serve.

4 portions

BEACH PARTY

Lobster Rolls
· · ·
Coleslaw
· · ·
Lemonade
· · ·
White Chocolate-
Macadamia-Chocolate
Cookies
· · ·
Watermelon

NUBBLE LIGHT SEAFOOD BAKE

SPECIAL BIRTHDAY CELEBRATION

Corn Chowder
. . .
Mesclun Salad with
Toasted Goat Cheese
. . .
Nubble Light
Seafood Bake
. . .
Rum Cake

This rich and extravagant dish is the quintessential stuffed-baked presentation. Resplendent with shrimp, scallops, and lobster meat and dusted with an Old Bay seasoned crumb mix that's divine, it makes a grand statement. This is serious party fare.

8 tablespoons unsalted butter
1 medium yellow onion, finely diced
1³/4 cups fresh French bread crumbs
1 tablespoon Old Bay Seasoning
1 pound cooked lobster meat, cut into 1-inch chunks
1 pound sea scallops, cut in half
1 pound raw extra-large shrimp, shelled

1. Preheat the oven to 400°.

2. Heat the butter in a skillet. Add the onion and sauté over medium heat until soft and translucent, about 5 minutes. Stir in the bread crumbs and Old Bay Seasoning and mix until evenly combined. Remove from the heat.

3. Pile the seafood in a large bowl. Add the crumb mixture and stir well. Transfer the mixture to a 9 x 13-inch baking dish.

4. Bake for 15 minutes until the seafood is cooked and the crumbs are golden. Serve at once.

6 to 8 portions

SHRIMP, BACON, AND TOMATOES

The hickory flavor of bacon and the lush sweetness of cherry tomatoes highlight shrimp in this simple sauté that will titillate your taste buds.

4 slices bacon
1¹/₂ pounds raw extra-large shrimp, shelled
salt and freshly ground pepper
16 cherry tomatoes, halved

1. In a large skillet, cook the bacon over medium heat until golden and crisp. Remove the bacon, reserving the fat in the pan. Coarsely chop the bacon.

2. Heat the bacon fat. Add the shrimp, season with salt and pepper, and stir-fry over medium-high heat for 3 to 4 minutes until the shrimp turn pink. Add the tomatoes and heat through for 1 minute. Sprinkle with the chopped bacon and serve.

4 portions

GRILLED SHRIMP WITH TOMATO-CUCUMBER SALSA

Grilled shrimp are enrobed in a dashing salsa, rich with cucumber, tomatoes, and red onion. This is a visually stunning entrée that's perfect for the dog days of summer. Try the salsa over grilled chicken as well.

2 pounds raw extra-large shrimp, shelled
3 tablespoons extra-virgin olive oil
salt and freshly ground pepper to taste
Tomato-Cucumber Salsa (recipe follows)

1. Skewer the shrimp. Brush with the olive oil and season with salt and pepper.

2. Grill over hot coals, 4 inches from the heat source, 2 to 3 minutes per side until cooked and lightly charred. Spoon the salsa over the shrimp and serve.

6 portions

Tomato-Cucumber Salsa:
1 cucumber, peeled and diced into $1/4$-inch cubes
2 cups cherry tomatoes, quartered
$1/4$ cup diced red onion
1 jalapeño pepper, seeded and finely diced
salt and freshly ground pepper to taste
$1/4$ teaspoon ground cumin
2 tablespoons lime juice
1 tablespoon extra-virgin olive oil

Combine all of the ingredients and mix well. Let marinate for 1 to 2 hours at room temperature.

SHRIMP CURRY

Perfumed with the traditional seasonings of a curry—garlic, ginger, coriander, cumin, and turmeric—and garnished with toasted coconut, this shrimp dish will dazzle and delight you. Serve the shrimp over a bed of fragrant basmati rice.

1 tablespoon vegetable oil
1 small yellow onion, chopped
1 to 2 jalapeño peppers, seeded and minced
3 large cloves garlic, crushed
1 tablespoon grated gingerroot
1 teaspoon ground coriander
1 teaspoon ground cumin
1 teaspoon turmeric
salt to taste
¹/₂ teaspoon freshly ground pepper
2 cups well-stirred unsweetened coconut milk
1¹/₃ pounds raw extra-large shrimp, shelled
2 tablespoons finely chopped fresh cilantro
¹/₄ cup toasted coconut for garnish

1. Heat the oil in a large skillet. Add the onion and sauté until soft and translucent. Add the jalapeños, garlic, ginger, spices, salt, and pepper and sauté for 1 minute.

2. Add the coconut milk and simmer, stirring occasionally, until slightly thickened, about 7 to 8 minutes. (Up to this point may be done several hours in advance and stored in the refrigerator. Reheat gently before proceeding.)

3. Add the shrimp and cook over medium heat, stirring occasionally, until shrimp are cooked and turn pink, about 5 minutes. Sprinkle with cilantro and spoon over basmati rice. Garnish with toasted coconut and serve.

4 portions

INDONESIAN
FARE

Gado Gado
. . .
Shrimp Curry
. . .
Basmati Rice
. . .
Fresh Pineapple
Chunks

RISOTTO WITH SHRIMP, GOAT CHEESE, AND SUN-DRIED TOMATOES

Risotto is the illustrious Italian rice dish known for its creamy texture. This is a baked version of risotto, stream-lining the classic preparation of slowly adding hot broth to the simmering rice while stirring constantly. This presentation is resplendent with plump shrimp, heady with goat cheese, and dotted with sun-dried tomatoes, creating a mouth-watering experience. It makes outstanding company fare!

2 tablespoons olive oil
1 cup chopped leeks (white part only)
2 cups Arborio rice
$1/2$ cup dry white wine
$3^1/2$ to $3^2/3$ cups simmering chicken broth
salt and freshly ground pepper to taste
$1/2$ cup grated Parmigiano-Reggiano cheese
5 ounces goat cheese, crumbled
$1/2$ cup coarsely chopped sun-dried tomatoes, rehydrated in hot water
    for 1 minute and drained
$3/4$ pound cooked extra-large shrimp

1. Preheat the oven to 425°.

2. Heat the oil in a large stockpot. Add the leeks and sauté until lightly golden. Add the rice and mix well until all the grains are evenly coated with the oil and the leeks.

3. Add the wine and continue to cook, stirring until the liquid is almost absorbed. Add 3 cups of the broth, stirring well to combine. Season with salt and pepper. Cover and place in the oven for 15 minutes. Cover the remaining broth and remove from the heat.

4. Remove the risotto from the oven. Stir in the remaining $1/2$ to $2/3$ cup warm broth—the amount depends on how creamy you like the rice. Add the cheeses and mix well. Stir in the sun-dried tomatoes and shrimp and serve at once.

4 to 6 main-course portions; 8 or more side portions

SHRIMP AND ASPARAGUS

Succulent shrimp and majestic asparagus spears make a vibrant and festive combination in this simple Oriental stir-fry that's finished with an oyster-flavored sauce.

3 tablespoons vegetable oil
$1/8$-inch thick slice gingerroot
$1^1/2$ pounds raw extra-large shrimp, shelled
1 pound mature asparagus, peeled and cut into $1^1/2$-inch lengths
2 scallions, cut into $1^1/2$-inch lengths
Oyster Sauce (recipe follows)

1. Heat the oil in a wok. When hot, add the ginger and cook for 1 minute.

2. Add the shrimp and asparagus and stir-fry over high heat for 3 to 4 minutes until the shrimp turn pink. Add the scallions and Oyster sauce and stir-fry for 1 minute more. Serve with a white rice accompaniment.

4 portions

Oyster Sauce:
2 tablespoons oyster sauce
3 tablespoons mirin (rice wine)
1 teaspoon sugar
$1/2$ teaspoon Oriental sesame oil

Combine all of the sauce ingredients and mix well.

CHINESE BANQUET

Chinese Hot and
Sour Soup
. . .
Shrimp and Asparagus
. . .
Lamb with Scallions
. . .
White Rice
. . .
Ginger Ice Cream

SOLE WITH HAZELNUT BUTTER

The simplicity of this dish makes it most appealing. Sweet filets of sole are quickly pan-seared in butter and garnished with chopped hazelnuts, adding a delicate, nutty flavor and crunch. This also works well with flounder and red snapper.

1¹/2 pounds filet of sole
salt and freshly ground pepper to taste
flour for dredging
7 tablespoons butter
²/3 cup coarsely chopped hazelnuts
¹/4 cup chopped fresh parsley

1. Season the filets with salt and pepper and dredge in flour.

2. Heat half of the butter (3¹/2 tablespoons) in a large non-stick skillet. When hot, add half of the fish filets and sauté over medium-high heat for 3 to 4 minutes until browned. Turn the filets over, add half of the nuts (¹/3 cup) and half of the parsley (2 tablespoons) and sauté for 3 minutes more, stirring the nuts so they do not burn. Remove to a platter and keep warm in a low oven. Repeat with the remaining ingredients. Serve at once.

4 portions

STRIPED BASS PROVENÇAL

Stacked with garlic, onion, almonds, fennel, and orange peel, these savory filets are steeped in the aromatic flavors common to Provence. This is also dashing with salmon and shrimp.

2 pounds striped bass filets
4 tablespoons extra-virgin olive oil
salt and freshly ground pepper to taste
1 large Vidalia (or other sweet) onion, chopped
1/4 cup slivered almonds, coarsely chopped
1 large clove garlic, minced
1 teaspoon fennel seeds
1 1/2 teaspoons finely grated orange peel

1. Preheat the oven to 400°. Grease a large baking dish.

2. Place the fish in the prepared pan. Brush the filets with 1 tablespoon of olive oil and season with salt and pepper.

3. Heat the remaining 3 tablespoons olive oil in a skillet. Add the onion and sauté over medium-high until golden. Stir in the almonds, garlic, fennel, and orange peel and remove from the heat. Spread the onion mixture evenly over the fish filets, along with any oil left in the skillet.

4. Bake for 20 to 25 minutes. Serve at once.

4 portions

ORANGE-MUSTARD SWORDFISH

This dish tops the charts in our house. Meaty swordfish is infused with orange essence, Dijon, and rosemary and grilled to a crusty turn. The marinade also works well with shrimp, salmon, and chicken.

> 2 pounds swordfish, 1 to 1¼-inches thick
> salt and freshly ground pepper to taste
> 1 teaspoon dried rosemary
> 2 tablespoons Dijon mustard
> 1 teaspoon mustard seeds
> 1 tablespoon orange marmalade
> 1 teaspoon finely grated orange peel
> ¼ cup orange juice
> 2 tablespoons extra-virgin olive oil

1. Put the swordfish in a baking dish or deep platter.

2. In a bowl, combine the salt, pepper, rosemary, Dijon, mustard seeds, marmalade, orange peel, orange juice, and olive oil. Pour the marinade over the fish and let sit in the refrigerator for 1 to 2 hours. Return the fish to room temperature to cook.

3. Brush the grill with oil. Grill the fish over hot coals, 3 to 4 minutes per side for medium, basting with the marinade. The swordfish will be moist and succulent. Serve hot off the grill.

4 to 6 portions

CUMIN-CRUSTED SWORDFISH

Swordfish steaks are embraced by a garlic and cumin-scented mayonnaise in this moist and tender grilled presentation.

2 pounds swordfish, 1 to 1¼-inches thick
6 tablespoons mayonnaise
salt and freshly ground pepper to taste
1 large clove garlic, crushed
1 tablespoon ground cumin

1. Put the swordfish on a large platter.

2. In a small bowl, combine the mayonnaise, salt, pepper, garlic, and cumin. Spread half of the mixture over the top and sides of the swordfish. Reserve the rest.

3. Place the swordfish on the grill, mayonnaise side down, 4 inches from the heat source. Spread the remaining mayonnaise over the top of the fish. Grill the swordfish about 3 to 4 minutes per side for medium. The fish will be moist and succulent. Slice and serve.

4 portions

SUMMER FARE

Mango Salad
. . .
Cumin-Crusted
Swordfish
. . .
Israeli Couscous
with Cranberries
and Almonds
. . .
Peach Kuchen

HOISIN-GLAZED SWORDFISH

The hoisin-based sauce glazes grilled swordfish, giving an Oriental flair to this meaty fish. This simple presentation is packed with flavor. It's also stunning on salmon and tuna.

freshly ground pepper to taste
1/4 cup hoisin sauce
2 tablespoons apricot preserves
2 teaspoons Oriental sesame oil
2 pounds swordfish, 1-inch thick

1. In a small bowl, combine the pepper, hoisin, apricot preserves, and sesame oil and mix well. Brush the mixture over the swordfish.

2. Grill or broil the fish, 4 inches from the heat source, 3 to 4 minutes per side on a well-oiled grill. Serve hot off the grill.

4 to 6 portions

GRILLED TUNA WITH MEDITERRANEAN TOMATO RELISH

MEDITERRANEAN
FLAIR

Mesclun Salad with
Basic Vinaigrette
. . .
Grilled Tuna with
Mediterranean Relish
. . .
Pasta Toscano
. . .
Cannoli

Seared tuna steaks are resplendent with a lusty tomato relish rich with the Mediterranean influences of garlic, capers, and Kalamata olives. I like to serve the tuna with freshly cooked linguine and spoon the relish over both. For a change of pace, try this with swordfish.

2 pounds tuna steaks, 1^1/$_4$-inches thick
salt and freshly ground pepper to taste
1 tablespoon balsamic vinegar
1 tablespoon extra-virgin olive oil
Tomato Relish (recipe follows)

1. Put the tuna on a serving dish.

2. In a small bowl, whisk the salt, pepper, balsamic, and olive oil. Brush the mixture over all surfaces of the fish.

3. Grill the tuna over hot coals, 4 inches from the heat source, 3 minutes per side for medium-rare. Slice and serve topped with spoonfuls of Tomato Relish.

4 portions

Tomato Relish:
2 dozen cherry tomatoes, quartered
12 Kalamata olives, pitted (see page 5)
1 tablespoon capers, rinsed
^{1}/$_4$ cup coarsely chopped Italian parsley
salt and freshly ground pepper to taste
1 medium-size clove garlic, minced
1 tablespoon balsamic vinegar
1 tablespoon extra-virgin olive oil

Combine all of the relish ingredients in a bowl and mix well. Let sit at room temperature for 1 to 2 hours for the flavors to blend.

SEARED TUNA WITH HORSERADISH CREAM

SEAFOOD SPLENDOR

Seared Tuna with Horseradish Cream
· · ·
Green Garden Salad
· · ·
White Bean Crostini
· · ·
Layered Sponge Cake

Thick, meaty tuna steaks are coated with a crumb crust, quickly pan-seared, and adorned with a luscious Dijon and horseradish-flavored cream sauce. The tuna is rare and delicately flavored with an assertive topping.

> *2 pounds tuna steaks, 1 to 1¹/₄-inches thick*
> *salt and freshly ground pepper to taste*
> *1 egg, beaten*
> *1 cup French bread crumbs*
> *4 tablespoons butter*
> *Horseradish Cream (recipe follows)*

1. Season the tuna with salt and pepper. Dip the tuna in the beaten egg and then coat with the bread crumbs. Place in the refrigerator for 30 minutes for the crumbs to adhere.

2. Heat the butter in a non-stick skillet. Add the tuna and sauté over high heat, 2 minutes per side until crumbs are golden. Remove to a platter and slice into ¹/₄-inch thick pieces. Serve with dollops of Horseradish Cream.

4 to 6 portions

> ***Horseradish Cream:***
> *¹/₂ cup sour cream*
> *2 tablespoons prepared white horseradish*
> *1 tablespoon Dijon mustard*

Combine all of the ingredients and mix well. Store in the refrigerator until needed.

GRILLED TUNA WITH WASABI MAYONNAISE

Wasabi is the Japanese horseradish powder that is sharp, pungent, and fiery. Tuna takes on an Oriental flair when topped with dollops of a wasabi-infused mayonnaise. The mayonnaise is also fabulous as a sauce for cold, poached lobster.

> 2 pounds tuna steaks, 1 to 1¹/4-inches thick
> 2 tablespoons soy sauce
> freshly ground pepper to taste
> 1 tablespoon grated gingerroot
> 2 tablespoons vegetable oil
> Wasabi Mayonnaise (recipe follows)
> 1 teaspoon sesame seeds, toasted

1. Put the tuna in a baking dish.

2. In a small bowl, combine the soy, pepper, ginger, and oil. Pour the marinade over the tuna and let sit for 30 minutes.

3. Grill the tuna over hot coals, 4 inches from the heat source, 3 minutes per side for medium-rare. Serve at once topped with dollops of Wasabi Mayonnaise and sprinkled with sesame seeds.

4 portions

> **Wasabi Mayonnaise:**
> 2 tablespoons wasabi powder (available in Oriental markets)
> 1¹/2 tablespoons warm water
> 2 teaspoons soy sauce
> ¹/2 cup mayonnaise

1. In a small bowl, mix the wasabi and warm water until it forms a dough-like consistency. Add the soy sauce and stir until evenly combined.

2. Add the wasabi mixture to the mayonnaise and mix thoroughly. Serve at room temperature or store in the refrigerator until needed.

VIBRANT VEGGIES

Do you remember your mother saying, "Eat your vegetables, they're good for you!" Well, she was right, they are. They're chock full of vitamins, nutrients, and anti-oxidants. Vegetables are the element that add color, varied texture, and vibrancy to the meal. The large variety and their crunchy, crispy quality make them especially appealing. I always try to choose vegetables that add a color note and complementary flavor to the main dish.

Whether they're from the backyard garden, the local farm stand, or the supermarket, vegetables need to be fresh, firm, and top of the line. Dry, withered, limp vegetables just don't make the grade. Simple roasting, grilling, or sautéing brings out the best of the bunch. So eat your veggies and enjoy.

ASPARAGUS AND RASPBERRIES

The delicate, much-prized queen of berries, the raspberry, is set against tender, green stalks of asparagus, creating a most colorful dish. All is finished in a raspberry-infused vinaigrette, complementing this favored perennial vegetable.

> 1 pound asparagus, peeled and poached until tender-crisp,
>   about 5 minutes
> 1 cup raspberries
>
> **Raspberry Vinaigrette:**
> salt and freshly ground pepper to taste
> 1 tablespoon raspberry preserves
> 2 tablespoons raspberry vinegar
> 1/3 cup olive oil (not extra-virgin)

1. Arrange the asparagus in a serving dish. Sprinkle with the raspberries.

2. In a small bowl, whisk together the salt, pepper, preserves, vinegar, and oil. Pour the vinaigrette over the asparagus and let marinate for 1 to 2 hours. Serve at room temperature.

4 portions

MAPLE-GLAZED RED CABBAGE

The slight peppery taste of the dark purple, red cabbage is tempered by a sweet-sour maple syrup glaze. I especially enjoy this with the lavish Thanksgiving meal.

3 tablespoons pure maple syrup
2 tablespoons balsamic vinegar
3 tablespoons butter
1/4 cup diced shallots
4 cups thinly sliced red cabbage
1/2 teaspoon salt
freshly ground pepper to taste

1. In a small bowl, combine the maple syrup and vinegar and set aside.

2. Heat the butter in a large skillet. Add the shallots and sauté over medium heat for 1 to 2 minutes until translucent.

3. Add the cabbage, season with the salt and pepper, and sauté for about 5 minutes, stirring constantly until the cabbage begins to wilt.

4. Pour the maple syrup mixture over the cabbage, mixing well, and simmer for 2 minutes until the cabbage is glazed. Serve at once.

4 portions

WINTER COMFORT FOOD

Roasted Turkey
Breast*
. . .
Baked-Stuffed Onions
. . .
Maple-Glazed
Red Cabbage
. . .
Pumpkin Bread
Pudding

ROASTED CARROTS

The high temperature roasting method locks in the flavor and brings out the natural sweetness of the carrots. Tossed with olive oil and seasoned with cumin, this dish comes together with almost no effort. Do not use the peeled baby carrots in this preparation, as they do not cook properly.

2 pounds carrots, peeled and cut into 2-inch lengths
1/4 cup extra-virgin olive oil
1 tablespoon ground cumin
salt and freshly ground pepper to taste

1. Preheat the oven to 450°.

2. In a large bowl, toss the carrots with the olive oil until evenly coated. Season with the cumin, salt, and pepper, mixing well.

3. Transfer the carrots to a baking sheet, along with any of the seasonings, spreading them out in a single layer.

4. Roast for 25 minutes, shaking the pan after 15 minutes. Serve hot or at room temperature.

6 portions

ROASTED CAULIFLOWER

This elegant member of the cabbage family does not get its just recognition. The creamy white variety is tossed with olive oil, then dressed in gremolata, rich with garlic, lemon, and parsley, and roasted until tender. It totes well to picnics and barbecues and lends new flavor dimension to freshly cooked pasta.

1 head cauliflower, broken into flowerets (large pieces cut in half)
1/4 cup extra-virgin olive oil
1 tablespoon lemon juice
1 teaspoon grated lemon peel
1 large clove garlic, minced
1/4 cup finely chopped fresh parsley
salt and freshly ground pepper to taste

1. Preheat the oven to 450°.

2. In a large bowl, toss the cauliflower with the olive oil until evenly coated. Add the remaining ingredients, mixing well.

3. Turn the flowerets onto a baking sheet, spreading them out in a single layer.

4. Roast for 20 minutes until the cauliflower softens and begins to brown, stirring after 15 minutes. Serve hot or at room temperature.

6 portions

ROAST BEEF
DINNER

Carrot and
Parsnip Soup
. . .
Roast Beef*
. . .
Roasted Cauliflower
. . .
Asparagus and
Cherry Tomatoes
. . .
Caramel Pineapple
Upside-Down Cake

GREEN BEANS WITH TOASTED HAZELNUTS

Hazelnuts, also known as filberts, sport creamy meat with a sweet, rich taste. Sautéing the nuts lends a nutty, toasted flavor, accenting these snappy green beans.

> 1 pound green beans, trimmed
> 2 tablespoons butter (no substitutions)
> 1/4 cup chopped hazelnuts
> salt and freshly ground pepper to taste

1. Cook the beans in boiling salted water for about 5 minutes until tender-crisp. Drain well and place in a serving dish.

2. Heat the butter in a small pan over high heat until foamy. Add the nuts and sauté for about 1 minute until golden. Pour the nut butter over the beans, season with salt and pepper, and serve at once.

4 portions

ROASTED GREEN BEANS

Roasting green beans is a simple way to prepare the vegetables with tasty results. Browned and crisp, these beans are always requested in our house.

1 pound green beans, stems removed
2 tablespoons extra-virgin olive oil
salt and freshly ground pepper to taste

1. Preheat the oven to 450°.

2. In a large bowl, toss the beans with the olive oil, salt, and pepper. Spread them out in a single layer in a large baking pan.

3. Roast for 10 to 12 minutes, shaking the pan after 5 minutes. Serve hot or at room temperature.

4 to 6 portions

DINNER PARTY FOR 8

Grilled Herbed
Leg of Lamb
· · ·
Roasted Green Beans
· · ·
Soubise Parmesan
· · ·
Chocolate
Cream Cake

MUSHROOM AND CHEESE STRATA

This savory bread pudding is real comfort food. The basic bread and egg custard is embellished with a riot of sautéed wild mushrooms and encrusted with cheddar cheese. This also makes a great brunch dish or luncheon choice.

8 ounces French bread, cut into 1-inch cubes
5 extra-large eggs
2¹/₂ cups whole milk
dash Worcestershire sauce
salt and freshly ground pepper to taste
1 tablespoon Dijon mustard
2 tablespoons butter
1 pound assorted mushrooms, sliced (shiitake, cremini, portobello, and oyster)
³/₄ pound sharp cheddar cheese, grated

1. Put the bread in a large bowl.

2. In a separate bowl, whisk together the eggs, milk, Worcestershire, salt, pepper, and Dijon. Pour the custard over the bread, mixing well to coat all of the cubes. Let sit at room temperature for 30 minutes to allow the bread to absorb the liquid.

3. Preheat the oven to 350°. Grease a 9 x 13-inch baking dish.

4. While the bread is soaking, sauté the mushrooms. In a large skillet, heat the butter. Add the mushrooms, season with salt and pepper, and sauté over medium heat, stirring occasionally, until golden.

5. Add the mushrooms and cheddar to the bread mixture, mixing until evenly combined. Turn into the prepared pan.

6. Bake for 45 to 50 minutes until set and golden. Let sit for 5 minutes before slicing and serving.

8 to 10 portions

ROASTED MUSHROOMS

Roasting mushrooms intensifies their taste, lending a rich, earthy flavor. These double as cocktail food, and make mouth-watering toppings for pasta and salad.

1¼ pounds white mushrooms, stems trimmed
6 tablespoons extra-virign olive oil
salt and freshly ground pepper to taste

1. Preheat the oven to 400°. Grease a large baking pan.

2. Put the mushrooms in a large bowl. Drizzle with the olive oil and season with salt and pepper. Toss well until evenly coated.

3. Spread the mushrooms out in a single layer in the prepared pan, stem side up. Roast for 15 minutes.

4. Turn the mushrooms over and roast for 10 minutes more. Toss with the pan juices, mixing well. Serve warm or at room temperature.

6 portions

TRIP TO ITALY

Roasted Mushrooms
. . .
Chicken Bianco
. . .
Baked Polenta
. . .
Lemon Ricotta Cake

BAKED-STUFFED ONIONS

Baked onions make an excellent accompaniment to roasted meats and poultry. These sweet Vidalias are encrusted with a fetching bread crumb topping, rich with feta and mint.

8 medium-size Vidalia (or other sweet) onions, peeled
2 to 3 tablespoons olive oil
salt and freshly ground pepper to taste
1 cup fresh bread crumbs
1/2 cup crumbled feta cheese
1/4 cup thinly sliced scallions
1/4 cup finely chopped fresh mint
2 tablespoons finely chopped fresh parsley
1/4 cup extra-virgin olive oil

1. Preheat the oven to 375°.

2. Cut 1-inch off from the tops of the onions. Trim the bottoms slightly so the onions will sit level. Scoop out the centers of the onions, leaving about 1/3-inch thick shells.

3. Place the shells in a baking dish. Drizzle the insides with 1 tablespoon olive oil and season with salt and pepper. Pour water into the pan until it is halfway up the sides of the onions.

4. Cover and bake for 35 to 40 minutes. Pour off the water.

5. Turn the onions over and brush the outsides with 1 to 2 tablespoons olive oil. Turn right side to.

6. In a bowl, combine the bread crumbs, feta, scallions, mint, parsley, and 1/4 cup olive oil. Mix well and season with salt and pepper.

7. Stuff the onions with the above mixture, pressing the filling into place.

8. Bake for 30 minutes until the stuffing is golden. Serve at once.

8 portions

SWEET PICKLED VIDALIAS

The much-prized Vidalia onion is cut into rings and steeped in a sweet, mustardy pickling mixture. Left to marinate overnight, this sweet onion relish is the perfect companion for sausages, burgers, grilled meats, and chicken.

1 1/2 pounds Vidalia onions, sliced into 1/4-inch thick rings
1 cup white vinegar
1 cup sugar
1 tablespoon coarse or kosher salt
1 teaspoon dry mustard
1 teaspoon turmeric
1 teaspoon celery seeds
1 1/2 teaspoons mustard seeds

1. In a large saucepan, combine all of the ingredients. Bring to a boil over medium heat, stirring until the sugar dissolves. Simmer for 5 minutes until the onions are translucent.

2. Transfer the pickles to clean pint jars, cover, and place on a rack to cool. When cool, refrigerate overnight before serving. These will keep for 1 month.

3 pints

ALL-AMERICAN
BACKYARD
BARBECUE

Grilled Burgers
· · ·
All-American
Potato Salad
· · ·
Sweet Pickled Vidalias
· · ·
Watermelon,
Cucumber, and
Jicama Salad
· · ·
Peanut Butter
Swirl Brownies
· · ·
Orange Creamsicle
Smoothies

MAPLE-PARSNIP PURÉE

The parsnip, a member of the carrot family, has creamy white flesh and a sweet, nutty flavor. This old-fashioned root vegetable takes on a new identity as a purée, laced with maple syrup and ginger. It's perfect with roast turkey for Thanksgiving.

1 pound parsnips, peeled and cut into 1-inch chunks
1/4 cup sour cream
2 tablespoons butter
1/4 cup pure maple syrup
1/2 teaspoon ground ginger
salt and freshly ground pepper to taste

1. Boil the parsnips in a pot of salted water for about 15 minutes until tender. Drain well.

2. Put the parsnips, sour cream, butter, maple syrup, ginger, salt, and pepper in the bowl of a food processor and purée. Serve at once.

4 portions

MASHED POTATOES AND CELERIAC

Celeriac, or celery root, is the brown, knobby, rather unattractive root of a special celery. Don't let its appearance fool you—underneath its tough skin is a firm-textured, white flesh with a glorious taste much like celery, only more intense. It pairs well with potato in this soul-satisfying comfort food.

> 1 pound celeriac, peeled (use a knife to peel off the tough rind) and cut into 1-inch cubes
> 2 pounds Idaho potatoes, peeled and cut into 1-inch cubes
> 1 cup warm milk
> 4 tablespoons butter
> salt and freshly ground pepper to taste

1. Boil the celeriac in a pot of salted water for 15 minutes or until tender. Drain well and place in a bowl.

2. While the celeriac is cooking, boil the potatoes in a pot of salted water for 10 to 15 minutes until tender. Drain well and add to the celeriac.

3. Mash the vegetables. Add the milk, butter, salt, and pepper, mixing until smooth. Serve at once.

6 portions

WINTER COMFORTS

Meatloaf
. . .
Mashed Potatoes and Celeriac
. . .
Roasted Carrots
. . .
Grape Nuts Custard

HORSERADISH-MASHED YUKON GOLDS

Mashed potatoes are probably the ultimate comfort food. The basic potato, butter, and milk theme is spiked with white horseradish, lending a new level of flavor to this already yummy dish.

2 pounds Yukon Gold potatoes, cut into 1-inch cubes
4 tablespoons butter
1/2 cup whole milk, at room temperature
2 tablespoons prepared white horseradish
salt and freshly ground pepper to taste

1. Boil the potatoes for 10 to 15 minutes until tender. Drain well and mash with their skins to a chunky consistency.

2. Add the butter, milk, horseradish, salt, and pepper and mix well. Serve at once.

6 portions

SMASHED POTATOES

These tasty taters will take center stage at the dinner table. They're actually a cross between roasted and mashed potatoes, capturing the best of both—a crusty outside and soft interior flesh.

2 pounds medium-size red skinned potatoes, halved
¼ cup extra-virgin olive oil
lots of salt and freshly ground pepper

1. Preheat the oven to 400°. Grease a large baking pan.

2. Place the potatoes cut side down on the prepared pan. Roast for 45 minutes.

3. Remove the pan from the oven. Smash the potatoes lightly to flatten, using a potato masher or meat tenderizer. Turn the potatoes flesh side up.

4. Drizzle with the olive oil and season with salt and pepper.

5. Roast for 20 minutes more until crisp. Serve hot from the oven.

6 portions

FATHER'S DAY DINNER

Bruschetta with Black
Olive Pesto
. . .
Stuffed Flank Steak
. . .
Smashed Potatoes
. . .
Chocolate Swirl
Poundcake

GARLIC MASHED POTATO CAKES

Boiled, mashed, formed into large pancakes, and sautéed until browned and crusty, this potato dish is sure to garner praise. It goes one step beyond the ever so humble hash-brown potato.

3 Idaho potatoes, peeled and cut into 1-inch cubes
2 large cloves garlic, crushed
1/2 cup milk
1/4 cup grated Parmesan cheese
1/3 cup thinly sliced scallions
salt and freshly ground pepper to taste
6 tablespoons olive oil (not extra-virgin)
sour cream for garnish

1. Boil the potatoes in a large pot of salted water for 10 to 15 minutes until tender. Drain well, then mash.

2. Add the garlic, milk, Parmesan, scallions, salt, and pepper and mix well.

3. Heat 3 tablespoons of oil in a large non-stick skillet. When hot, add half of the batter, spreading it out into a large pancake. Cook over medium-high heat until browned, turning portions as the bottom gets crusty. The pancake will not stay in one piece, so you will end up with clusters of crusty mashed potato. Turn the potato often to end up with lots of crust. Keep the first batch warm in a low oven while you repeat with the remaining oil and potato mixture. Serve hot with dollops of sour cream.

4 to 6 portions

HONEYED BUTTERNUT SQUASH

The sweet orange flesh of this winter squash is glorious with honey and brown sugar. It makes a marvelous addition to the Thanksgiving meal, but it's actually delicious with any roasted poultry, pork, or ham.

1¹/₂ pounds peeled, cleaned butternut squash, cut into 1-inch pieces
salt to taste
4 tablespoons butter
2 tablespoons honey
2 tablespoons firmly packed dark brown sugar

1. Boil the squash in a pot of salted water for about 10 to 15 minutes until tender. Drain well and mash.

2. Add the salt, butter, honey, and brown sugar and mix well. Serve at once.

4 to 6 portions

THANKSGIVING FEAST

Dilled Onion Crostini
· · ·
Succulent
Roast Turkey*
· · ·
Honeyed-Butternut
Squash
· · ·
Cornbread Stuffing
· · ·
Roasted Asparagus**
· · ·
Cranberry Chutney**
· · ·
Pumpkin Cheesecake

MASHED APPLES AND SWEET POTATOES

This pumpkin-colored, nutmeg-scented mash of fall offerings makes a wonderful pairing with roast chicken, turkey, or pork.

3 medium-size sweet potatoes, peeled and chopped into 1-inch chunks
2 Granny Smith apples, peeled, cored, and coarsely chopped
1 medium yellow onion, diced
4 tablespoons butter
6 tablespoons packed dark brown sugar
$^1/_2$ teaspoon nutmeg
salt and freshly ground pepper to taste

1. Boil the potatoes, apples, and onions in a large pot of salted water for about 10 minutes until tender. Drain well; then mash to a chunky consistency.

2. Add the butter, brown sugar, nutmeg, salt, and pepper and mix well. Serve at once.

6 to 8 portions

ROASTED SWEET POTATOES

Roasted potatoes are definite comfort food. Roasting chunks of sweet potatoes allows them to form a crisp crust with a tender interior flesh. Serve them alongside roasted chicken, beef, or pork. For a dramatic presentation, use a medley of potatoes—sweet, red-skinned, and purple.

> *2 pounds sweet potatoes, cut into 1^1/$_2$-inch chunks with their skin*
> *3 tablespoons olive oil (not extra-virgin)*
> *1 teaspoon dried thyme*
> *1 teaspoon paprika*
> *salt and freshly ground pepper to taste*

1. Preheat the oven to 400°.

2. Arrange the potatoes in a single layer in a large baking dish. Drizzle with the olive oil and toss until evenly coated. Season with thyme, paprika, salt, and pepper.

3. Roast for 45 to 50 minutes until tender, stirring every 15 minutes. Serve hot or at room temperature.

5 to 6 portions

ROMANTIC
DINNER FOR
TWO

Salad Marly
. . .
Curry-Mustard
Rack of Lamb
. . .
Roasted Sweet
Potatoes
. . .
Raspberry Torte

SMOKEY MASHED SWEET POTATOES

These orange-hued potatoes will capture your attention with their sweet, slightly smokey, and spicy aroma.

2 pounds sweet potatoes, peeled and cut into 1-inch chunks
salt and freshly ground pepper to taste
¹/₄ teaspoon liquid smoke
¹/₂ teaspoon cayenne pepper
3 tablespoons butter, at room temperature
¹/₂ cup light cream, at room temperature

1. Boil the potatoes in a large pot of salted water for 10 to 12 minutes until fork tender. Drain well and mash.

2. Add the salt, pepper, liquid smoke, cayenne, butter, and light cream and mix until completely incorporated. Serve at once.

6 portions

MASHED ROOT VEGETABLES

Mashed vegetables are definitely in vogue, as nutritious, comfort food. The humble root vegetables—the mild-mannered potato, the sweet parsnip, and the distinct-flavored turnip—combine to make a most tasty mash.

2 Idaho potatoes, peeled and cut into 1-inch chunks
3/4 pound parsnips, peeled and cut into 1-inch chunks
3/4 pound turnips, peeled and cut into 1-inch chunks
4 tablespoons butter
1/2 cup light cream, warmed
1/4 cup grated Parmigiano-Reggiano cheese
salt and freshly ground pepper to taste

1. Boil the potatoes, parsnips, and turnips in a large pot of salted water for 10 to 15 minutes until tender. Drain well; then mash to a chunky consistency.

2. Add the butter, cream, cheese, salt, and pepper and mix well. Serve at once.

6 to 8 portions

HARVEST DINNER

Harvest Beet Salad
· · ·
Roast Pork
· · ·
Mashed Root
Vegetables
· · ·
Caramel Apple Cake

HALF-SOUR PICKLED TOMATOES

If you find yourself with a glut of tomatoes, transform the green ones into half-sour pickles. These zesty, garlicky, dill-pickled tomatoes are lip-smacking good.

> 2 pounds green tomatoes, quartered (or green cherry tomatoes, halved)
> 2 large cloves garlic, smashed
> 1/4 cup coarse or kosher salt
> 1 teaspoon pickling spices
> 1/4 teaspoon dill seed
> 1/4 cup white vinegar
> boiling water

1. Put the green tomatoes in a 2-quart jar. Add the garlic, seasonings, and vinegar.

2. Pour boiling water over the tomatoes to fill the jar. Cover and let sit at room temperature for 24 hours; then refrigerate for 2 weeks before eating. (Cherry tomatoes only need 1 week to pickle.)

about 2 quarts

VEGETABLE PANCAKES

This adaptation of a great classic, the potato pancake, will surprise and delight you. Grated carrots, potato, and zucchini are interlaced in these crusty pancakes that are peppered with dill. They're great as a side dish topped with dill-sour cream and make an outstanding addition to the hors d'oeuvre table.

VALENTINE'S
DINNER

Vegetable Pancakes
. . .
Spinach, Brie, and
Sun-Dried Tomatoes
. . .
Herbed Rack
of Lamb*
. . .
German Sweet
Chocolate Pie

1 large Idaho potato, coarsely grated
2 large carrots, coarsely grated
1 medium-size zucchini, coarsely grated
1/4 cup thinly sliced scallions
1/4 cup all-purpose flour
1 teaspoon dried dill
1 teaspoon salt
freshly ground pepper to taste
3 eggs, beaten
6 tablespoons vegetable oil
Dill-Sour Cream (recipe follows)

1. In a large bowl, combine the potato, carrots, zucchini, scallions, flour, dill, salt, and pepper and mix well.

2. Add the eggs and stir until evenly combined.

3. Heat 3 tablespoons of oil in a large skillet. Drop large spoonfuls of batter into the pan, making 3-inch rounds. Fry the pancakes over medium heat until brown and crisp on both sides. Remove to a platter and keep warm in a low oven. Repeat, adding the remaining oil and batter to the pan. Serve with Dill-Sour Cream.

14 pancakes; 6 to 8 portions

Dill-Sour Cream:
3/4 cup sour cream
2 tablespoons finely chopped fresh dill
freshly ground pepper to taste

Combine all of the ingredients and mix well. Refrigerate until needed.

PARMESAN-CRUSTED ZUCCHINI

Zucchini is an extremely versatile member of the squash family. When you have an abundance of zucchini in the summer, try roasting rounds of the vegetable dusted with Parmesan, for a fresh Italian taste.

2 medium-size zucchini, cut into 1-inch thick rounds
1½ to 2 tablespoons extra-virgin olive oil
¼ teaspoon garlic powder
salt and freshly ground pepper to taste
2 tablespoons grated Parmigiano-Reggiano cheese

1. Preheat the oven to 450°. Grease a large baking sheet.

2. In a large bowl, toss the zucchini with the olive oil. Season with the garlic powder, salt, and pepper and mix well.

3. Turn the rounds out onto the prepared pan. Drizzle with any of the oil from the bowl. Sprinkle with the Parmesan.

4. Roast for 15 minutes. Serve hot or at room temperature.

4 portions

STYLISH GRAINS

Grains have found a place of importance in the culinary world. They're considered a most stylish food, gracing the tables in trendy restaurants. Preparing grains—rice, couscous, bulgur, barley, wild rice, and corn—in the home kitchen can be both fun and exciting. They provide a marvelous base for stacking layers of complex flavors and textures. Whether adding sautéed vegetables, dried fruits and nuts, grilled seafood, roasted meats, or sautéed chicken, you're sure to create a satisfying mélange. Challenge yourself and cook them in both traditional and creative ways to add interest and intrigue to mealtime.

CORN PUDDING

This is actually a revised version of the stellar recipe from *The Uncommon Gourmet*. I've reduced the amount of butter and salt and made minor adjustments without compromising the results. I think you'll agree, it's still a winner and it's better for you!

4 cups corn kernels (frozen or canned)
$1/2$ cup flour
8 eggs, beaten
2 cups whole milk
$1^1/2$ cups sugar
$1/2$ cup butter, melted and cooled
1 tablespoon vanilla
$1/2$ teaspoon salt

1. Preheat the oven to 350°. Grease a 9 x 13-inch baking dish.

2. In a small bowl, mix the corn and flour until evenly blended.

3. In a large bowl, whisk together the eggs and milk. Beat in the sugar, butter, vanilla, and salt. Stir in the corn mixture.

4. Turn the custard into the prepared pan.

5. Bake for 1 hour until golden brown and bubbly. Let sit for 5 to 10 minutes, then cut into squares and serve.

8 to 10 portions

ROASTED CORN

Corn on the cob is one of the glories of summer. I have fond childhood memories of nibbling on ears of corn slathered with butter and sprinkled with salt. The simple roasting process in this recipe brings out the best of the ear, allowing the flavor to deepen and the kernel to remain juicy and sweet. This partners well with grilled steak, chicken, burgers and salmon.

> 6 ears of corn, shucked
> 3 tablespoons extra-virgin olive oil
> salt and freshly ground pepper to taste

1. Preheat the oven to 450°.
2. Brush the ears of corn with the olive oil, coating completely. Place on a baking sheet and season with salt and pepper.
3. Roast for 15 minutes, turning the ears after 10 minutes. Serve hot or at room temperature.

6 portions

BACKYARD
GET-TOGETHER

The 47 House Salad
· · ·
London Broil
· · ·
Roasted Corn
· · ·
Double Fudge
Brownies

CORN SOUFFLÉ

SPECIAL
OCCASION
DINNER

Asparagus Bundles
· · ·
Soft-Shell
Crab Remoulade
· · ·
Corn Soufflé
· · ·
Romaine with
Tomato Relish
· · ·
Fruits with
Raspberry Sauce

This dish is actually a crustless corn quiche. The savory custard of eggs and cream is laced with corn and a duo of cheeses, and then baked to a turn. This is a good companion to roast chicken and turkey.

3 eggs, slightly beaten
1 cup light cream
4 tablespoons butter, melted and cooled
2 cups corn kernels (frozen or canned)
1/2 pound grated sharp cheddar cheese
2 tablespoons snipped chives
1/4 teaspoon cayenne pepper
salt and freshly ground pepper to taste
1/4 cup grated Parmigiano-Reggiano cheese

1. Preheat the oven to 350°. Grease a 1½-quart casserole.

2. In a large mixing bowl, combine the eggs, cream, and butter. Add the corn, cheddar, chives, cayenne, salt, and pepper, and mix well.

3. Turn the custard into the prepared pan. Sprinkle with the Parmesan cheese.

4. Bake for about 45 minutes until set. Remove from the oven and let sit for 5 to 10 minutes before cutting and serving.

6 portions

CORNBREAD STUFFING

The Thanksgiving feast would be incomplete without stuffing.
Steeped in tradition, cornbread stuffing is real comfort food. I've
updated the classic savory dressing by incorporating corn kernels,
bacon, dried cranberries, and pecans. It's most definitely holiday
quality, but should be enjoyed year round!

1 recipe of cornbread (see page 111), cut into $3/4$-inch cubes
6 tablespoons butter
2 cups chopped yellow onions
4 large ribs celery, peeled and chopped
1 large red pepper, chopped
1 teaspoon dried sage
1 teaspoon dried thyme
1 teaspoon dried marjoram
$1/2$ cup chopped fresh parsley
salt and freshly ground pepper to taste
1 pound bacon, cooked and crumbled
1 cup corn kernels (frozen or canned)
1 cup chopped pecans
$3/4$ cup dried cranberries
$1/2$ cup Port wine
1 cup chicken broth

1. Preheat the oven to 350°.

2. Spread the cornbread out on a baking sheet in a single layer. Bake
for 25 to 30 minutes until golden. Let cool, then transfer to a large
mixing bowl.

3. Reset the oven to 325°.

4. Heat the butter in a large skillet. Add the onions, celery, red
pepper, and seasonings. Sauté over medium heat until the vegetables
are soft, about 10 minutes, stirring occasionally.

5. Add the cooked vegetables, bacon, corn kernels, pecans,
cranberries, wine, and chicken broth to the cornbread. Toss well
until evenly mixed. Turn into a large baking dish or casserole.

6. Cover and bake for 30 minutes; uncover and bake for 15 minutes
more to brown. Serve hot from the oven.

10 to 12 portions

THANKSGIVING
FEAST

Dilled Onion Crostini
. . .
Succulent Roast
Turkey*
. . .
Honeyed-Butternut
Squash
. . .
Cornbread Stuffing
. . .
Roasted Asparagus**
. . .
Cranberry Chutney**
. . .
Pumpkin Cheesecake

BAKED POLENTA

This version of the cornmeal mush native to Northern Italy makes polenta quick and easy to fix. It can be enjoyed warm and creamy, fresh from the oven, or chilled, then sliced, and reheated. Try it unadorned, or also embellished with various toppings—grilled or roasted poultry, seafood, vegetables, and sauces.

> 1 cup yellow cornmeal
> 5 cups water
> 2 tablespoons butter
> 1 teaspoon salt
> $^1/_4$ cup grated Parmigiano-Reggiano cheese

1. Preheat the oven to 325°.

2. In a small bowl, mix the cornmeal with 1 cup cold water until evenly combined.

3. In a 3-quart saucepan bring 4 cups water, butter, and salt to a boil. Add the cornmeal, stirring constantly, until completely incorporated and slightly thickened.

4. Cover and bake for 20 minutes. Remove from the oven, whisk in the cheese, and serve at once for soft polenta. (Keep the saucepan covered until serving so the polenta remains soft.) For firm polenta, spread the mixture into a greased 9 x 13-inch pan and refrigerate until firm, about 2 hours. Then slice, broil, grill, or sauté and serve.

6 to 8 portions

TOPPING IDEAS FOR POLENTA

For a satisfying meal, top soft or firm polenta with any of the following combinations:

- Roasted butternut squash
- Sautéed sausages and vinegar peppers
- Caramelized onions with rosemary and Parmesan
- Mushroom ragout
- Marinara sauce finished with goat cheese
- Pesto
- Grilled assorted shellfish
- Grilled chicken and Pecorino Romano cheese
- Thinly sliced prosciutto, provolone, and salami
- Chopped tomatoes, buffalo mozzarella, and basil drizzled with extra-virigin olive oil
- Marinated olive mélange
- Roasted peppers, capers, and artichoke hearts with olive oil and balsamic vinegar
- Grilled assorted vegetables—peppers, onions, mushrooms, zucchini, and eggplant
- Roasted asparagus and fontina cheese

COUSCOUS AND PEAS

The favored semolina grain is paired with peas, punctuated with pine nuts, and seasoned with tarragon in this delicate presentation.

1¹/₃ cups water
2 tablespoons butter
¹/₂ teaspoon salt
1 cup instant couscous
³/₄ cup fresh or frozen peas, blanched
3 tablespoons pine nuts, toasted
¹/₄ cup thinly sliced scallions
1 teaspoon dried tarragon
freshly ground pepper to taste

1. In a 2-quart saucepan, bring the water, butter, and salt to a boil. Stir in the couscous, cover, and remove from the heat. Let sit for 5 minutes, then fluff with a fork.

2. Add the remaining ingredients and mix well. Serve at once.

4 portions

COUSCOUS GENOVESE

Couscous takes on Italian flavors in this heavenly dish. The small, cereal grain is rippled with pesto, the lusty Genovese basil sauce. It makes a savory accompaniment to roasted or grilled chicken and fish.

1¹/3 cups water
¹/2 teaspoon salt
1 cup instant couscous
¹/2 cup pesto (see page 12)

1. In a 2-quart saucepan, bring the water and salt to a boil. Stir in the couscous, cover, and remove from the heat. Let sit for 5 minutes, then fluff with a fork.

2. Add the pesto and mix until evenly distributed. Serve warm or at room temperature.

4 to 6 portions

CASUAL FAMILY
DINNER

Salad Mezzaluna
· · ·
Baked Bluefish with
Olive Crumbs
· · ·
Couscous Genovese
· · ·
Apricot Cheesecake
Muffins

ISRAELI COUSCOUS

Israeli couscous is the giant-size pearls of semolina we find irresistible. It's delicate taste and texture make it a refreshing alternative to pasta or rice.

> $1^1/_4$ *cups chicken broth*
> *1 tablespoon butter*
> $^1/_2$ *teaspoon salt*
> *1 cup Israeli couscous*

1. In a 2-quart saucepan, bring the chicken broth, butter, and salt to a boil. Stir in the couscous, cover, remove from the heat, and let sit for 20 minutes.

2. Stir until remaining liquid is absorbed. Serve at once.

4 portions

ISRAELI COUSCOUS WITH CRANBERRIES AND ALMONDS

Israeli couscous is offset by a variety of flavors and textures—dried cranberries, toasted almonds, and orange peel—in this fragrant grain dish. It's glorious with poultry, pork, and fish.

1¼ cups chicken broth
2 tablespoons butter
½ teaspoon salt
1 cup Israeli couscous
⅓ cup dried cranberries
⅓ cup slivered almonds, toasted
1 tablespoon grated orange peel

1. In a 2-quart saucepan, bring the broth, butter, and salt to a boil. Stir in the couscous, cover, remove from the heat, and let sit for 20 minutes.

2. Stir until the remaining liquid is absorbed. Add the cranberries, almonds, and orange peel, mixing until evenly distributed. Serve at once.

4 portions

ISRAELI COUSCOUS ADD-INS

Couscous provides the perfect backdrop for a myriad of toppings. Try adding these embellishments to freshly cooked couscous for a sparkling, gustatory experience.

- Peas, ham, and Parmigiano-Reggiano cheese
- Fresh or dried figs, prosciutto, and pistachio nuts
- Dried apricots and toasted slivered almonds
- Herbs de Provence and chives
- Crumbled Blue cheese and toasted walnuts
- Sautéed assorted peppers
- Chopped tomatoes, fresh basil, and buffalo mozzarella
- Sun-dried tomatoes, Kalamata olives, and artichoke hearts seasoned with oregano
- Roasted red peppers and roasted potatoes sprinkled with thyme
- Pesto and goat cheese
- Sautéed assorted mushrooms splashed with Port wine
- Grilled shrimp, sausages, and corn
- Caramelized onions and Parmesan cheese
- Chopped tomatoes and scallions, fresh mint, parsley, feta cheese, lemon juice, and olive oil
- Ratatouille
- Roasted asparagus, toasted pine nuts, Romano cheese, balsamic vinegar, and extra-virgin olive oil

BAKED RISOTTO

This is an easy, baked version of the classic, slow-simmering rice dish native to Northern Italy. It features Arborio rice which lends a delectable creaminess to the dish, while the grain remains al dente. The timing of the preparation is important to the success of the dish, so have all of your ingredients ready!

1 tablespoon butter
1 tablespoon olive oil
1 medium-size yellow onion, diced
2 cups Arborio rice
$^1/_2$ cup dry white wine
$3^1/_2$ to $3^2/_3$ cups simmering chicken broth
salt and freshly ground pepper to taste
$^1/_2$ cup freshly grated Parmigiano-Reggiano cheese

1. Preheat the oven to 425°.

2. Heat the butter and oil in a 4-quart casserole. Add the onion and cook over medium heat until soft and translucent. Stir in the rice and mix well, until the grains are evenly coated with the fat.

3. Add the wine and continue to cook, stirring, until the liquid is mostly absorbed. Add 3 cups of the broth, stirring well to combine. Season with salt and pepper. Cover with a secure lid and bake for 15 minutes.

4. Remove the risotto from the oven. Stir in the remaining $^1/_2$ to $^2/_3$ cup hot broth, depending on how dry the rice appears—you want it to be very creamy. Stir in the cheese and mix well. Serve at once. (At this point, you may choose to add any favorite ingredient to embellish the risotto—sautéed vegetables, grilled chicken or meats, poached shellfish, condiments, etc.—to make it your signature dish.)

6 to 8 side portions; 4 to 6 main-course portions with additions

ITALIAN IMPORT

Salad Romano
· · ·
Osso Buco
· · ·
Baked Risotto
· · ·
Gelato

BASMATI RICE PILAF

Basmati rice is indigenous to Indian cuisine. It has been cultivated in the foothills of the Himalayas for centuries. The long grain has a lovely perfume and nut-like flavor that is sure to win your fancy.

1 cup basmati rice
2 tablespoons butter
1 medium yellow onion, chopped
2 cups chicken broth
salt to taste

1. Rinse the basmati rice well under cold water and drain.

2. Heat the butter in a 2-quart saucepan. Add the onion and sauté over medium heat until soft and translucent.

3. Add the rice and stir well until all of the grains are coated with the butter.

4. Add the chicken broth and salt.

5. Bring to a boil, cover, lower the heat, and simmer for 15 minutes until all the liquid is absorbed. Fluff with a fork and serve.

4 to 6 portions

SAFFRON RICE

Saffron, the dried stigmas of the crocus plant, is the most expensive spice in the world. Each flower bears only three stigmas which must be hand-picked before being dried. It's a labor-intensive process as each ounce of saffron contains more than 14,000 stigmas! This spice lends an ethereal fragrance to the rice elevating it to the exotic.

$1/8$ teaspoon crushed saffron threads
$1/4$ cup warm water
2 tablespoons butter
1 medium yellow onion, chopped
1 large clove garlic, minced
1 cup long-grain rice
$1^3/4$ cups chicken broth
salt and freshly ground pepper to taste

1. Put the saffron in a small bowl. Pour the water over the threads and let steep for 10 minutes.

2. Heat the butter in a 2-quart saucepan. Add the onion and sauté until soft and translucent. Add the garlic and sauté for 1 minute more.

3. Add the rice and stir until the grains are evenly coated with the butter.

4. Add the chicken broth, salt, pepper, and saffron liquid.

5. Bring to a boil, cover, lower the heat, and simmer for 20 minutes until all the liquid is absorbed. Fluff with a fork and serve.

4 to 6 portions

MEMORIES ARE
MADE OF THIS

Spinach and
Chèvre Turnovers
· · ·
Sole with
Hazelnut Butter
· · ·
Saffron Rice
· · ·
Slow-Roasted
Tomatoes**
· · ·
Raspberry Torte

SOUBISE PARMESAN

Soubise is a side-dish that showcases an abundance of cooked onions and rice. Its unique preparation excludes any cooking liquid for the rice. The onions and rice cook together in a low oven; as the onions sweat, they create moisture that is absorbed by the rice. All is finished with a dusting of Parmesan, creating a creamy, savory rice.

1/2 cup raw long-grain rice
salt to taste
5 cups diced sweet onions
4 tablespoons butter, melted
1/2 teaspoon salt
1/2 cup grated Parmesan cheese

1. Preheat the oven to 325°.

2. Put the rice in a pot of salted boiling water and boil for 5 minutes. Drain well.

3. In a 3-quart casserole, combine the rice, onions, butter, and 1/2 teaspoon salt and mix well. Cover and bake for 1 hour.

4. Add the Parmesan, mix well, and serve at once.

5 to 6 portions

SPINACH, FETA, AND RICE BAKE

This casserole features long-grain rice mixed with a Greek-inspired palette of spinach, feta, and dill, laced with custard, and baked until set.

2 cups cooked long-grain rice
10-ounce package frozen chopped spinach, thawed and squeezed dry
1/4 cup grated Parmigiano-Reggiano cheese
1/4 cup crumbled feta cheese
1/4 cup thinly sliced scallions
2 tablespoons chopped fresh dill
salt and freshly ground pepper to taste
3 eggs
1 cup milk
4 tablespoons butter, melted and cooled

1. Preheat the oven to 400°. Grease a 2-quart casserole.

2. In a large bowl, combine the rice, spinach, cheeses, scallions, dill, salt, and pepper and mix well.

3. In a separate small bowl, whisk together the eggs, milk, and butter.

4. Add the custard to the spinach mixture, stirring until evenly combined. Turn the mixture into the prepared pan.

5. Bake for 35 to 40 minutes until set. Serve at once.

6 portions

LABOR DAY BRUNCH

Assorted Bagels
. . .
Cream Cheese
. . .
Gravlax*
. . .
Herring with Mustard Sauce
. . .
Cucumber Salad
. . .
Spinach, Feta, and Rice Bake
. . .
Fruits with Raspberry Sauce
. . .
Streusel Coffeecake

CAROLINA RICE

**SASSY NEW
ORLEANS-STYLE
MENU**

Muffuletta**
. . .
Grilled Shrimp
. . .
Carolina Rice
. . .
Glazed Peaches

This rice dish is big on flavor, featuring long-grain rice embellished with zesty seasonings and a symphony of sautéed vegetables—red onion, green pepper, and cremini mushrooms.

*2 cups water
1 teaspoon salt
1 cup long-grain rice
3 tablespoons olive oil (not extra-virgin)
1 small red onion, chopped
1 medium green pepper, chopped
$1/2$ pound cremini mushrooms, sliced
1 large clove garlic, crushed
$1/2$ teaspoon dried thyme
2 teaspoons Worcestershire sauce
salt and freshly ground pepper to taste*

1. Bring the water and 1 teaspoon salt to a boil in a 2-quart saucepan. Stir in the rice, cover, lower the heat, and simmer for 20 minutes until all the liquid is absorbed. Fluff with a fork.

2. While the rice is cooking, sauté the vegetables. In a large non-stick skillet, heat the oil. Add the onion, green pepper, mushrooms, garlic, and seasonings. Sauté over medium-high heat for 10 minutes, stirring occasionally, until the vegetables are tender and lightly browned.

3. Stir the vegetables into the cooked rice and serve.

6 portions

MADRAS RICE

The heavenly flavor of basmati rice is further enriched with Indian condiments—raisins, toasted coconut, and almonds—elevating the grain to new heights.

1 cup basmati rice
2 tablespoons butter
1 medium yellow onion, chopped
2 cups chicken broth
salt and freshly ground pepper to taste
3 tablespoons golden raisins
3 tablespoons sweetened, shredded coconut, toasted
1/4 cup slivered almonds, toasted

1. Rinse the basmati rice well under cold water and drain.

2. Heat the butter in a 2-quart saucepan. Add the onion and sauté over medium heat until soft and translucent.

3. Add the rice and stir well until all of the grains are coated with the butter.

4. Add the chicken broth, salt, and pepper.

5. Bring to a boil, cover, lower the heat, and simmer for 15 minutes until all the liquid is absorbed. Fluff with a fork. Stir in the raisins, coconut, and almonds and serve.

6 portions

INDIAN-STYLE
FAVORITES

Chicken Tikka
. . .
Madras Rice
. . .
Grilled Assorted
Vegetables—Onions,
Peppers, and
Tomatoes
. . .
Grape Nuts Custard

FRIED RICE

Chinese fried rice was conceived as a way to use up leftovers. This authentic dish is simple and unadulterated. It's wonderful as is or also served in combination with other Oriental dishes.

5 tablespoons vegetable oil
2 eggs, beaten
1 cup bean sprouts
3 scallions, chopped
$^1/_2$ cup frozen peas, thawed
3 cups cold, cooked white rice
1 teaspoon salt
$^1/_2$ to 1 teaspoon sugar

1. Heat 2 tablespoons oil in a wok. When hot, add the eggs, and lightly scramble. Push to one side of the pan and add the remaining 3 tablespoons oil.

2. When hot, add the bean sprouts, scallions, and peas and stir-fry for 1 minute.

3. Add the rice, season with the salt and sugar, and stir-fry for 1 minute, tossing gently until the rice is heated. Serve at once.

6 to 8 portions

RICE WITH GREEN CHILIES

Mexican flavors prevail in this creamy rice dish accented with sour cream and green chilies.

2 cups water
1 teaspoon salt
1 cup long-grain rice
³/4 cup sour cream, at room temperature
4-ounce can mild green chilies, drained and chopped
¹/3 cup thinly sliced scallions
freshly ground pepper to taste

1. Bring the water and salt to a boil in a 2-quart saucepan. Stir in the rice, lower the heat, and simmer for 20 minutes until all the liquid is absorbed. Fluff with a fork.

2. Add the sour cream, chilies, scallions, and pepper and mix until evenly combined. Serve at once.

4 to 6 portions

MEXICAN FLAIR

Gazpacho Latino
. . .
Carne Asada
. . .
Rice with
Green Chilies
. . .
Ice Cream

RICE WITH BLACK BEANS AND SALSA FRESCA

SOUTH-OF-THE-BORDER FIESTA

Pork Tenderloin
Cubano

. . .

Rice with Black Beans
and Salsa

. . .

Roasted Corn

. . .

Flan

Salsa is the Mexican word for sauce. Salsa fresca, or pico de gallo, is a happy marriage of bold flavors—ripe tomatoes, chilies, onion, garlic, and lime juice. It graces the table daily in Mexican households, adding vibrancy to meals. Coupled with black beans, this salsa-infused rice is sure to set your taste buds dancing!

> *3 cups cooked long-grain white rice*
> *15-ounce can black beans, rinsed and drained*
> *Salsa Fresca (recipe follows)*

In a large bowl, combine the rice, beans, and Salsa Fresca and mix well. Serve at room temperature.

6 portions

> *Salsa Fresca:*
> *4 large plum tomatoes, diced or (28-ounce can diced tomatoes, drained)*
> *1/2 small yellow onion, diced*
> *1 jalapeño pepper, seeded and minced*
> *1 large clove garlic, minced*
> *1/4 cup chopped fresh cilantro*
> *1 tablespoon lime juice*
> *salt and freshly ground pepper to taste*

Combine all of the ingredients in a non-reactive bowl and stir until evenly mixed.

WILD RICE PILAF

This elegant dish of grains boasts a white and wild rice base trimmed with sautéed onion and toasted pecans.

1/3 cup wild rice
3 cups water
salt to taste
2 tablespoons butter
1 medium yellow onion, chopped
1 cup long-grain rice
2 cups chicken broth
3/4 cup pecans, toasted and coarsely chopped

1. Rinse the wild rice under cold water and drain. In a large saucepan, bring the water and salt to a boil. Add the rice, cover, lower the heat, and simmer gently for 35 to 40 minutes. Drain well and set aside.

2. While the wild rice is cooking, prepare the white rice. Heat the butter in a 3-quart saucepan. Add the onion and sauté over medium heat until soft and translucent.

3. Add the rice and stir until the grains are evenly coated with the butter.

4. Add the chicken broth and season with salt.

5. Bring to a boil, cover, lower the heat, and simmer for 20 minutes until all the liquid is absorbed. Fluff with a fork.

6. Stir in the cooked wild rice and pecans and serve.

6 to 8 portions

EASY
ENTERTAINING

Baby Spinach and
Shiitake Mushrooms
· · ·
Pan-Roasted
Duck Breast
· · ·
Wild Rice Pilaf
· · ·
Almond Cream Cake

GRAND FINALES

There's always room for dessert! Just the mention of the word conjures up images of divine cakes and pies, crispy, chewy cookies, rich puddings, luscious fruit cobblers, and outrageous chocolate indulgences. Desserts are the memorable part of the meal. It's what we recall with enthusiasm and fondness.

Desserts should dazzle, be enticing and sublime. Whether it's a big, rich cake or a simple cookie, who doesn't love home-baked goodies? It's hard to resist something that's sweet, utterly delicious, and totally satisfying. Cap off your meal with some splendid temptation and make the dinner a heavenly occasion.

FRUITS AND PUDDINGS

ORANGES BALSAMIC

ITALIAN MANIA

White Bean Crostini
. . .
Risotto with Shrimp,
Goat Cheese, and
Sun-Dried Tomatoes
. . .
Mesclun Salad with
Sherry Vinaigrette
. . .
Oranges Balsamic

Vinegar with dessert? Certainly, when you're using balsamic vinegar. Balsamic is the exquisite vinegar hailed from Italy's town of Modena. It's made from Trebbiano grapes, and gets its dark color and sweetness from aging in barrels for several years. The pungent sweetness of the balsamic complements the juicy, sweet orange citrus.

6 navel oranges, peeled and cut into $1/2$-inch thick slices
4 tablespoons balsamic vinegar
2 tablespoons sugar

1. Place the orange slices on individual plates.
2. In a small bowl, combine the vinegar and sugar, stirring until the sugar dissolves. Drizzle the mixture over the orange slices. Let marinate at room temperature for 30 minutes before serving.

6 portions

GLAZED PEACHES

This dessert bursts with the glorious fragrance and sweet taste of peaches. Peach halves are crowned with a lush brown sugar-sour cream sauce and roasted until glazed. Dollop each portion with a scoop of vanilla ice cream for a heavenly finale.

4 ripe peaches, cut in half and pitted
$^1/_4$ cup sour cream
$^1/_4$ cup packed dark brown sugar
$^1/_8$ teaspoon cinnamon
2 tablespoons Grand Marnier

1. Preheat the oven to 450°. Line a 9-inch square pan with foil and grease the foil.

2. Nestle the peaches in the pan, cut side up.

3. In a small bowl, mix the sour cream, brown sugar, and cinnamon. Stir in the Grand Marnier.

4. Spoon the sour cream topping over each peach half.

5. Bake for 20 minutes. Let cool slightly and serve warm or at room temperature drizzled with the pan juices and topped with vanilla ice cream.

4 portions

SOUTHERN
COMFORTS

Summer Bean Salad
. . .
Shrimp and
Crab Gumbo
. . .
Rice
. . .
Glazed Peaches

FRUITS WITH RASPBERRY SAUCE

SPECIAL
OCCASION
DINNER

Asparagus Bundles
· · ·
Soft-Shell Crab
Remoulade
· · ·
Corn Soufflé
· · ·
Romaine with
Tomato Relish
· · ·
Fruits with
Raspberry Sauce

There are occasions when you serve fruit and want to sauce the ingredients without adding liqueur or alcohol. This dessert is the perfect solution—melted raspberry sorbet envelopes a riot of fruits, providing the quintessential sauce.

2^1/$_2$ cups cantaloupe, cut into 1-inch chunks
2^1/$_2$ cups honeydew melon, cut into 1-inch chunks
2^1/$_2$ cups seedless watermelon, cut into 1-inch chunks
2^1/$_2$ cups pineapple, cut into 1-inch chunks
2^1/$_2$ cups strawberries, hulled
2 cups red grapes
1 pint raspberry sorbet, thawed

1. Heap the fruits in a large glass bowl.

2. Pour the melted sorbet over the fruits, mix gently, and serve. (This may be prepared 4 to 6 hours in advance and refrigerated until needed. Return to room temperature to serve.)

8 to 10 portions

BAKED BANANAS PRALINE

Bananas are an all-time favorite fruit. Dessert doesn't get better than this! Lengthwise-sliced bananas are baked in a luscious brown sugar-pecan topping and served with vanilla ice cream.

3 large bananas, peeled and cut in half lengthwise
3 tablespoons butter
$1/4$ cup well-packed dark brown sugar
2 tablespoons heavy cream
$1/2$ teaspoon cinnamon
$1/2$ teaspoon dried orange peel
$1/2$ cup coarsely chopped pecans

1. Preheat the oven to 350°. Grease a 9 x 13-inch pan.
2. Place the bananas in the prepared pan.
3. In a small saucepan, combine the butter, sugar, cream, cinnamon, and orange peel. Heat over low until the butter and sugar melt. Stir in the pecans and remove from the heat.
4. Pour the pecan mixture over the bananas.
5. Bake for 20 minutes. Serve warm with scoops of vanilla ice cream.

6 portions

AUTUMN REPAST

Salad Christine
. . .
Grilled Shrimps
and Scallops
. . .
Couscous and Peas
. . .
Baked Bananas Praline

STUFFED STRAWBERRIES

Strawberries rank as an American favorite. These plump red berries are a member of the rose family and therefore, should smell sweet and fragrant. Let your nose be your guide when selecting this harbinger of summer. This strawberries and cream theme is sure to put a smile on your face.

1 quart very large, ripe strawberries
4 ounces mascarpone cheese
2 tablespoons sugar
1 generous tablespoon minced crystallized candied ginger
$1/3$ cup semi-sweet mini chocolate chips
3 tablespoons finely chopped almonds, toasted

1. Hull the strawberries, making a deep cavity in each berry.

2. In a bowl, combine the mascarpone, sugar, candied ginger, and chocolate chips and mix well.

3. Fill each strawberry with the cheese mixture. Dip the stuffed end of the berries into the chopped almonds. Chill until serving time; return the berries to room temperature to serve. These are best served the same day as made.

6 to 8 portions

MIXED BERRY PAVLOVA

A Pavlova is a meringue shell with a fruit and whipped cream topping. This spectacular dessert is crowned with a riot of plump summer berries—strawberries, blueberries, raspberries, and blackberries—and clouds of whipped cream.

Topping:
3 cups mixed berries, sliced (strawberries, blueberries, raspberries, and blackberries)
$1/2$ cup sugar
1 cup heavy cream

Meringue:
3 egg whites (from extra-large eggs)
$1/8$ teaspoon cream of tartar
1 teaspoon vanilla
$3/4$ cup sugar

1. In a large mixing bowl, combine the berries and $1/4$ cup sugar and mix well. Let sit at room temperature for 2 to 3 hours, stirring occasionally, allowing a sauce to form.

2. Preheat the oven to 275°. Line a large cookie sheet with parchment paper. Mark off a 7 x 9-inch rectangle on the paper.

3. Make the meringue crust. In a large bowl with an electric mixer, beat the egg whites until frothy. Add the cream of tartar and vanilla and beat to soft peaks. Add the sugar 1 tablespoon at a time, beating constantly. Beat until whites are stiff and glossy, but not dry.

4. Spread the mixture out onto the parchment paper in the shape of the rectangle.

5. Bake for 1 hour and 15 minutes. Remove the meringue from the cookie sheet to a rack to cool completely. The outside will be lightly brown and crusty while the inside of the meringue will remain moist.

6. Make the whipped cream. In a mixing bowl with an electric mixer, beat the heavy cream and $1/4$ cup sugar until stiff peaks form. Refrigerate until needed.

7. To serve, cut the meringue into 8 portions. Spoon the berry mixture over the meringue along with any accumulated juices and top with dollops of whipped cream.

8 portions

**DINNER PARTY
FOR 6**

Spinach, Bacon, and
Fig Salad
. . .
Scallops with Sun-
Dried Tomato Pesto
. . .
Rice Pilaf*
. . .
Mixed Berry Pavlova

PEAR CRISP

Crisps and crumbles are as satisfying as a pie but don't require a crust. They consist of sweetened fruit that's covered with a crumbly topping of flour, butter, sugar, and sometimes oats and nuts and baked to a turn. This autumn crisp of succulent pears punctuated with tart cranberries turns this humble dessert into the extraordinary.

3 firm, ripe pears, peeled, cored, and cut into 1 1/4-inch chunks
1 cup cranberries
1/2 teaspoon almond extract
3 tablespoons dark brown sugar
2 tablespoons all-purpose flour

Topping:
1/2 cup all-purpose flour
6 tablespoons butter, cut into 1/2-inch cubes
1/2 cup dark brown sugar
1 teaspoon cinnamon
1/2 cup old-fashioned rolled oats

1. Preheat the oven to 350°. Grease a 9-inch deep-dish pie pan.

2. Put the pears and cranberries in a large bowl. Drizzle with the extract and sprinkle with the sugar. Mix well until evenly coated.

3. Sprinkle with 2 tablespoons flour and mix thoroughly. Spread the mixture into the prepared pan along with any accumulated juices.

4. In another bowl, make the topping. Mix the flour, butter, brown sugar, and cinnamon until the texture of coarse meal. Stir in the oats.

5. Cover the pear mixture with the crumb topping.

6. Bake for 45 minutes until the pears are soft and topping is lightly browned and bubbly. Serve hot or at room temperature with whipped cream or vanilla ice cream.

6 to 8 portions

PEACH KUCHEN

What better way to celebrate summer's bounty than with this open-faced peach pie! Fragrant peach halves are housed on a buttery pastry base, dusted with cinnamon and sugar, cloaked in a custard topping, and baked until browned and bubbly.

Pastry:
2 cups all-purpose flour
1/4 cup sugar
1/4 teaspoon baking powder
1/2 teaspoon salt
1/2 cup butter

Filling:
4 large freestone peaches, peeled† and halved
1/2 cup sugar
1 teaspoon cinnamon

Topping:
2 egg yolks
1/2 cup heavy cream

1. Preheat the oven to 400°.
2. Prepare the crust. In a large mixing bowl, sift the flour, sugar, baking powder, and salt. Cut the butter into the flour mixture until the texture of coarse meal. Pat the mixture onto the bottom and halfway up the sides of a 9-inch springform pan.
3. Arrange the peaches cut side down on the pastry crust.
4. In a small bowl, mix the sugar and cinnamon until evenly combined. Sprinkle over the peaches, coating generously.
5. Bake for 30 minutes.
6. While the peaches are baking, prepare the topping. In a small bowl, beat the egg yolks. Add the cream and mix well.
7. Pour the topping over the peaches and bake for 25 minutes more. Serve hot, warm, or at room temperature.

6 to 8 portions

† To peel peaches—drop the peaches into a pot of boiling water to cover. Boil about 2 minutes. Remove the peaches with a slotted spoon and plunge them into a bowl of cold water. Rub the skins off with your fingers, starting at the stem end.

SUMMER FARE

Mango Salad
· · ·
Cumin-Crusted
Swordfish
· · ·
Israeli Couscous with
Cranberries and
Almonds
· · ·
Peach Kuchen

STRAWBERRY-RHUBARB COBBLER

I love to combine the complementary, tart flavor of rhubarb with the sweet succulence of strawberries in this old-fashioned, deep-dish dessert that's crowned with a buttery crust and baked until bubbly.

2 cups rhubarb, cut into 1-inch chunks
2 cups halved strawberries (quartered if large)
1/3 cup all-purpose flour
1 cup sugar
1 teaspoon cinnamon
1 tablespoon grated orange peel

Topping:
1 cup sugar
1/2 cup butter, melted and cooled
1 teaspoon vanilla
1 egg, beaten
1 cup all-purpose flour

1. Preheat the oven to 350°. Grease and flour a 9-inch deep-dish pie pan.

2. In a mixing bowl, combine the rhubarb, strawberries, flour, sugar, cinnamon, and orange peel and mix well. Turn the mixture into the prepared pan.

3. In a separate bowl, make the topping. Combine the sugar, butter, and vanilla. Add the egg. Stir in the flour, mixing until evenly combined.

4. Pour the topping evenly over the filling, making sure all of the fruit is covered by the batter.

5. Bake for 45 minutes. Serve hot, warm, or at room temperature. (It's especially delicious topped with vanilla ice cream.)

6 to 8 portions

MIXED BERRY GALETTE

A galette is a flat, open-faced, free-form rustic tart. The crust is rolled into a large circle, the berry filling is spooned into the center, and the dough is folded over the edges of the fruit, forming a pleated border. Baked to a turn, this exquisite pie bursts with summer's berries. In the fall, substitute peeled, chopped apples for a spectacular harvest treat.

Crust:
1¹/2 cups all-purpose flour
¹/3 cup sugar
¹/4 teaspoon salt
10 tablespoons cold unsalted butter, cut into ¹/2-inch pieces
  (no substitutions)
¹/4 cup cold water

1. Put the flour, sugar, and salt in the bowl of a food processor and pulse to combine. Add the butter and pulse until the texture of coarse crumbs.

2. Add the water and pulse only until moist crumbs form. Remove the dough to a board and shape it into a smooth 6-inch round. Cover in plastic wrap and chill at least 2 hours and as much as overnight.

3. On a floured board, roll the dough into a 14-inch circle. Transfer to a parchment paper-lined baking sheet.

Berry Filling:
4 cups mixed berries (I use 2 cups blueberries, 1 cup raspberries,
  and 1 cup blackberries)
¹/2 cup plus 1 teaspoon sugar
¹/4 cup all-purpose flour
1 tablespoon butter, melted

1. Preheat the oven to 400°.

2. In a bowl, mix the berries, ¹/2 cup sugar, and the flour.

3. Mound the berry mixture in the middle of the dough, leaving a 3-inch border all around. Fold the dough up over the edges of the filling, making pleats to accommodate the extra pastry.

4. Brush the pastry with the melted butter and sprinkle with 1 teaspoon sugar.

5. Bake for 35 to 40 minutes until crust is golden. Serve hot, warm, or at room temperature.

8 portions

LIGHT SUMMER DINNER

Deviled Crab Cakes
. . .
BLT Salad with Blue Cheese Dressing
. . .
French Bread
. . .
Mixed Berry Galette

GINGER ICE CREAM

Ginger preserves are slightly pungent and sweet. When rippled into vanilla ice cream, the jam lends a refreshing taste to the frozen dessert, elevating it to new heights. This simple recipe is especially good to complete an Oriental meal.

1 quart favorite vanilla ice cream
1/3 cup ginger preserves

1. Transfer the ice cream to a large container and let soften.

2. Add the preserves and mix through. Place in the freezer until hardened.

3. When ready to serve, scoop into bowls and present.

6 portions

GRAPE NUTS CUSTARD

This baked pudding offers blissful comfort. The egg custard is enriched with Grape Nuts cereal and dusted with nutmeg.

3/4 cup Grape Nuts cereal
6 eggs
3/4 cup sugar
1 quart whole milk
1 teaspoon vanilla
pinch of salt
1/4 teaspoon nutmeg

1. Preheat the oven to 350°. Grease a 9-inch square pan.

2. Sprinkle the cereal over the bottom of the pan.

3. In a large mixing bowl with a wire whisk, beat the eggs, sugar, milk, vanilla, and salt.

4. Pour the custard over the Grape Nuts. Sprinkle with the nutmeg.

5. Bake for 50 to 55 minutes until set—a knife inserted in the center will come out clean. Cool before serving. Store in the refrigerator.

9 or more portions

WINTER COMFORTS

Meatloaf
. . .
Mashed Potatoes and Celeriac
. . .
Roasted Carrots
. . .
Grape Nuts Custard

ARBORIO RICE PUDDING

Rice pudding ranks high on the list of comfort foods. It utilizes simple ingredients, combining Arborio rice with milk, sugar, and vanilla and becomes lusciously creamy during baking.

2 tablespoons butter
1 cup Arborio rice
4 cups whole milk
$1/2$ cup sugar
1 tablespoon vanilla
$1/8$ teaspoon salt
$1/2$ cup heavy cream
$1/2$ teaspoon cinnamon

1. Preheat the oven to 425°.

2. In a 4-quart casserole or baking dish, melt the butter over medium heat. Add the rice and stir to coat the grains completely with the butter.

3. Add the milk, sugar, vanilla, and salt and stir well. Turn the heat to medium-high and cook until the milk begins to simmer. Cover, turn off the heat, and place in the oven for 30 minutes.

4. Remove from the oven and mix well. Stir in the heavy cream and cinnamon. (The rice will be quite soupy, but will thicken as it cools.) Cover and let cool for 45 to 60 minutes, stirring occasionally. Refrigerate. Serve chilled or at room temperature.

6 to 8 portions

INDIAN PUDDING

This old-fashioned dessert is a New England classic. The pudding is defined by a ginger-scented, cornmeal custard, rich with molasses and brown sugar. It's especially delicious topped with vanilla ice cream.

2 eggs
¼ cup mild-flavored molasses
½ cup packed light brown sugar
½ teaspoon salt
1 teaspoon ground ginger
½ teaspoon cinnamon
pinch of nutmeg
1 quart whole milk
½ cup yellow cornmeal
¼ cup butter, cut into chunks

1. Preheat the oven to 350°. Grease a 9-inch square pan.

2. In a large mixing bowl, whisk the eggs, molasses, brown sugar, salt, ginger, cinnamon, and nutmeg. Set aside.

3. Combine the milk and cornmeal in a heavy saucepan. Whisk over medium heat until mixture comes to a boil. Lower heat and cook until mixture is very thick and creamy, about 5 minutes, stirring constantly. Whisk in the butter, then remove from the heat.

4. Gradually add the hot cornmeal to the egg mixture, whisking until evenly combined. Pour the custard into the prepared pan.

5. Bake for 1 hour until set. The custard will seem a little loose when you remove it from the oven; it continues to set as it cools. Serve warm or at room temperature with scoops of vanilla ice cream.

9 portions

IRISH-STYLE
MENU

Glazed Corned Beef
· · ·
Irish Soda Bread
· · ·
Indian Pudding

FLAN

Hailed as one of the great Spanish desserts, flan is here to stay. It's actually a custard that's been baked in a caramel-coated pan. When chilled, the flan is inverted onto a serving plate, the caramel glazes the top, forming a delectable sauce.

1¼ cups sugar
3 tablespoons water
6 eggs
¼ teaspoon salt
1 tablespoon vanilla
2 cups evaporated whole milk

1. Put ¾ cup sugar and the water in a small, heavy saucepan. Heat over low until the solution becomes clear. (Do not stir the mixture, but swirl it instead.) Raise the heat and cook until the syrup turns a light amber color. Immediately pour the caramel into a 9-inch souffle dish or deep-dish pie pan, tilting the pan to coat the bottom and halfway up the sides evenly. The syrup will harden as it cools. Let cool completely.

2. Preheat the oven to 350°.

3. In a large mixing bowl, beat the eggs. Add the remaining ½ cup sugar, salt, vanilla, and evaporated milk and mix well.

4. Pour the custard into the pie pan. Place the pan in a larger pan and fill the larger one with hot water to come halfway up the sides of the pie pan. (This is known as a water bath.)

5. Place in the oven and bake for 40 to 50 minutes until a knife inserted in the center comes out clean. The center will be slightly jiggly and will continue to set as it cools. Remove the pan from the water bath to a rack to cool completely; then cover and refrigerate at least 2 hours and preferably overnight.

6. To unmold, run a knife around the edge of the pan to loosen the flan. Cover with a plate and invert. Pour the remaining caramel over the custard. Cut into wedges and serve.

6 to 8 portions

PUMPKIN BREAD PUDDING

Bread pudding is the quintessential comfort food. The essential ingredients of this favorite include bread, milk, eggs, and sugar. This rendition is also flavored with pumpkin purée, laced with maple syrup, and studded with dried cranberries for a most gratifying experience.

3/4 pound soft French or Italian bread, cut into 1-inch chunks
15-ounce can pumpkin purée
1 cup sugar
1 cup pure maple syrup
2 teaspoons cinnamon
1 1/2 teaspoons vanilla
4 eggs, beaten
1 quart whole milk
4 tablespoons butter, melted and cooled
1/2 cup dried cranberries or craisins

1. Preheat the oven to 350°. Grease a 9 x 13-inch baking dish.

2. Put the bread in a large mixing bowl.

3. In a separate bowl, combine the pumpkin, sugar, maple syrup, cinnamon, and vanilla and mix well. Add the eggs, milk, and butter and stir until evenly combined. Pour the custard over the bread chunks, mix until evenly coated, and let sit for 10 to 15 minutes so that the bread can absorb the liquid.

4. Stir in the dried cranberries. Turn the bread mixture into the prepared pan.

5. Bake for 45 to 50 minutes until set. Serve the pudding warm or at room temperature drizzled with maple syrup.

12 or more portions

**WINTER
COMFORT FOOD**

Roasted Turkey
Breast*
· · ·
Baked-Stuffed Onions
· · ·
Maple-Glazed
Red Cabbage
· · ·
Pumpkin Bread
Pudding

BLUEBERRY CHEESECAKE BREAD PUDDING

Comfort food doesn't get better than this! This stellar bread pudding is rich with sweet blueberries and is rippled with a vanilla-flavored cream cheese batter, making it an outrageous dessert.

3/4 pound day old challah, cut into 1-inch chunks
4 eggs, beaten
1 quart whole milk
1 cup sugar
1 tablespoon vanilla
pinch of salt
4 tablespoons butter, melted and cooled
2 cups blueberries
1/4 cup sugar mixed with 1 teaspoon cinnamon for topping

Cheesecake Swirl:
8 ounces cream cheese, at room temperature
1/4 cup sugar
1 egg
1/2 teaspoon vanilla

1. Preheat the oven to 350°. Grease a 9 x 13-inch pan.

2. Put the bread in a large mixing bowl.

3. In a separate bowl, combine the eggs, milk, sugar, vanilla, salt, and melted butter and mix well. Pour the custard over the bread chunks, stir until evenly combined, and let sit for 15 to 20 minutes so that the bread can absorb the liquid.

4. Stir in the blueberries. Turn the bread mixture into the prepared pan.

5. Make the cheesecake swirl. In a mixing bowl, with an electric mixer, beat the cream cheese and sugar until soft. Add the egg and vanilla and beat until smooth.

6. Spoon the cheesecake batter over the bread. Swirl with a knife to achieve a rippling effect. Sprinkle the top with the cinnamon-sugar mixture.

7. Bake for 45 to 50 minutes until set. Serve hot, warm, or at room temperature.

12 or more portions

COOKIES AND PASTRIES

APRICOT SHORTBREADS

Buttery shortbread pastry is lavished with apricot preserves and encrusted with chopped almonds, making these bars perfect for dessert. For a luscious treat, substitute raspberry preserves.

1 cup butter (no substitutions)
1/2 cup sugar
1 tablespoon vanilla
2 cups all-purpose flour
1/4 teaspoon salt
3/4 cup apricot preserves
1/2 cup slivered almonds, chopped

1. Preheat the oven to 375°. Line a 9 x 13-inch pan with parchment paper, leaving an overlap on the ends.

2. In a large bowl, cream the butter and sugar. Add the vanilla and mix well.

3. Add the flour and salt and mix until the texture of coarse meal. Spread the dough into the prepared pan, pressing it evenly into place.

4. Spread the preserves over the dough to within 1/2-inch of the edges.

5. Sprinkle the nuts over the jam.

6. Bake for 20 to 25 minutes until the edges are lightly golden. Remove the parchment paper from the pan to a rack to cool for 20 minutes. Transfer to a cutting board and while still warm, using a sharp knife, cut the pastry into squares. Return the pastry to the rack to cool completely.

4 dozen shortbread

PECAN BUTTERBALLS

Lots of butter and pecans make these powdery cookies the perfect goody for teatime.

¹/₂ cup butter
¹/₂ cup confectioners' sugar
1 tablespoon vanilla
1 cup all-purpose flour
¹/₄ teaspoon salt
1 cup finely ground pecans (use a food processor)
confectioners' sugar for coating

1. In a bowl, cream the butter and sugar. Add the vanilla. Stir in the flour and salt.

2. Add the pecans and stir until evenly mixed. Chill the dough in the refrigerator for 1 to 2 hours.

3. Preheat the oven to 300°.

4. Remove the dough from the refrigerator and shape into balls the size of a quarter. Place on ungreased baking sheets, 2 inches apart.

5. Bake for 25 to 30 minutes until lightly golden. Let the cookies cool slightly on the baking sheets, then roll them in confectioners' sugar. Set them on a rack to cool completely. When cool, re-roll the cookies in confectioners' sugar, coating well.

27 cookies

COOKIE TRAY

Chocolate-Hazelnut Biscotti

. . .

Chocolate-Fig Clusters

. . .

Meringues*

. . .

Coconut Macaroons

. . .

Pecan Butterballs

. . .

Mini Carrot Cake Muffins

GINGER CRISPS

Reminiscent of old-fashioned ginger snaps, these crunchy, ginger-spiced crisps have an additional blast of flavor from candied ginger.

1/2 cup butter
1 1/4 cups firmly packed dark brown sugar
1 egg
2 teaspoons ground ginger
1 tablespoon minced crystallized candied ginger
1 3/4 cups all-purpose flour
1/2 teaspoon baking soda
1/2 teaspoon salt

1. In a large mixing bowl, cream the butter and sugar. Add the egg, ground ginger, and candied ginger and mix well.

2. Sift together the flour, baking soda, and salt and add to the batter. Mix until the dough comes together.

3. Form the dough into a log, 12 inches long. Wrap in plastic wrap and refrigerate at least 4 hours and as much as overnight.

4. Preheat the oven to 375°.

5. Slice the dough into 1/4-inch thick rounds and place 2 inches apart on ungreased cookie sheets.

6. Bake for 10 minutes. Transfer the cookies to racks to cool completely.

4 dozen crisps

LEMON ICEBOX COOKIES

These crispy, lemon-flavored wafers are the perfect accompaniment to tea. I like to keep a batch of dough in the freezer for spontaneous entertaining!

1 cup all-purpose flour
¹/₂ cup sugar
1 tablespoon finely grated lemon peel
¹/₂ cup butter, cut into small pieces (no substitutions)
1 tablespoon sugar for garnish

1. Put the flour, sugar, and lemon peel in the bowl of a food processor and pulse until evenly mixed.

2. Add the butter and pulse only until the dough begins to come together. Transfer the dough to a piece of wax paper and form into a log, 6 inches long.

3. Roll the log in the 1 tablespoon sugar. Wrap in plastic wrap and refrigerate at least 4 hours and as much as overnight.

4. Preheat the oven to 375°.

5. Slice the dough into ¹/₄-inch thick rounds and place 2 inches apart on ungreased cookie sheets.

6. Bake for 10 minutes until cookies are lightly golden—the edges will brown slightly more. Transfer the cookies to racks to cool completely.

2 dozen wafers

BUTTERSCOTCH FOGGIES

These chewy, crispy butterscotch-flavored cookies outshine the infamous chocolate chipper. Chock full of chocolate chips, butterscotch chips, coconut, and pecans, they're the stuff of which dreams are made.

$1/2$ cup butter
$1/2$ cup firmly packed dark brown sugar
$3/8$ cup granulated sugar
1 egg
1 teaspoon vanilla
1 cup all-purpose flour
$1/2$ teaspoon baking soda
$1/4$ teaspoon salt
$1/2$ cup semi-sweet chocolate chips
$1/2$ cup butterscotch chips
$1/2$ cup sweetened, shredded coconut
$1/2$ cup chopped pecans

1. Preheat the oven to 375°.

2. In a large mixing bowl, cream the butter and sugars. Add the egg and vanilla and mix well.

3. Sift the flour, baking soda, and salt and add the dry ingredients to the batter.

4. Stir in the chips, coconut, and pecans.

5. Using a level tablespoonful of dough, drop the batter onto ungreased cookie sheets, 2 inches apart.

6. Bake for 9 to 11 minutes until lightly golden. Let the cookies sit on the baking sheets for 1 minute before removing them to racks to cool completely.

$3^1/2$ dozen cookies

TOFFEE CRISPS

These light, crunchy, butterscotch-flavored wafers are studded with bits of English toffee, creating the perfect nibble.

1/2 cup butter
1 1/4 cups packed light brown sugar
1 egg
2 teaspoons vanilla
1 3/4 cups all-purpose flour
1/2 teaspoon baking soda
1/2 teaspoon salt
1/2 cup English Toffee Bits or crushed Heath Bars

1. In a large mixing bowl, cream the butter and sugar. Add the egg and vanilla.

2. Add the flour, baking soda, and salt and mix well. Stir in the toffee bits.

3. Form the dough into a log, 12 inches long. Refrigerate at least 4 hours and as much as overnight.

4. Preheat the oven to 375°.

5. Slice the dough into 1/4-inch thick rounds. Place 2 inches apart on ungreased cookie sheets. Bake for 10 minutes. Let cookies sit on sheets for 1 minute before removing them to racks to cool.

4 dozen wafers

LEMON COOLERS

Delicate, buttery, and lemony best describe these dainty tea cookies that are coated with confectioners' sugar. They disappear like soap bubbles!

1/2 cup butter
1/2 cup confectioners' sugar
1 tablespoon finely grated lemon peel
1 tablespoon lemon juice
1 cup all-purpose flour
confectioners' sugar for dusting

1. In a large bowl, cream the butter and sugar. Add the lemon peel, lemon juice, and flour and mix well.

2. Preheat the oven to 300°.

3. Using 1 tablespoon of dough, form the mixture into quarter-size balls.

4. Place the balls on ungreased cookie sheets, 2 inches apart.

5. Bake for 23 to 25 minutes until puffed and golden around the edges. Remove the cookies to a rack.

6. While the cookies are still warm, roll them in confectioners' sugar. Set them on a rack to cool completely. Once cool, re-roll the cookies in more confectioners' sugar, coating well.

19 coolers

PEANUT BUTTER-WHITE CHOCOLATE CHIPPERS

These old-fashioned peanut butter cookies take on a new personality when peppered with white chocolate chips. One cookie just isn't enough!

MID-DAY
PICK-ME-UP

Banana-Rum Raisin
Smoothie
. . .
Peanut Butter-White
Chocolate Chippers

1/2 cup butter
1/2 cup granulated sugar
1/2 cup packed light brown sugar
1/2 cup smooth peanut butter
1 egg
1 teaspoon vanilla
1 1/4 cups all-purpose flour
3/4 teaspoon baking soda
1/4 teaspoon salt
1 1/8 cups white chocolate chips

1. Preheat the oven to 375°. Grease two cookie sheets.

2. In a large mixing bowl, cream the butter, sugars, and peanut butter. Add the egg and vanilla.

3. Sift together the flour, baking soda, and salt and add to the batter, stirring until well mixed.

4. Stir in the white chocolate chips.

5. Using a tablespoon, drop the batter onto the prepared baking sheets, 2 inches apart.

6. Bake for 7 to 8 minutes until lightly golden. Let the cookies sit on the baking sheets for 2 minutes; then remove the cookies to racks to cool completely.

5 dozen cookies

COCONUT MACAROONS

These chewy, almond-laced coconut mounds are just right for an afternoon snack or a sweet nibble.

2 egg whites
1/3 cup sugar
1 teaspoon almond extract
1 1/2 cups sweetened, shredded coconut

1. Preheat the oven to 300°. Line two cookie sheets with parchment paper.

2. In a bowl with an electric mixer, beat the egg whites until frothy. Gradually add the sugar, 1 tablespoon at a time, beating until whites are glossy and form stiff peaks.

3. Gently fold in the vanilla and coconut.

4. Drop the batter by heaping tablespoonfuls onto the prepared cookie sheets, 2 inches apart.

5. Bake for about 18 minutes until golden. Turn off the oven, leave the oven door ajar, and let the cookies remain in the oven for 20 minutes more. Remove from the oven and carefully transfer the cookies from the parchment paper to a rack to cool completely.

20 to 22 cookies

CONGO BARS

These butterscotch squares are moist, dense, and slightly chewy. They're studded with pecans and butterscotch chips, making them rich and extravagant!

1/2 cup butter
1 1/4 cups packed light brown sugar
1 egg
1 tablespoon vanilla
1 cup all-purpose flour
1/4 teaspoon salt
3/4 cup chopped pecans
2/3 cup butterscotch chips

1. Preheat the oven to 350°. Grease an 8-inch square pan.

2. In a large bowl, cream the butter and sugar until fluffy. Add the egg and vanilla.

3. Stir in the flour and salt and mix well.

4. Add the nuts and chips, stirring until evenly combined. Spread the mixture in the prepared pan.

5. Bake for 30 to 35 minutes until golden and a toothpick inserted in the center comes out clean. Cool on a rack before cutting.

16 squares

SOUTHWESTERN
BASH

Five Spice-Rubbed
Ribs
· · ·
Smokey Mashed
Sweet Potatoes
· · ·
Onion Slaw
· · ·
Congo Bars

ORANGE TEA CAKES

**AL FRESCO
DINNER**

Cold Cucumber Soup
· · ·
Potato and
Mussel Salad
· · ·
Sourdough Bread
· · ·
Orange Tea Cakes
· · ·
Assorted Berries

These moist, dainty, orange-scented squares are dusted with a sugary topping. What a lovely accompaniment to Sunday brunch! (If you're a lemon-lover, substitute lemon peel and juice for the orange peel and juice.)

1/2 cup butter, melted
1 cup sugar
2 eggs, beaten
1 tablespoon finely grated orange peel
2 tablespoons orange juice
1 cup all-purpose flour
1 teaspoon baking powder
pinch of salt
2 tablespoons sugar for dusting

1. Preheat the oven to 325°. Grease a 9-inch square baking pan.

2. In a large mixing bowl, combine the butter and sugar. Add the eggs, orange peel, and orange juice and mix well.

3. Sift the flour, baking powder, and salt and add to the batter, stirring until evenly combined. Turn the batter into the prepared pan.

4. Sprinkle the top with 2 tablespoons sugar.

5. Bake for 25 to 30 minutes until a toothpick inserted in the center comes out clean. The cake should be slightly moist. Remove to a rack to cool completely before cutting.

25 squares

SEVEN LAYER BARS

I am always asked for this recipe whenever I serve these outrageous squares. These bars have been around for years; everyone has sampled them in one form or another. I wanted to share my version of this popular confection. I always keep a batch of these in the freezer for unexpected guests.

1/2 cup butter, melted
1 1/4 cups graham cracker crumbs
3 1/2 ounces sweetened, shredded coconut
1 cup (6 ounces) semi-sweet chocolate chips
1 cup (6 ounces) butterscotch chips
14-ounce can sweetened condensed milk
2 cups pecans

1. Preheat the oven to 325°. Grease a 9 x 13-inch pan.

2. Pour the butter into the prepared pan. Sprinkle the graham cracker crumbs evenly over the butter.

3. Cover the crumbs with the coconut. Sprinkle the chocolate and butterscotch chips over the coconut.

4. Pour the condensed milk over the chips, spreading it out evenly. Top with the pecans. Using a metal spatula, press the nuts down.

5. Bake for 30 minutes. While warm, run a knife around the edges of the pan. Set on a rack to cool completely before cutting into bars.

4 dozen bars

SUNDAY SIPPER

Piña Colada Smoothie
. . .
Seven Layer Bars

SPICED-WALNUT BISCOTTI

Biscotti have become the darlings of the cookie world. They're crisp, crunchy, and not too sweet, but especially satisfying with a mug of hot coffee or a cup of tea. These walnut-studded, spice-scented cookies are sure to win raves.

2 eggs, beaten
$3/4$ cup sugar
$1/2$ cup vegetable oil
2 cups all-purpose flour
$1^1/2$ teaspoons baking powder
$1/4$ teaspoon salt
1 teaspoon cinnamon
$1/2$ teaspoon ground ginger
$1/4$ teaspoon nutmeg
$1/8$ teaspoon ground cloves
1 cup chopped walnuts, toasted

1. Preheat the oven to 325°. Line two baking sheets with parchment paper.

2. In a large mixing bowl, combine the eggs, sugar, and oil.

3. Add the flour, baking powder, salt, and spices and mix well.

4. Stir in the walnuts.

5. Divide the dough in half. Turn each half out onto a cookie sheet and form into a log, 3 inches wide and 12 inches long.

6. Bake for 30 minutes. Remove the logs from the cookie sheets and let cool for 3 minutes. Slice each log into $3/4$-inch wide pieces. Place a rack on each cookie sheet and place the slices on the racks, $1/2$-inch apart.

7. Return to the oven and bake for 15 minutes more. Remove the racks from the baking sheets and let biscotti cool completely. Store in an airtight tin.

32 biscotti

LEMON-POPPY SEED BISCOTTI

The sparkle of lemon and the nuttiness of poppy seeds makes a special flavor statement. Showcased in these crunchy Italian-style cookies, the combination will become a family favorite.

2 eggs, beaten
³/4 cup sugar
¹/2 cup vegetable oil
1 tablespoon finely grated lemon peel
2 tablespoons poppy seeds
2 cups all-purpose flour
1¹/2 teaspoons baking powder
¹/4 teaspoon salt

1. Preheat the oven to 325°. Line two baking sheets with parchment paper.

2. In a large mixing bowl, combine the eggs, sugar, oil, lemon peel, and poppy seeds.

3. Add the flour, baking powder, and salt and mix well.

4. Divide the dough in half. Turn each half out onto the prepared baking sheet and form into a log, 3 inches wide and 10 inches long.

5. Bake for 30 minutes. Remove the logs from the cookie sheets and let cool for 3 minutes. Slice each log into ³/4-inch wide pieces. Place a rack on each cookie sheet and place the slices on the racks, ¹/2-inch apart.

6. Return to the oven and bake for 15 minutes more. Remove the racks from the baking sheets and let biscotti cool completely. Store in an airtight tin.

28 biscotti

COFFEE AND . . .

Streusel-Topped
Muffins
. . .
Lemon-Poppy
Seed Biscotti
. . .
Linzer Torte Muffins

DATE WONTONS

These wonton pillows are chock full of dates and walnuts and a sprinkling of candied ginger for a fruit-filled treat.

1 cup pitted dates, finely chopped
$1/2$ cup walnuts, finely chopped
2 tablespoons minced crystallized candied ginger
2 teaspoons finely grated orange peel
32 wonton wraps
2 tablespoons butter, melted
confectioners' sugar for garnish

1. Preheat the oven to 350°. Grease two baking sheets.

2. In a bowl, combine the dates, walnuts, candied ginger, and orange peel and mix well.

3. Place $1/2$ tablespoon of the filling in the middle of a wonton skin. Slightly dampen the outer edges of two adjacent sides with cold water. Fold over to form a triangle, pressing the edges together to seal. Place on the prepared baking sheet. Repeat with the remaining filling and wonton wraps.

4. Brush the top of the wontons with melted butter.

5. Bake for 10 to 12 minutes until lightly golden. Remove wontons to a rack to cool completely. Once cooled, dust with confectioners' sugar and serve.

32 wontons

COCONUT-ALMOND TRUFFLES

HOLIDAY GIFTS

Raspberry Vinegar
· · ·
Half-Sour Pickled
Tomatoes
· · ·
Chili-Spiced
Mixed Nuts
· · ·
Peanut Butter Fudge
· · ·
Coconut-Almond
Truffles

Truffles are those exquisite confections we have come to adore. These darling nuggets sport an almond-flavored coconut filling that's rolled in cocoa, making them irresistible.

3 cups sweetened, shredded coconut
1¹/₂ cups confectioners' sugar
¹/₄ cup heavy cream
1 teaspoon almond extract
2 tablespoons unsweetened cocoa
2 tablespoons packed confectioners' sugar
1 teaspoon cinnamon

1. Put the coconut in the bowl of a food processor and pulse until it is finely chopped. Transfer the coconut to a bowl.

2. Add the 1¹/₂ cups confectioners' sugar, cream, and almond extract and mix well. Refrigerate for 30 minutes.

3. While the coconut mixture is chilling, prepare the coating. In a small bowl, combine the cocoa, the 2 tablespoons confectioners' sugar, and cinnamon and mix well.

4. Using 1 tablespoon of coconut filling, roll the mixture into 1-inch balls. Roll the balls in the cocoa mixture, coating completely. Store in the refrigerator.

about 3 dozen truffles

CANNOLI

A cannoli is the fabulous Italian dessert consisting of a fried tube-shaped pastry shell encasing a cream filling. I've streamlined the recipe by using baked egg roll wraps to house the treasured chocolate-studded ricotta cream.

MEDITERRANEAN FLAIR

Mesclun Salad with
Basic Vinaigrette
· · ·
Grilled Tuna with
Mediterranean Relish
· · ·
Pasta Toscano
· · ·
Cannoli

6 egg roll wraps
cooking oil spray
8 ounces ricotta cheese
1 cup confectioners' sugar
1 tablespoon Grand Marnier
¼ cup chopped bittersweet chocolate
2 tablespoons finely chopped pistachio nuts for garnish
confectioners' sugar for garnish

1. Preheat the oven to 350°. Grease a regular-size muffin pan.

2. Make the dessert cups. Place an egg roll wrap in a muffin cup, pressing it gently to conform to the shape of the pan. The sides will form some pleats and the edges will overlap the top of the muffin pan. Coat the wraps with the cooking oil spray.

3. Bake for 7 to 8 minutes until golden. Remove the cups from the muffin pan to a rack to cool completely. (These may be made in advance and frozen.)

4. In a mixing bowl, combine the ricotta, sugar, Grand Marnier, and chocolate and mix well. Store in the refrigerator until serving time.

5. When ready to serve, fill the dessert cups with the ricotta mixture. Sprinkle the tops with the chopped nuts, dust the shells with confectioners' sugar, and present.

6 portions

DESSERT CUPS

For a specialty dessert, use the baked egg roll wraps and fill them with any one of the following ideas:

- Chocolate mousse
- Pot de crème
- Custard, tapioca pudding, or rice pudding
- Assorted berries with whipped cream
- Ice cream or frozen yogurt drizzled with sauce
- Sorbet or sherbet with fruits
- Mascarpone mixed with dried fruits

SPRING-SUMMER LUNCHEON

Parmesan Bites
. . .
Arugula, Tomatoes, and White Beans
. . .
Deviled Salmon Cakes
. . .
Dessert Cups with Assorted Berries and Whipped Cream

PEANUT BUTTER FUDGE

Peanut butter aficionados take heed! The heavenly peanut butter flavor and smooth, creamy texture of this fudge will knock off your socks. It makes a great lunch box treat.

1 pound peanut butter chips
14-ounce can sweetened condensed milk
1 teaspoon vanilla
pinch of salt

1. Line an 8-inch square pan with silver foil.

2. Put the chips and condensed milk in a saucepan and cook over low heat, stirring occasionally until the chips are melted. When smooth, add the vanilla and salt and mix well.

3. Spread the fudge into the prepared pan. Chill for 2 hours or more until firm. Remove the fudge from the pan by lifting the foil. Peel away the foil and cut into squares. Store in the refrigerator.

2 pounds fudge; about 4 dozen pieces

CAKES
AND PIES

ALMOND CREAM CAKE

This light, almond-scented yellow cake is the epitome of simple elegance. Rather than butter, the batter is infused with heavy cream. The cream provides the richness, making this a moist, luscious cake that suits any occasion.

1 1/2 cups sugar
4 eggs
1 teaspoon almond extract
1 3/4 cups all-purpose flour
2 teaspoons baking powder
1/8 teaspoon salt
1 cup heavy cream
confectioners' sugar for garnish

1. Preheat the oven to 400°. Grease and flour a 10-inch tube pan.

2. In a large bowl with an electric mixer, beat the sugar and eggs until thick and pale lemon colored. Add the almond extract.

3. Sift together the flour, baking powder, and salt. Add the dry ingredients alternately with the cream to the batter. Turn the batter into the prepared pan.

4. Bake for 15 minutes. Reduce the oven temperature to 300° and bake for 30 minutes more until a toothpick inserted in the center comes out clean. Remove to a rack to cool for 10 minutes. Remove the tube from the pan and let the cake cool completely.

5. Run a knife under the bottom of the cake to release it from the pan. Invert the cake onto a plate, then using a second plate, turn the cake right side up. Dust with confectioners' sugar and serve.

8 to 10 portions

BUTTERMILK POUNDCAKE

The true poundcake was originally made with one pound each of butter, sugar, flour, and eggs. However, this yields a heavy, dry cake. This version is a moist, buttermilk-laced cake scented with vanilla. It is truly reminiscent of old-fashioned goodness.

1 cup butter, at room temperature
2 cups sugar
4 eggs
1 tablespoon vanilla
3 cups all-purpose flour
1 teaspoon baking powder
1/2 teaspoon baking soda
1/4 teaspoon salt
1 cup buttermilk

1. Preheat the oven to 350°. Grease a 10-inch bundt pan.

2. In a large bowl with an electric mixer, cream the butter and sugar. Add the eggs, one at a time, beating well after each addition. Add the vanilla.

3. Sift together the flour, baking powder, baking soda, and salt. Add the dry ingredients alternately with the buttermilk to the batter. Turn the batter into the prepared pan.

4. Bake for 50 to 55 minutes until a toothpick inserted in the center comes out clean. Remove to a rack to cool for 15 to 20 minutes; then remove the cake from the pan to the rack to cool completely before serving.

12 or more portions

APRÈS SKI
GATHERING

Prunes Purcell
. . .
Cheese Scones
. . .
Portuguese Kale Soup
. . .
Buttermilk Poundcake

CARAMEL APPLE CAKE

When it's autumn, be sure to earmark some freshly picked apples for this spectacular cake. It goes one step beyond caramel apples that we all remember from our childhood. The cake struts a buttermilk batter dappled with chunks of apple and glazed with a pecan-caramel sauce that's divine.

$^1/_2$ cup butter
1 cup sugar
1 egg
1 tablespoon vanilla
$2^1/_2$ cups all-purpose flour
1 teaspoon baking soda
$^1/_2$ teaspoon salt
1 cup buttermilk
3 cups peeled and chopped apples, cut into $^1/_2$-inch cubes
    (I use MacIntosh.)

Caramel Topping:
$^1/_2$ cup butter, melted
$^3/_4$ cup firmly packed light brown sugar
$^1/_2$ cup heavy cream
1 teaspoon vanilla
1 cup chopped pecans, toasted

1. Preheat the oven to 350°. Grease and flour a 9 x 13-inch baking dish.

2. In a large bowl, cream the butter and sugar. Add the egg and vanilla and mix well.

3. Sift together the flour, baking soda, and salt and add the dry ingredients alternately with the buttermilk to the batter.

4. Fold in the apple chunks. Turn the batter into the prepared pan, spreading it evenly.

5. Bake for about 40 minutes until a toothpick inserted in the center comes out clean. Prick the cake all over with a toothpick.

6. While the cake is still hot, prepare the caramel topping. In a small saucepan, combine the butter, brown sugar, cream, and vanilla. Bring to a boil and boil for 3 minutes, stirring often. Mix in the pecans.

7. Pour the warm topping evenly over the hot cake, spreading it with a spatula. Serve warm or at room temperature.

10 to 12 portions

STREUSEL COFFEECAKE

There's nothing better than this coffeecake to top off brunch. Infused with a brown sugar batter, crowned with a heavenly, crumbly, cinnamon-pecan topping, and drizzled with a vanilla glaze, this is the stuff of which dreams are made.

1/2 cup butter
1 1/2 cups firmly packed light brown sugar
1 egg
1 tablespoon vanilla
2 cups all-purpose flour
1 teaspoon baking soda
1/4 teaspoon salt
1 cup buttermilk
Streusel (recipe follows)
Glaze (recipe follows)

1. Preheat the oven to 350°. Grease and flour a 10-inch tube pan.

2. In a large bowl with an electric mixer, cream the butter and sugar. Add the egg and vanilla and beat until fluffy.

3. Sift together the flour, baking soda, and salt. Add the dry ingredients alternately with the buttermilk to the batter. Turn the batter into the prepared pan. Sprinkle the streusel evenly over the top.

4. Bake for 50 minutes or until a toothpick inserted in the center comes out clean. Remove the tube from the pan and set the cake on a rack to cool. When cool, remove the tube from the cake. Drizzle the glaze over the top of the cake. Let the glaze set before serving.

8 to 10 portions

Streusel:
1/3 cup self-rising flour
3 tablespoons butter, cut into pieces
3 tablespoons sugar
1 teaspoon cinnamon
1/2 cup chopped pecans

Combine the flour, butter, sugar, and cinnamon in a bowl and mix until the texture of coarse meal. Stir in the pecans.

LABOR DAY BRUNCH

Assorted Bagels
. . .
Cream Cheese
. . .
Gravlax*
. . .
Herring with
Mustard Sauce
. . .
Cucumber Salad
. . .
Spinach, Feta, and
Rice Bake
. . .
Fruits with
Raspberry Sauce
. . .
Streusel Coffeecake

Glaze:
1 cup confectioners' sugar
1 to 2 tablespoons water
1 teaspoon vanilla

Mix all of the glaze ingredients together until smooth.

LEMON RICOTTA CAKE

The fresh light flavor of lemon shines in this moist and satisfying cake that's sure to become an all-time favorite.

1/2 cup butter
1 1/4 cups sugar
2 eggs
2 tablespoons grated lemon peel
1/4 cup lemon juice
1 cup whole milk ricotta cheese
2 cups all-purpose flour
1 teaspoon baking powder
1 teaspoon baking soda
1/2 teaspoon salt
1/2 cup whole milk
confectioners' sugar for garnish

1. Preheat the oven to 350°. Grease a 10-inch tube pan.

2. In a large bowl with an electric mixer, cream the butter and sugar. Add the eggs and beat until thick and pale lemon colored.

3. Add the lemon peel, lemon juice, and ricotta, beating until smooth.

4. Sift together the flour, baking powder, baking soda, and salt. Add the dry ingredients alternately with the milk to the batter. Turn the batter into the prepared pan.

5. Bake for 40 to 45 minutes until a toothpick inserted in the center comes out clean. Remove the tube from the pan to a rack and let the cake cool completely.

6. Run a knife under the bottom of the cake to release it from the pan. Invert the cake onto a plate, then using a second plate, turn the cake right side up. Dust with confectioners' sugar and serve.

8 to 10 portions

TRIP TO ITALY

Roasted Mushrooms
. . .
Chicken Bianco
. . .
Baked Polenta
. . .
Lemon Ricotta Cake

RAISIN POUNDCAKE

DINING AL FRESCO

Mixed Greens with
Balsamic Vinaigrette*
. . .
Grilled Chicken with
Salsa Verde
. . .
Pasta Sette Mezzo
. . .
Raisin Poundcake
à la Mode

This buttery, sour cream poundcake is moist, dense, and lavishly speckled with golden raisins, making it reminiscent of home-baked goodness.

1 1/2 cups golden raisins
1 tablespoon all-purpose flour
1 cup butter, melted and cooled
2 3/4 cups sugar
6 eggs
1 tablespoon vanilla
3 cups all-purpose flour
1/4 teaspoon baking soda
1/2 teaspoon salt
1 cup sour cream

1. Preheat the oven to 325°. Grease and flour a 10-inch tube pan.

2. Put the raisins in a bowl and sprinkle with 1 tablespoon flour. Toss until evenly coated.

3. In a large mixing bowl with an electric mixer, cream the butter and sugar. Add the eggs and vanilla and beat until fluffy.

4. Sift together the flour, baking soda, and salt. Add the dry ingredients alternately with the sour cream to the batter.

5. Stir in the raisins.

6. Turn the batter into the prepared pan and bake for 1 hour and 20 to 30 minutes until a toothpick inserted in the center comes out clean. Remove to a rack to cool for 10 minutes. Run a knife around the outer edge of the pan; then remove the cake from the pan to the rack to cool completely.

12 or more portions

BLUEBERRY-CORNMEAL CAKE

When blueberries are in season, this cake is a real treat. The moist, vanilla-scented cornmeal batter is chock full of plump, succulent blueberries. It's absolutely divine for dessert and a sweet success served warm for breakfast or brunch.

1 cup blueberries
2 cups plus 1 tablespoon all-purpose flour
1 cup cornmeal
1 cup sugar
2 teaspoons baking powder
$1/2$ teaspoon baking soda
$1/2$ teaspoon salt
2 eggs, lightly beaten
$1^1/2$ teaspoons vanilla
$1^1/2$ cups buttermilk
$1/3$ cup vegetable oil

1. Preheat the oven to 350°. Grease a 9-inch springform pan.

2. Rinse the blueberries and dust them with 1 tablespoon flour.

3. In a large mixing bowl, combine the 2 cups flour, cornmeal, sugar, baking powder, baking soda, and salt.

4. In a separate bowl, mix the eggs, vanilla, buttermilk, and oil.

5. Add the buttermilk mixture to the dry ingredients, mixing until evenly combined. Gently fold in the blueberries. Turn the batter into the prepared pan.

6. Bake for 50 to 55 minutes until a toothpick inserted in the center comes out clean. Serve warm or at room temperature.

8 to 10 portions

COFFEE GINGERSNAP ICEBOX CAKE

Icebox cakes are not baked but are assembled layers of cookies and whipped cream. They're meant to be made in advance and refrigerated so that the cookies can soften and the flavors mellow. The combination of coffee whipped cream and gingersnap cookies is an aphrodisiac.

> $2^1/4$ cups heavy cream
> $1^1/2$ tablespoons instant coffee powder
> $1/3$ cup confectioners' sugar
> 28 whole gingersnaps
> $1/4$ cup crushed gingersnaps

1. Line a 9 x 5-inch loaf pan with two pieces of overlapping plastic wrap, long enough to overhang the edges.

2. In a mixing bowl, combine the cream and coffee. Let sit for 15 minutes for the coffee to dissolve. Add the confectioners' sugar.

3. With an electric mixer, whip the cream, coffee powder, and sugar until stiff peaks form.

4. Spread $2/3$ of the whipped cream in the loaf pan. Starting at the long side of the pan, sink the cookies in the cream, lining them up in four rows, 7 cookies per row. Press the cookies down as you work. Spread the remaining whipped cream over the cookies, filling in any gaps between them.

5. Cover the pan with plastic wrap and refrigerate for 24 hours.

6. To serve, remove the plastic wrap from the top, then place a tray over the top of the loaf pan. Invert the cake onto the tray. Lift off the pan and gently peel away the plastic wrap. Sprinkle the cookie crumbs over the top of the cake, slice, and serve. Refrigerate any leftover cake.

8 portions

STRAWBERRY SHORTCAKE

There's no better way to celebrate summer than with this old-time favorite. This all-American dessert struts a scone-like biscuit that's resplendent with lush berries and crowned with pillows of whipped cream. This is the soul of home cooking!

Fruit Filling:
1 quart (4 cups) strawberries, hulled and halved
¼ cup strawberry preserves

In a bowl, mix the berries and preserves together and set aside.

Whipped Cream:
1 cup heavy cream
3 to 4 tablespoons confectioners' sugar
½ teaspoon vanilla

In a bowl with an electric mixer, beat the cream, sugar, and vanilla until peaks form. Cover and refrigerate for up to 2 hours.

Biscuit:
2 cups all-purpose flour
3 tablespoons sugar
1 tablespoon baking powder
½ teaspoon salt
6 tablespoons cold, unsalted butter, cut into pieces
¾ cup whole milk

1. Preheat the oven to 450°. Grease a baking sheet.

2. Put the flour, sugar, baking powder, and salt in the bowl of a food processor and pulse to mix. Add the butter and pulse only until the texture of coarse meal. Add the milk and pulse slightly until dough forms small clumps.

3. Remove the dough to a lightly floured board and knead to gather the dough into a ball. (Do not overwork the dough or the biscuit will not be fluffy.) Gently pat the dough into a rectangle ¾-inch thick. Cut the dough into half lengthwise. Cut each half into thirds. Place pieces 2 inches apart on the prepared baking sheet.

4. Bake for 10 to 12 minutes until lightly golden. Remove the scones to a rack to cool for 15 minutes.

5. To serve, split the warm biscuits in half horizontally. Place the bottom halves on individual plates. Spoon the berries and their juice over the biscuits. Cover with dollops of whipped cream and the biscuit tops. Serve at once.

6 portions

MAX'S VANILLA CUPCAKES

I made these happy little cakes for my grandson's first birthday. He loved poking his fingers into the cupcake and licking them. Adults will also find them irresistible!

1/2 cup butter (no substitutions)
1 cup sugar
2 eggs
11/2 teaspoons vanilla
3/4 cup self-rising flour
1/2 cup plus 2 tablespoons all-purpose flour
1/2 cup milk
Vanilla Buttercream Icing (recipe follows)

1. Preheat the oven to 350°. Line a 12-cup muffin pan with paper baking cups.

2. In a large bowl with an electric mixer, cream the butter and sugar. Add the eggs and vanilla and mix well.

3. Combine the flours and add them alternately with the milk to the batter, mixing until smooth.

4. Spoon the batter into the muffin cups, filling them 3/4 full.

5. Bake for 20 to 23 minutes until a toothpick inserted in the center comes out clean. Remove the cupcakes from the pan to a rack to cool completely. Spread the Vanilla Buttercream Icing over the tops of the cupcakes and serve.

10 cupcakes

Vanilla Buttercream Icing:
2 tablespoons butter
3/4 cup confectioners' sugar
11/2 to 2 tablespoons milk
1/2 teaspoon vanilla
2 to 3 drops of food coloring (optional)

With an electric mixer, beat the butter, sugar, milk, vanilla, and food coloring until smooth and creamy. Refrigerate until needed.

LUNCH BOX TREATS

Curried Nuts
. . .
Blue Cheese-Cheddar Wafers
. . .
Chocolate Chip-Peanut Butter Muffins
. . .
Max's Vanilla Cupcakes
. . .
Macadamia Nut Fudge

LAYERED SPONGE CAKE

Sponge cakes are known for their feather-light texture. They get their lightness and volume from egg whites that are whipped separately with sugar and are then gently folded into the batter. These sponge layers are drizzled with Chambord and filled with raspberry preserves, adding a special touch of sophistication.

6 eggs, separated
1 cup sugar
1¹/₂ teaspoons vanilla
1 cup sifted cake flour
¹/₂ teaspoon baking powder
¹/₄ teaspoon salt
¹/₄ cup Chambord (raspberry liqueur)
¹/₂ cup raspberry preserves
whipped cream for garnish

1. Preheat the oven to 375°. Line the bottoms of two 9-inch round layer cake pans with parchment paper.

2. In a large mixing bowl with an electric mixer, beat the egg whites until frothy. Gradually add ¹/₂ cup sugar and continue beating until the whites are stiff and glossy, about 3 to 4 minutes. Set aside.

3. In a separate mixing bowl with an electric mixer, beat the egg yolks and remaining ¹/₂ cup sugar until thick and pale lemon colored. Add the vanilla.

4. Sift the flour, baking powder, and salt over the top of the batter. Using a spatula, fold the dry ingredients into the batter.

5. Using a spatula, gently fold in the beaten egg whites. Turn equal amounts of batter into each pan.

6. Bake for about 18 minutes or until the cake is golden and rebounds when lightly pressed in the center. Remove to a rack and while still warm, drizzle each layer with 2 tablespoons Chambord. Once the Chambord has been absorbed, let cool slightly; then run a knife around the edges of the pan to release the cakes from the pans. Remove the layers from the sides of the pans to cool completely.

7. Once cooled, peel off the parchment paper. Spread the preserves over the top of one layer. Assemble the cake, covering the preserves with the second cake layer. Serve with dollops of whipped cream.

8 portions

BUTTERSCOTCH PUDDING CAKE

This cake forms its own pudding sauce as it bakes. The warm vanilla sponge cake is set atop a cloyingly sweet butterscotch pudding that's lip-smacking good!

Cake:
1 cup all-purpose flour
2/3 cup sugar
1 1/2 teaspoons baking powder
1/4 teaspoon salt
1/2 cup milk
4 tablespoons butter, melted
1 tablespoon vanilla

Pudding:
3/4 cup light brown sugar
1 1/4 cups boiling water

1. Preheat the oven to 350°.

2. In a mixing bowl, combine the flour, sugar, baking powder, and salt and mix well.

3. Add the milk, butter, and vanilla and stir until evenly combined. Transfer the batter to an ungreased 8-inch square pan.

4. In a small bowl, combine the brown sugar and water, stirring until the sugar dissolves. Pour this mixture over the cake batter—do not stir!

5. Bake for 30 to 35 minutes until the top is golden and the cake begins to pull away from the sides of the pan. Serve warm with the pudding spooned over the cake. Top with vanilla ice cream.

6 portions

AUTUMN NITE SUP

Warm Cabbage, Apple, and Goat Cheese Salad
. . .
French Bread
. . .
Butterscotch Pudding Cake

CARAMEL PINEAPPLE UPSIDE-DOWN CAKE

This cake never fails to win raves. I've updated the retro recipe to feature a vanilla-flavored buttermilk cake capped with a sweet, gooey, caramel glaze studded with fresh pineapple rings.

Caramel Topping:
4 tablespoons butter, melted
2 tablespoons heavy cream
1/2 cup packed dark brown sugar
6 to 7 fresh pineapple slices, cut 1/2-inch thick

1/2 cup butter
1 cup granulated sugar
2 eggs
1 tablespoon vanilla
1 3/4 cups all-purpose flour
1 1/2 teaspoons baking powder
1/2 teaspoon salt
2/3 cup buttermilk

1. Preheat the oven to 350°. Grease the sides of a 9-inch round cake pan. Line the bottom with parchment paper.

2. Prepare the topping. In a bowl, combine the melted butter, cream, and brown sugar. Spread the mixture evenly on the bottom of the prepared pan. Lay the pineapple rings on the caramel, starting around the edge of the pan. Fill in the middle—you may have to slice some of the rings in half to fit into the pan.

3. In a large bowl, cream the butter and sugar. Add the eggs and vanilla.

4. Sift together the flour, baking powder, and salt. Add the dry ingredients alternately with the buttermilk to the batter. Spread the batter evenly over the pineapple rings.

5. Bake for 55 to 60 minutes until a toothpick inserted in the center comes out clean. Remove to a rack to cool for 15 minutes; then run a knife around the edge of the pan. Invert the cake onto a large plate. Peel off the parchment paper. Serve warm or at room temperature.

8 to 10 portions

RUM CAKE

The essence of rum dominates this light and spongy cake that's finished with a coffee whipped cream.

1/2 cup whole milk
1/4 cup dark rum
3 eggs, separated
1 1/2 cups sugar
6 tablespoons butter
1 1/2 teaspoons vanilla
1 1/2 cups all-purpose flour
2 teaspoons baking powder
1/4 teaspoon salt
Coffee Whipped Cream (recipe follows)

1. Preheat the oven to 325°. Grease a 10-inch tube pan.

2. In a small bowl, combine the milk and rum and set aside.

3. In a large bowl with an electric mixer, beat the egg whites to soft peaks. Gradually add 1/2 cup sugar and continue beating until the whites are stiff and glossy, but not dry, about 3 to 4 minutes. Set aside.

4. In a separate bowl with an electric mixer, cream the butter and 1 cup sugar until fluffy. Add the egg yolks and vanilla and beat until thick and pale lemon colored.

5. Sift together the flour, baking powder, and salt. Add the dry ingredients alternately with the milk mixture to the batter.

6. Using a spatula, gently fold the beaten egg whites into the batter until there are no traces of white. Turn the batter into the prepared pan.

7. Bake for 45 to 50 minutes until a toothpick inserted in the center comes out clean. Remove to a rack to cool for 10 minutes. Remove the tube from the pan and let the cake cool completely.

8. Run a knife under the bottom of the cake to release it from the pan. Invert the cake onto a plate, then using a second plate, turn the cake right side up. Serve with dollops of Coffee Whipped Cream.

10 to 12 portions

SPECIAL
BIRTHDAY
CELEBRATION

Corn Chowder
· · ·
Mesclun Salad with
Toasted Goat Cheese
· · ·
Nubble Light
Seafood Bake
· · ·
Rum Cake

Coffee Whipped Cream:
1 cup heavy cream
1 tablespoon instant coffee granules
$^1/_4$ cup confectioners' sugar

1. In a mixing bowl, combine the cream and coffee. Let sit for 15 minutes for the coffee to dissolve. Add the confectioners' sugar.

2. With an electric mixer, whip the ingredients until stiff peaks form. Refrigerate until needed.

SPICE POUNDCAKE

This homestyle, light-textured cake brings together a potpourri of aromatic spices, making it the perfect choice with mugs of hot coffee.

1¹/₈ cups (2¹/₂ sticks) butter
1 cup granulated sugar
1 cup packed dark brown sugar
4 eggs
2 teaspoons vanilla
3 cups all-purpose flour
2 teaspoons baking powder
1 teaspoon baking soda
¹/₂ teaspoon salt
1¹/₂ teaspoons cinnamon
1 teaspoon ground ginger
¹/₂ teaspoon allspice
¹/₂ teaspoon nutmeg
¹/₄ teaspoon ground cloves
1¹/₃ cups buttermilk
whipped cream for garnish

1. Preheat the oven to 350°. Grease a 10-inch bundt pan.

2. In a large mixing bowl with an electric mixer, cream the butter and sugars until light and fluffy. Add the eggs and vanilla.

3. Sift together the flour, baking powder, baking soda, salt, and spices. Add the dry ingredients alternately with the buttermilk to the batter. Turn the batter into the prepared pan.

4. Bake for 50 to 55 minutes until a toothpick inserted in the center comes out clean. Remove to a rack to cool for 15 minutes; then remove the cake from the pan to the rack to cool completely. Serve with dollops of whipped cream.

12 or more portions

GRADUATION
DINNER

Honey-Mustard Dip
with Crudités
. . .
Stuffed Leg of Lamb
. . .
Garlic Mashed
Potato Cakes
. . .
Roasted Asparagus**
. . .
Spice Poundcake

KAHLUA AND CREAM CAKE

Americans' love affair with coffee is booming. There's no better way to celebrate the passion for this universal flavor than in a light-textured coffee and cream cake.

1 tablespoon instant coffee powder
1/2 cup light cream
1/4 cup Kahlua
3 eggs, separated
1 1/2 cups sugar
6 tablespoons butter
1 1/2 cups all-purpose flour
2 teaspoons baking powder
1/4 teaspoon salt

1. Preheat the oven to 325°. Grease a 10-inch tube pan.

2. Combine the coffee powder, cream, and Kahlua and mix well. Let sit for 20 minutes for the coffee granules to dissolve.

3. In a large bowl with an electric mixer, beat the egg whites until soft peaks form. Gradually add 1/2 cup sugar and continue beating until whites are stiff and glossy, but not dry, about 3 to 4 minutes. Set aside.

4. In a separate bowl with an electric mixer, cream the butter and 1 cup sugar until fluffy. Add the egg yolks and beat until thick and pale lemon colored.

5. Sift together the flour, baking powder, and salt. Add the dry ingredients alternately with the coffee cream to the batter.

6. Using a spatula, gently fold the beaten egg whites into the batter until there are no traces of white. Turn the batter into the prepared pan.

7. Bake for 45 to 50 minutes until a toothpick inserted in the center comes out clean. Remove to a rack to cool for 30 minutes. Remove the tube from the pan and let the cake cool completely.

8. Run a knife under the bottom of the cake to release it from the pan. Invert the cake onto a plate, then using a second plate, turn the cake right side up. Serve with dollops of whipped cream.

10 to 12 portions

ALL BUTTER-SOUR CREAM CRUMB CAKE

FAVORITES FOR FAMILY AND FRIENDS

Shrimp, Bacon, and Tomatoes
. . .
Linguine with Walnut Crumbs
. . .
All Butter-Sour Cream Crumb Cake

This absolutely rivals the Crumb Cake recipe in *The Uncommon Gourmet* and could easily win over my family's hearts as their number one favorite. This gets 5 stars!

Topping:
1/2 cup butter, melted
1 cup sugar
1 cup all-purpose flour
1/2 teaspoon cinnamon

Cake:
1/2 cup butter
1 cup sugar
2 eggs
1 tablespoon vanilla
2 cups all-purpose flour
1 teaspoon baking powder
1/4 teaspoon baking soda
1/4 teaspoon salt
1 cup sour cream

1. Preheat the oven to 350°. Grease a 9 x 13-inch baking pan.

2. Prepare the topping. Combine all of the ingredients in a bowl and mix with a fork to form coarse crumbs. Set aside.

3. In a bowl with an electric mixer, cream the butter and sugar until pale and fluffy. Add the eggs and vanilla and mix well.

4. Sift together the flour, baking powder, baking soda, and salt. Add the dry ingredients alternately with the sour cream to the batter. Beat at low speed only until evenly combined. Turn the batter into the prepared pan.

5. Crumble the topping mixture evenly over the batter.

6. Bake for 35 to 40 minutes until a toothpick inserted in the center comes out clean. Transfer the pan to a rack to cool completely.

12 or more portions

PUMPKIN CHEESECAKE

This is the perfect finale to the Thanksgiving meal! Cheesecake is always a hit. This one sports a velvety smooth, creamy pumpkin batter nestled in a gingersnap crust, providing classic comfort.

Crust:
$1^{1}/_2$ cups gingersnap crumbs
3 tablespoons sugar
5 tablespoons butter, melted

Filling:
$1^{1}/_2$ pounds cream cheese, at room temperature
$^{3}/_4$ cup granulated sugar
$^{3}/_4$ cup firmly packed light brown sugar
1 teaspoon vanilla
5 eggs
16-ounce can pumpkin purée
$1^{1}/_2$ teaspoons cinnamon
1 teaspoon ground ginger
$^{1}/_2$ teaspoon allspice
$^{1}/_2$ teaspoon ground cloves

1. Preheat the oven to 375°.

2. Prepare the crust. Combine the gingersnap crumbs, sugar, and butter in a mixing bowl and stir until evenly blended. Press the mixture firmly over the bottom of a 9-inch springform pan.

3. Bake the crust for 5 to 7 minutes on the bottom rack of the oven until golden. Remove to a rack to cool completely.

4. Reduce the oven to 325°.

5. Prepare the filling. In a large mixing bowl with an electric mixer, beat the cream cheese, sugars, and vanilla until light and fluffy. Add the eggs, one at a time, beating well after each addition.

6. Add the pumpkin and spices and mix until well blended. Pour the batter into the cooled crust.

7. Bake in the middle of the oven for $1^{1}/_2$ hours. Transfer to a rack to cool completely. Refrigerate at least 4 hours before serving. (Run a knife around the edge of the pan before removing the cake from the pan.)

8 to 10 portions

LEMON MERINGUE PIE

This is not your average Joe lemon meringue pie. This easy-style pie gets a 10-star rating with its luscious, lemony, creamy custard piled high with meringue.

Crust:
1¼ cups all-purpose flour
¼ cup confectioners' sugar
½ cup butter, cut into chunks

1. Preheat the oven to 400°.

2. Put the flour and sugar in the bowl of a food processor and pulse to mix. Add the butter and pulse until mixture is the texture of coarse crumbs.

3. Remove the dough to a 9-inch deep-dish pie pan and pat into place. Prick the bottom of the crust with a fork. Bake for 12 to 14 minutes until lightly golden. Let cool completely before filling.

Filling:
3 egg yolks
14-ounce can sweetened condensed milk
1 tablespoon grated lemon peel
½ cup lemon juice

1. In a bowl with an electric mixer, beat the egg yolks until thick and lemon colored.

2. Add the condensed milk, lemon peel, and lemon juice and beat until thick and creamy. Pour the mixture into the pre-baked pie shell. Prepare the meringue.

SUNDAY DINNER FOR FRIENDS

Roasted Cornish Hens
· · ·
Mashed Apples and Sweet Potatoes
· · ·
Green Beans with Toasted Hazelnuts
· · ·
Lemon Meringue Pie

Meringue:
3 egg whites
¹/₄ teaspoon cream of tartar
1 teaspoon vanilla   .
¹/₂ cup sugar

1. Preheat the oven to 350°.

2. In a bowl with an electric mixer, beat the egg whites until frothy. Add the cream of tartar and vanilla and beat to soft peaks. Add the sugar 1 tablespoon at a time, beating constantly. Beat until whites are stiff and glossy, but not dry.

3. Pile the meringue on the pie, spreading it from the edges of the crust towards the middle, making sure to seal the meringue to the crust so that no filling is visible.

4. Bake for 15 minutes. Remove to a rack to cool; then refrigerate for 2 to 3 hours. Serve chilled.

6 to 8 portions

COFFEE MASCARPONE-RASPBERRY TART

Fresh fruit tarts are the crown jewels of summer. This exceptional pastry is spread with a lush coffee-flavored mascarpone filling and encrusted with plump, juicy raspberries. For variations on the theme, try vanilla mascarpone by substituting 1 teaspoon vanilla for the instant coffee and top with a variety of berries—raspberries, blackberries, and blueberries—or whole strawberries.

Crust:
1 cup all-purpose flour
2 tablespoons sugar
pinch of salt
6 tablespoons cold butter, cut into cubes
2$^1/_2$ tablespoons ice water

1. Put the flour, sugar, and salt in the bowl of a food processor and pulse. Add the butter and pulse until the texture of coarse meal. With the motor running, add the water and process until the dough comes together and forms a ball. Remove the dough and form it into a flat disk. Cover with plastic wrap and refrigerate for 2 to 3 hours.

2. Preheat the oven to 425°.

3. On a lightly floured board, roll the dough into an 11-inch circle. Place in a 9-inch pie pan. Flute the edges and prick the bottom of the pastry with a fork. Bake for 12 to 14 minutes until golden. Remove to a rack to cool completely before filling. (This may be prepared 1 day ahead.)

Filling:
8 ounces mascarpone cheese
$^1/_4$ cup sugar
1 tablespoon instant coffee

1. In a bowl, mix the mascarpone, sugar, and coffee until evenly combined. Let sit for 15 minutes for the coffee granules to fully dissolve; stir again before filling the tart.

2. Spread the coffee mascarpone over the pastry.

Fruit Topping:
1 pint raspberries
confectioners' sugar

Cover the filling with the raspberries. Refrigerate until needed. Dust the berries with confectioners' sugar before serving.

6 to 8 portions

RASPBERRY TORTE

This is a modified version of the apple torte in *The Uncommon Gourmet Cookbook*. I think the substitution of raspberries makes this an exquisite dessert!

> *¹/₂ cup butter*
> *1¹/₄ cups sugar*
> *2 eggs*
> *1¹/₂ teaspoons vanilla*
> *1 cup all-purpose flour*
> *1 teaspoon baking powder*
> *¹/₄ teaspoon salt*
> *¹/₂ pint raspberries*
> *confectioners' sugar for garnish*

1. Preheat the oven to 350°. Grease a 9-inch springform pan.

2. In a mixing bowl, cream the butter and 1 cup sugar until light and fluffy. Add the eggs and vanilla and mix well.

3. Sift together the flour, baking powder, and salt and add to the batter, stirring until evenly incorporated.

4. Turn the batter into the prepared pan. Spread the raspberries over the top, reserving 3 berries for garnish. Sprinkle the raspberries with the ¹/₄ cup sugar.

5. Bake for 50 minutes. Remove the pan to a rack to cool. While the torte is still warm, run a knife around the edge of the pan. Once cooled, remove the torte from the springform to a platter. Dust the top with confectioners' sugar, place the reserved raspberries in the center of the torte, and serve.

6 to 8 portions

ROMANTIC
DINNER FOR
TWO

Salad Marly
. . .
Curry-Mustard Rack
of Lamb
. . .
Roasted Sweet
Potatoes
. . .
Raspberry Torte

CHOCOLATE
FANTASIES

CHOCOLATE-HAZELNUT BISCOTTI

Biscotti actually means "twice baked". The dough gets baked, then sliced, and is then returned to the oven for a second baking to crisp. They're quite easy to make, taking the mystique out of this delightful pastry. These double chocolate treats strut a chocolate base that's studded with ground chocolate and hazelnuts.

6 ounces semi-sweet chocolate (not chips)
1/2 cup butter
3/4 cup sugar
2 eggs
1 teaspoon vanilla
2 cups all-purpose flour
1 1/2 teaspoons baking powder
1/4 teaspoon salt
1 cup hazelnuts, toasted and ground in a food processor
1 cup semi-sweet chocolate chips, finely ground in a food processor

1. Preheat the oven to 325°. Line two baking sheets with parchment paper.

2. In the top of a double boiler, melt the chocolate. Stir until smooth, then remove from the heat and let cool.

3. In a large mixing bowl, cream the butter and sugar. Add the eggs and vanilla and mix well.

4. Stir in the cooled, melted chocolate.

5. Add the flour, baking powder, and salt and mix well. Stir in the ground nuts and ground chocolate chips.

6. Divide the dough in half. Turn each half out onto a cookie sheet and form into a log, 3 inches wide and 13 inches long.

7. Bake for 30 minutes. Remove the logs from the cookie sheets and let cool for 3 minutes. Slice each log into 3/4-inch wide pieces. Place a rack on each cookie sheet and place the slices on the racks, 1/2-inch apart.

8. Return to the oven and bake for 10 minutes more. Remove the racks from the baking sheets and let biscotti cool completely.

36 biscotti

CHOCOLATE RUGELACH

This is an old Jewish recipe that's a holiday tradition. What distinguishes rugelach is the cream cheese dough which makes a tender, flaky pastry. Chilling the dough overnight is essential for successful results! These are finished with a cinnamon-laced chocolate filling, making them out of this world.

Pastry:
1 cup butter
1/2 pound cream cheese, at room temperature
2 tablespoons sugar
1/2 teaspoon salt
2 cups sifted all-purpose flour

1. In a bowl with an electric mixer, cream the butter and cream cheese until smooth. Add the sugar and salt.

2. Gradually blend in the flour until the texture of coarse meal. Remove the dough to a board and form into a log. Divide the dough into 4 portions. Cover each portion with plastic wrap and flatten each into a rectangle. Chill overnight.

Filling:
1/2 cup sugar
1 1/2 teaspoons cinnamon
4 tablespoons butter, melted
1 cup mini semi-sweet chocolate chips

Glaze:
1 egg yolk beaten with 1 teaspoon cold water

1. Preheat the oven to 350°. Line two baking sheets with parchment paper.

2. In a small bowl, combine the sugar and cinnamon.

3. Lightly dust a board with flour. Roll a chilled portion of dough into an 8 x 12-inch rectangle. Flip the dough often to prevent sticking. (It's okay if the edges of the dough are ragged.)

4. Brush the dough with 1 tablespoon butter. Sprinkle with 2 tablespoons of the cinnamon-sugar mixture and 1/4 cup chocolate chips. Using a rolling pin, press the filling into the dough. Starting at the long side, roll the dough into a tight cylinder. Trim off 1/4 inch from each end. Cut the roll into 10 pieces. Place the pieces seam side down on the prepared baking sheets. Repeat with the remaining dough and filling.

5. Brush the pastry with the egg glaze. Bake for 20 minutes, turning the pans from front to back after 10 minutes. Remove to racks to cool before serving.

40 rugelach

WHITE CHOCOLATE-MACADAMIA-CHOCOLATE COOKIES

These inside out chocolate chippers sport a chocolate batter rich with white chocolate chips and macadamia nuts. No one can eat just one!

> 3 tablespoons butter
> 1 1/2 cups semi-sweet chocolate chips
> 3/4 cup sugar
> 2 eggs
> 1 teaspoon vanilla
> 1/4 cup all-purpose flour
> 1/4 teaspoon baking powder
> pinch of salt
> 1 cup white chocolate chips
> 1 cup dry-roasted macadamia nuts, coarsely chopped

1. Preheat the oven to 350°. Grease two cookie sheets.

2. In a small saucepan, heat the butter and chocolate over low until melted. Stir well and remove from heat to cool.

3. In a large bowl, beat the sugar, eggs, and vanilla. Add the cooled chocolate and mix well.

4. Sift together the flour, baking powder, and salt and add to the batter.

5. Fold in the chips and nuts.

6. Drop the batter by heaping tablespoonfuls onto the cookie sheets, 2 inches apart.

7. Bake for 10 to 12 minutes until cracked on top. The cookies will puff during baking. Remove the sheets to racks to cool for 4 minutes; then remove the cookies to racks to cool completely. The cookies will be very moist and will set as they cool.

3 1/2 dozen cookies

BEACH PARTY

Lobster Rolls
· · ·
Coleslaw
· · ·
Lemonade
· · ·
White Chocolate-Macadamia-Chocolate Cookies
· · ·
Watermelon

DOUBLE FUDGE BROWNIES

This is an updated version of my truffle brownies in *The All-Occasion Cookbook*. These are even more decadent and fudgier, making them absolutely outrageous. They're a little piece of heaven!

8 ounces bittersweet chocolate
1/2 cup butter (no substitutions)
2 tablespoons heavy cream
2 eggs
3/4 cup sugar
1 teaspoon vanilla
1/4 cup all-purpose flour
1 cup semi-sweet chocolate chips

1. Preheat the oven to 375°. Line an 8-inch square baking pan with silver foil and grease the foil.

2. Put the bittersweet chocolate, butter, and heavy cream in a saucepan. Melt the chocolate over low heat. Once melted, stir until smooth, remove from the heat, and let cool.

3. With an electric mixer, beat the eggs, sugar, and vanilla until thick and pale lemon colored. Add the cooled, melted chocolate and mix well.

4. Stir in the flour and chocolate chips. Turn the batter into the prepared pan, spreading it out evenly.

5. Bake for 25 to 28 minutes until set. The top will be crusted and a toothpick inserted in the center will be coated with moist batter. Let cool on a rack completely; then refrigerate for 4 hours until firm. Lift the foil out of the pan and peel it away from the brownies. Cut into squares and keep refrigerated until ready to serve.

25 brownies

PEANUT BUTTER SWIRL BROWNIES

Reese's fans take heed! These brownies combine the best of both world— super chocolaty, fudgy brownies with a peanut butter-cheesecake swirl. They're moist, chock full of chocolate chips, and sheer decadence.

4 ounces unsweetened chocolate
2 ounces semi-sweet chocolate
1 cup butter
2 cups sugar
4 eggs
1 teaspoon vanilla
1 cup all-purpose flour
3/4 cup semi-sweet chocolate chips
Peanut Butter Swirl (recipe follows)

1. Preheat the oven to 350°. Line a 9 x 13-inch pan with parchment paper.

2. Melt the unsweetened and semi-sweet chocolates in the top of a double boiler. Let cool.

3. In a large mixing bowl, cream the butter and sugar. Add the eggs and vanilla. Add the cooled chocolate to the batter and mix well.

4. Stir in the flour.

5. Mix in the chocolate chips. Turn the batter into the prepared pan.

6. Drop spoonfuls of the Peanut Butter Swirl onto the batter. Swirl the mixture through the batter with a knife to achieve a rippling effect.

7. Bake for 28 to 30 minutes until the top is set and the middle is still slightly moist. The batter will adhere somewhat to a toothpick inserted in the center. Cool completely; then refrigerate for 2 to 3 hours to chill. Remove the brownies from the pan by lifting the parchment paper. Cut the brownies into squares and serve. Store in the refrigerator.

4 dozen brownies

Peanut Butter Swirl:

2/3 cup smooth peanut butter
4 ounces cream cheese, at room temperature
1 egg
1/4 cup packed light brown sugar
2/3 cup dry roasted salted peanuts, chopped

In a bowl with an electric mixer, beat the peanut butter and cream cheese. Add the egg and sugar and beat until the mixture is fluffy. Stir in the peanuts.

CHOCOLATE-FIG CLUSTERS

I love to combine chocolate with dried fruits and nuts. Rather than dipping the fruits or nuts in melted chocolate, I've mixed them together, creating decadent chocolate confections studded with dried figs and pistachio nuts. These make a wonderful holiday or hostess gift.

6 ounces semi-sweet chocolate (not chips)
1¼ cups diced dried figs (cut into ½-inch pieces)
½ cup shelled pistachio nuts

1. Line a large baking pan with wax paper.
2. Melt the chocolate in the top of a double boiler. When smooth, add the figs and nuts and stir until evenly combined.
3. Using a small spoon, scoop out heaping teaspoons of the mixture and place on the prepared baking pan. Make sure you use all of the chocolate.
4. Refrigerate for 2 hours until set. Store in the refrigerator in an airtight container for up to 2 weeks.

30 clusters

COOKIE TRAY

Chocolate-Hazelnut
Biscotti
. . .
Chocolate-Fig Clusters
. . .
Meringues*
. . .
Coconut Macaroons
. . .
Pecan Butterballs
. . .
Mini Carrot Cake
Muffins

MACADAMIA NUT FUDGE

This old-fashioned favorite is updated with the extravagance of buttery macadamia nuts. This rich, dark, velvety chocolate experience is absolutely divine.

18 ounces (1 pound 2 ounces) semi-sweet baking chocolate
14-ounce can sweetened condensed milk
2 teaspoons vanilla
pinch of salt
1 cup coarsely chopped macadamia nuts

1. Line an 8-inch square pan with silver foil.

2. Heat the chocolate in the top of a double boiler until melted. Add the condensed milk, vanilla, and salt and mix well. Stir in the nuts.

3. Spread the fudge in the prepared pan. Chill for 2 hours or more until firm. Remove the fudge from the pan by lifting the foil. Peel away the foil and cut into squares. Store in the refrigerator.

2^1/$_4$ pounds fudge; about 4 dozen pieces

SPICED CHOCOLATE CHIP CAKE

There's no better way to cap off a brunch than with this moist brown sugar and spice cake. The ground chocolate chip-laced batter is fragrant with cloves and adorned with vanilla icing.

TAIL-GATING PARTY

Cold Roasted Chicken
. . .
Corn and Barley Salad
. . .
Moroccan Salad
. . .
Spiced Chocolate
Chip Cake

$^1/_2$ cup butter
1 cup lightly packed light brown sugar
2 eggs
1 tablespoon vanilla
1 cup whole milk ricotta cheese
2 cups all-purpose flour
1 teaspoon baking powder
1 teaspoon baking soda
$^1/_2$ teaspoon salt
$^1/_2$ teaspoon ground ginger
$^1/_2$ teaspoon ground cloves
$^3/_4$ cup whole milk
$1^1/_4$ cups semi-sweet chocolate chips, ground in a food processor
Vanilla Icing (recipe follows)
shaved semi-sweet chocolate for garnish

1. Preheat the oven to 350°. Grease a 10-inch tube pan.

2. In a large bowl with an electric mixer, cream the butter and sugar until fluffy. Add the eggs and vanilla.

3. Add the ricotta, beating until smooth.

4. Sift together the flour, baking powder, baking soda, salt, ginger, and cloves. Add the dry ingredients alternately with the milk to the batter.

5. Mix in the ground chocolate chips. Turn the batter into the prepared pan.

6. Bake for 45 minutes or until a toothpick inserted in the center comes out clean. Remove the tube from the pan and set the cake on a rack to cool.

7. Run a knife between the bottom of the cake and the pan. Invert the cake onto a plate, then using a second plate, turn the cake right side up. Glaze with the Vanilla Icing and decorate with shaved chocolate before serving.

8 to 10 portions

Vanilla Icing:
2 cups confectioners' sugar
2 tablespoons butter, melted
1 teaspoon vanilla
2 tablespoons boiling water

Combine all of the ingredients and mix well until smooth. Spread over the top and sides of the cake.

CHOCOLATE PUDDING CAKE

This is a most unusual, magical cake. As the cake bakes, the bottom becomes a smooth, velvety chocolate pudding while the top turns into a chocolate sponge cake. The pudding is served as a rich, fudgy sauce spooned over the cake, making it a heavenly chocolate experience.

Cake:
1 cup all-purpose flour
3/4 cup sugar
1/4 cup unsweetened cocoa
1 1/2 teaspoons baking powder
1/4 teaspoon salt
1/2 cup whole milk
4 tablespoons butter, melted
2 teaspoons vanilla

Pudding:
1 cup sugar
1/4 cup unsweetened cocoa
1 1/3 cups boiling water

1. Preheat the oven to 350°.

2. In a large mixing bowl, combine the flour, sugar, cocoa, baking powder, and salt and mix well.

3. Add the milk, butter, and vanilla and stir until evenly mixed. Transfer the batter to an ungreased 8-inch square pan.

4. In a small bowl, make the pudding. Combine the sugar and cocoa and stir until evenly mixed. Add the boiling water and stir until the cocoa is dissolved. Pour this mixture over the cake batter—do not stir!

5. Bake for 30 to 35 minutes until the top is set. Let cool for 15 minutes. (The pudding will thicken as it cools.) Serve warm with the pudding spooned over the cake. Top with whipped cream or vanilla ice cream.

8 portions

LIGHT REPAST

Minted Pea Soup
. . .
Grilled Salmon
. . .
Penne with Tomatoes
and White Beans
. . .
Chocolate
Pudding Cake

CHOCOLATE SWIRL POUNDCAKE

Even though this is included in the chocolate section, it has a widespread appeal! Ribbons of chocolate are laced through a light almond-scented poundcake. Serve this with mugs of hot coffee for a homestyle treat.

1/2 cup semi-sweet chocolate chips
1/2 cup butter
1 cup sugar
2 eggs
1 teaspoon vanilla
1/2 teaspoon almond extract
2 cups all-purpose flour
2 teaspoons baking powder
1/2 teaspoon salt
3/4 cup whole milk

1. Preheat the oven to 350°. Grease and flour the sides of a 9 x 5-inch loaf pan. Line the bottom of the pan with parchment paper.

2. Melt the chocolate chips in the top of a double boiler. Turn off the heat and let sit to keep warm while preparing the batter.

3. In a large mixing bowl, cream the butter and sugar. Add the eggs and vanilla and almond extracts.

4. Sift together the flour, baking powder, and salt and add the dry ingredients alternately with the milk to the batter.

5. Turn 1/3 of the batter into the prepared pan. Drizzle half of the melted chocolate over the top. Cover with the remaining batter; drizzle the rest of the chocolate over all. With a knife, swirl the chocolate through the batter to achieve a rippling effect.

6. Bake for 50 to 55 minutes until a toothpick inserted in the center comes out clean. Run a knife around the edge of the cake while still warm. Let cool on a rack completely before removing from the pan.

1 loaf

GERMAN SWEET CHOCOLATE PIE

The classic German chocolate cake takes on a new identity in this rendition. A buttery, deep-dish crust is filled with a chocolaty, fudgy batter spiked with pecans and baked just until set. Capped with a caramel coconut-pecan frosting, this luscious dessert is guaranteed to put a smile on your face.

9-inch deep-dish pie crust, pre-baked (see page 502)
8 ounces sweet chocolate, broken into pieces
6 tablespoons butter
1/4 cup sugar
2 eggs
1 teaspoon vanilla
1/2 cup chopped pecans
Caramel Coconut-Pecan Frosting (recipe follows)

1. Preheat the oven to 350°.

2. In a small saucepan, melt the chocolate and butter over low heat, stirring occasionally until smooth. Remove from the heat and cool completely.

3. In a bowl, whisk together the sugar, eggs, vanilla, and pecans. Add the cooled chocolate, stirring until evenly combined. Pour the mixture into the prepared crust.

4. Bake about 25 minutes until the center of the filling is set. Transfer to a rack to cool completely.

5. Spread the warm Caramel Coconut-Pecan Frosting over the cooled pie. Chill to set, about 1 hour. Keep refrigerated until serving time.

8 portions

VALENTINE'S DINNER

Vegetable Pancakes
. . .
Spinach, Brie, and Sun-Dried Tomatoes

Herbed Rack of Lamb*
. . .
German Sweet Chocolate Pie

Caramel Coconut-Pecan Frosting:
6 tablespoons sugar
2 tablespoons water
6 tablespoons butter, cut into 6 pieces
$^1/_2$ cup sweetened, shredded coconut
$^1/_2$ cup chopped pecans, toasted

1. Combine the sugar and water in a 1-quart saucepan. Swirl over medium-high heat until sugar is dissolved. Let syrup boil until it turns an amber color, about 3 to 4 minutes, swirling pan occasionally.

2. Remove from the heat and immediately swirl in the chunks of butter. When melted, mix in the coconut and pecans.

CHOCOLATE CREAM CAKE

This light-textured cake has a rich, fudgy chocolate flavor. I like to dust the top with confectioners' sugar and serve it with whipped cream and fresh raspberries for a grand finale.

2 cups sugar
4 eggs
1 teaspoon vanilla
1 3/4 cups all-purpose flour
2 teaspoons baking powder
1/8 teaspoon salt
3/4 cup unsweetened cocoa
1 1/4 cups heavy cream
confectioners' sugar for garnish

1. Preheat the oven to 400°. Grease a 10-inch tube pan and dust it with cocoa.

2. In a large mixing bowl, with an electric mixer, beat the sugar and eggs until thick and pale lemon colored. Add the vanilla.

3. Sift together the flour, baking powder, salt, and cocoa. Add the dry ingredients alternately with the cream to the batter. Turn the batter into the prepared pan.

4. Bake for 15 minutes. Reduce the oven temperature to 300° and bake for about 40 minutes longer. A toothpick inserted in the center should have some crumbs adhering to it. (For a fudgier cake, bake for about 37 minutes.) Remove to a rack to cool for 10 minutes; then remove the tube from the pan and let the cake cool completely.

5. Run a knife under the bottom of the cake to release it from the pan. Invert the cake onto a plate, then using a second plate, turn the cake right side up. Dust with confectioners' sugar and serve.

10 to 12 portions

INDEX